OLD CROWN DERBY CHINA WORKS
THE KING STREET FACTORY
1849 – 1935

Robin Blackwood & Cherryl Head

This photograph, dated 1914, shows that part of the factory that faced onto King Street. The premises to the right of the "Old Crown Derby" sign on the front of the building, are not part of the factory, but were occupied by other firms.

   This less than prepossessing building and other similar ones shown in this book, should not be taken as an indication that inferior products were produced, and this is demonstrated by the illustrations presented in Chapters Two and Six.

This book is dedicated to the founder
partners and entire workforce of
The Old Crown Derby China Works,
King Street,
Derby.

Opposite page: Seasons figures, Spring and Autumn.
Private collection.

OLD CROWN DERBY CHINA WORKS
THE KING STREET FACTORY
1849 – 1935

Robin Blackwood & Cherryl Head

Published by

Ashbourne Hall, Cokayne Ave
Ashbourne, Derbyshire DE6 1EJ England
Tel: (01335) 347349 Fax: (01335) 347303
e-mail: landmark@clara.net
web site: www.landmarkpublishing.co.uk

1st edition

ISBN 1 84306 091 4

Printed by Gutenburg Press Ltd, Malta

Design & reproduction by James Allsopp

Cover captions:

Front cover: Bottle and Stopper. Private collection

Back cover Left top: Basket of modelled flowers. Private collection

Right top: Dish, painted with a landscape view of Derby and signed W. E. Mosley. Private collection.

Main photograph: Dish, painted with flowers and butterflies and signed H. S. Hancock.
Private collection.

CONTENTS

PREFACE

This book is the result of many years of research on the part of Robin Blackwood and Cherryl Head. Until now the King Street Factory has been the Cinderella of the Derby porcelain concerns: no major monograph has been devoted to this works and its products. Many previous publications discuss the King Street Factory in a chapter or two, and deal chiefly with the earlier Nottingham Road works or the later Royal Crown Derby Porcelain Company.

This new book therefore meets a need, and it contains much new evidence. It is a most welcome contribution to the study of Derby porcelain history.

Anneke Bambery
Principal Curator, Derby Museums and Art Gallery.

I am delighted to welcome Robin Blackwood and Cherryl Head's book on the China factory in King Street, Derby. Although quite small, the factory is very important in the history of Derby porcelain, for two main reasons. First, it provides the artistic and corporate link between the original Nottingham Road factory, and the present Royal Crown Derby. Second, the consistent high quality of design and production, and the faithful development of the "Derby" style were remarkable. The authors' diligent research and elegant prose will close an important gap in our knowledge.

Hugh Gibson
Chief Executive, Royal Crown Derby.

ACKNOWLEDGEMENTS

Many people have supported the authors in their search for that additional piece of information that is so important in the writing of a book of this type.

Hugh Gibson, the Chief Executive of the Royal Crown Derby Porcelain Company Limited and members of staff have provided endless help and particular thanks go to Jacqueline Banks, the Museum Curator, Caroline Salmon and Bryan Bourne. The Company's help in giving the authors access to the King Street Archives and for allowing photographs to be taken of porcelain in the Museum has been of considerable benefit and for this they are most grateful.

Anneke Bambery, the Principal Curator at the Museum and Art Gallery, Derby, has been unsparing in the time that she has devoted to assisting the authors and for this they are most grateful. The Museum's permission to reproduce photographs of items in this collection has been of great assistance.

The experience of Linda Owen, former Senior Librarian at The Local Studies Library, Derby, has been most welcome, especially in the arduous task of indexing. The authors wish to thank Peter Owen for the support he gave to his wife.

This book would be incomplete if it were not for the participation of many owners who allowed their homes to be visited for details and photographs to be taken of their prized wares from the King Street factory.

Whether one of those named in the book, or amongst those, who when given the choice, decided to remain anonymous, the contribution made by all these kind people is acknowledged with gratitude.

Grateful thanks go to Hubert King of W. W. Winter, the Derby photographers for producing such consistently excellent photographs.

John Twitchett's generous gesture in giving the authors access to material from his publications is greatly appreciated.

Frequent help and encouragement has been provided by the porcelain enthusiasts Colin and Freda Wharf, who so often manage to supply information to the authors, which is hard to come by elsewhere.

The authors also acknowledge, with gratitude, the valuable assistance accorded to them by the following people:

Martin Bennett
Aileen Dawson, the Curator of the Department of Medieval and Modern Europe, the British Museum, and the staff in this department
Joan D'Arcy of The Derby Archaeological Society
James Hamilton Fairley
Nicholas Gent
Brian and Joan George
Ora Gordon
Tony Horsley
Mark Law and Nicholas Lyne, Law Fine Art Ltd.
Andrew Ledger

Mike Morris
Basil Mosenthal
Thimbleby and Shorland

Acknowledgements of a more personal note are due to Ken and Richard Head, husband and son of author Cherryl Head, for all the support they have given her. Robin Blackwood is appreciative of the help given by Pat and Graham Holt during the numerous trips that took him away from home whilst the writing of this book progressed.

Grateful thanks are also due to members of the Hancock family who have generously allowed the authors access to their family treasures, and to the nephew of Elsie Larcombe, who kindly allowed the authors access to William Larcombe's papers.

INTRODUCTION

The china works situated at 26 King Street, Derby, was in production from 1849 until its closure in 1935. Although the smallest of the three porcelain factories which have operated in the town of Derby, it formed an important link between the Nottingham Road factory which closed in 1848 and the present day Royal Crown Derby factory which commenced production on its present site in Osmaston Road in 1877, and which ran concurrently with the King Street factory for 58 years.

King Street is the name by which the factory is generally known today. This avoids any confusion with the present factory which started life as the Derby Crown Porcelain Company, later to become the Royal Crown Derby Porcelain Company. The factory on King Street had called itself, at different times, both the Old Derby Crown China Works and the Old Crown Derby China Works, both names not dissimilar to those used by the present factory. Throughout this book, the factory that is being considered will be referred to as King Street.

John Twitchett with Betty Bailey (1) and Brayshaw Gilhespy, with Dorothy Budd (2), have devoted a chapter each to the King Street factory in books that they have written. Other authors have made mention of the factory in their works, and the Derby Porcelain International Society has published various short articles on this subject.

The aim of this publication is to cover all aspects of production at the factory, including notes on its proprietors, modellers and artists and a chapter is devoted to marks.

A large part of Chapter Six is devoted to providing information and illustrations of a wide range of shapes and decoration turned out by the King Street factory.

Where an artist's work can be attributed to him or her, details of these pieces, accompanied by illustrations, are placed in Chapter Two in the entry dealing with that particular artist.

In 1993, the Museum and Art Gallery, supported by the Derby Porcelain International Society, organised a very successful exhibition in Derby of products from King Street. Since that date, some further interesting pieces have come to light and these are included.

Sadly, records relating to the factory are sparse and those covering sales almost non- existent. Those documents that remain cover mainly the 1860s – 1880s, with some bearing dates before King Street was founded. These are all held by the Museum at Royal Crown Derby and were sorted into groups by John Twitchett, the then Curator of the Museum, who titled them the King Street Archives. His book, *"In Account with Sampson Hancock 1860s-1880s"* contains details of these remaining records(3). Two pattern books remain in the British Museum and the contents of another is in the Museum at Royal Crown Derby. These and other sources of information on shapes and patterns are considered in Chapter Six.

Assisted by their own research material, the authors hope they have, to some small degree, overcome the handicap created by the lack of records of what the factory produced.

Whilst aiming to include as many important facts as possible it is hoped readers will perceive this as a friendly book. Both authors would be pleased to receive any queries or comments arising from this publication which could further advance the knowledge of the King Street factory.

The claims made by the King Street factory *"established in 1750"* and *"we bought Bow in 1776, or thereabouts,"* both of which readers will find mentioned in this book, are perhaps a little excessive, but show a keenness to be associated with porcelain manufacture of the past in Derby.

Perhaps this small concern felt a need to boost its confidence when faced with some of the slightly belittling remarks that were made about it. However, one of the few people to heap praise on this small factory was the historian Llewellyn Jewitt, when he wrote in January 1862 these encouraging words, which must have been most welcome to the management and workers (4).

> "Mr. Locker died in 1859, and the works have since been carried on under the style of "Stevenson and Co.," and bid fair, if not to rival the early glory and success of the works at least to do credit to the town of Derby, in which they are situated. Great difficulties have had to be encountered by this band of workmen, but their zeal and determination have so far overcome them; and I doubt not, with a fair measure of support accorded to them, that the works will again rise to an enviable eminence. The place has every element of success about it – long experience, great skill, untiring attention, and zeal and energy in abundance – and some of the productions are highly creditable to the taste and skill of the men, and show that "ye art of making English china" imparted to William Duesbury in 1750, is not forgotten, but remains with his successors to the present day."

Note: Locker and Stevenson were both proprietors at King Street and Duesbury was founder of the Nottingham Road factory.

It would be immensely satisfying had the authors been able to provide answers to all the questions raised during the writing of this book. In the case of a few, this has not proved possible, but this will present a challenge to any future researchers with an interest in the King Street factory.

For the convenience of readers, references are placed at the close of each chapter, rather than in a longer list, at the end of the book.

John Twitchett's excellent definitions regarding restoration, which are given below, are used throughout the book and it is the authors' view that it would be beneficial if they were more widely used:

"Repairing:" Means putting back an original piece that has
   broken off.
"Restoring:" Is the making of a new piece or any new decoration.

INTRODUCTION REFERENCES

1) Twitchett, J., & Bailey, B., *"Royal Crown Derby China,"* 1988, Antique Collectors' Club.
2) Gilhespy, F. B., & Budd, D., *"Royal Crown Derby China,"* 1964, C. Skilton.
3) Twitchett, J., *"In Account with Sampson Hancock, 1860s-1880s."* 1996, D. J.C. Books.
4) Jewitt, L., *"Old Derby China, A History of the Derby China Works,"* *The Art Journal,* 1862, p.4.

Note: Concerning the above references, the authors have tried without success, to contact the copyright owners, C. Skilton.

ILLUSTRATIONS

Sampson Henry Hancock and Harry Sampson Hancock were one and the same person. It appears in order to prevent confusion with his grandfather Sampson Hancock, Sampson Henry Hancock changed the order of his Christian names. Very early pieces decorated by him were signed S. H. Hancock for Sampson Henry Hancock, however later he was known as Harry Sampson Hancock.

MONOCHROME

3. MARKS

COLOUR

MONOCHROME

4. NINETEENTH CENTURY INVOICES

COLOUR

MONOCHROME

5. RECIPES

6. THE PRODUCTS, THEIR SHAPES AND PATTERNS

As explained in Chapter Three, when dealing with marks, it is now considered with a degree of certainty, that Harry Sampson Hancock used the mark of two parallel lines on his work that was not signed with his name in full, this being fully covered in Chapter Two.

On the decorated wares listed and illustrated in Chapter Six, all of which are not artist signed, around a quarter of the entries covered in the period that H. S. Hancock was employed at King Street, bear the mark of "//" and this is noted against each entry that bears this mark. This provides an indication of the wide variety of wares decorated by this artist.

MONOCHROME

7. SALES

FACTORY SALES CATALOGUE 1934-35
COLOUR PLATES

8. QUALITY CONTROL

COLOUR PLATES

1. HISTORY OF THE FACTORY

This initial chapter covers the setting up of the factory on King Street, with a detailed look at the site and buildings. It also provides notes on the founder partners and on the subsequent proprietors. It does not deal with the products turned out during the life span of the factory, these being considered in depth in Chapter Six and also in Chapter Two where the work of particular artists is examined.

CLOSURE OF NOTTINGHAM ROAD FACTORY

Before dealing with the setting up of the King Street factory, it is useful to set the scene by briefly looking at the circumstances that led up to this.

The china manufactory situated on Nottingham Road, Derby had been in production for more than ninety years. After the death of proprietor Robert Bloor, his successors attempted to sell the business, or attract some fresh capital. These efforts failed and a notice was placed in the *Derby Mercury* in July 1847, to the effect that the Executors of the late Robert Bloor had taken the decision to close the works.

A further notice in the *Derby Mercury*, dated 14 February 1849 confirmed that the business had been disposed of to Messrs. Boyle and Sons, Fenton, Staffordshire.

It is not known if any effort was made by the Nottingham Road employees to continue the business on that site, perhaps by way of a management buy out. However, it is clear that there was considerable support for the continuance of porcelain manufacture in Derby and this was to take place on a different site, in King Street.

SETTING UP THE NEW FACTORY

Sampson Hancock, one of the six founder partners who started the works at King Street, summed up the situation clearly during an interview in 1894, at which time he was proprietor, stating:

"But six working – men employed at the Old Factory put their wits together and started my Works" (1)

In 1994, Colin and Freda Wharf, and Robin Blackwood, wrote an article which dealt with the closure of the Nottingham Road factory and the opening of King Street. As no fresh evidence regarding the latter has come to light, there follows an extract from that article. (2):

The Opening of King Street.
The researcher of the history of the King Street factory is immediately confronted with the problem that eminent writers seem to be at odds over the date when the factory was founded. Thus:

A) John Haslem[1] (writing less than 20 years after the attributed dates):

"On the close of the old factory on Nottingham Road in 1848, William Locker.....Samuel Fearn, John Henson and Samuel Sharpe, potters, and Sampson Hancock and James Hill, painters and gilders, all of whom had been engaged, and, with the exception of Mr. Hancock, had been apprenticed at the old works, commenced the manufacture of china on premises in King Street, and for the last twenty-seven years the concern has been carried on...".

We know that Haslem's book "The Old Crown Derby China Factory" was published in 1876 and this date less the twenty-seven years he mentions, brings us back to 1849, but we do not know exactly when Haslem wrote his chapter titled "The Present China Works in Derby", from which this passage is taken.

B) Sampson Hancock [2] in a press interview in 1894:

During the course of this interview, Sampson Hancock is asked about the start of the King Street manufactory and states,

"I succeeded Robert Bloor, transplanting the Nottingham Road works to my present factory."

When asked the question, "it was then you started your own works!" (sic). he replied "yes in 1848".

C) Gilhespy and Budd[3] (published in 1964):

"In 1849 William Locker, who had been the last manager at "The Old Derby Factory", opened a manufactory in King Street."

D) Hilda Moore [4] (writing in 1983):

"... the date 1848 is somewhat puzzling, because the 18th century Crown Derby factory closed, we are told, at the end of 1848 and it would seem doubtful if the original factory could close and a "follow-on" factory open in the same year."

Hilda Moore also recalls that in 1970 she was told by Mrs. Woodhouse, great grand-daughter of founder proprietor William Locker, that there had been a gap of two years before the opening of the new works, which would bring us to 1850.

Perhaps the confusion arises from the fact (as later demonstrated in this article) that although manufacture did not commence in 1848, the premises were probably leased in that year. Unfortunately the lack of King Street records makes the latter part of the preceding sentence more difficult to prove although it is hoped that further research may provide evidence to support this conjecture.

What recent research has established is that manufacture did not start before 1849. This is borne out by the following two newspaper extracts: an entry from a local directory is also recorded:

a) The Derby Mercury January 3rd 1849 (news column).

"Manufacture of China – We understand that although the Derby China Works are closed as far as the manufacture of china is concerned, arrangements are in progress to commence the making in our town by a party connected with the establishment of the late Mr. Bloor and that in a week or two the public will be acquainted with the fact."

b) The Derby and Chesterfield Reporter (advertisement).
William Locker and Co.
China Manufacturers and Dealers in
Earthenware and Glass,
26 King Street,
(Next door to Mr. Hall's Spar Manufactory),

Beg to inform the Nobility, Clergy, Gentry and Inhabitants of Derby and the surrounding Counties, that they have taken the above Premises and are having them altered, to suit the Manufacturing of China, which will occupy some weeks in completing, when they hope to be favoured with the support of their Friends, and a generous Public, as it will ever be their study to produce as good and cheap Articles as any furnished by the Trade.

SETS of CHINA bought from the late Mr. Bloor, can be MATCHED on application to W. Locker.
Derby, Jan. 23rd 1849."

c) The History and Directory of the Borough of Derby, intended as a Guide to Strangers Visiting the Town. (fourth edition 1849).

This guide shows the occupant of 26 King Street to be:

"Locker, William & Co. China Manufacturers & dealers in earthenware and glass."

This is inconclusive regarding the initial date of occupancy, but a directory of this type may well have been compiled prior to the year of printing. In the section dealing with the history of the Borough there is a long paragraph devoted to the Nottingham Road operation, but not yet any mention of production at King Street. Sadly, there is no version of this History and Directory for 1848.

If, as now seems likely, we have 26 King Street (re-numbered 85 from 1900) being leased in 1848 and manufacture in 1849, perhaps the majority of earlier writers were not incorrect, depending on whether their interpretation of when the factory "started" was the date upon which the premises were acquired or when manufacture commenced.

These findings in no way alter the accepted role played by the King Street factory in providing continuity of porcelain production in Derby, being the "link" between Nottingham Road and the present Royal Crown Derby factory on Osmaston Road, which started production in 1877, trading as the Derby Crown Porcelain Company.

Notes and References for the above article.

(In all instances "Haslem" refers to "The Old Derby China Factory" – first published 1876).

1 Haslem. p.237.
2 Hancock, Sampson – "The Story of Old Crown Derby China", from papers belonging to John Twitchett. Published in D.P.I.S. newsletter No. 17, December 1989 with annotation by John Twitchett.
3 Gilhespy, F. Brayshaw and Budd, Dorothy M. – "Royal Crown Derby China" (1964) – p.21.
4 Moore, Hilda M. - "The Old Crown Derby China Works", D.P.I.S. Newsletter No. 8, April 1987.

Note: In the above references D.P.I.S. stands for the Derby Porcelain International Society.

PLANT AND MATERIALS

Doubts have been expressed covering what plant and materials these six workers took with them to King Street, bearing in mind that the Nottingham Road works had been sold to Messrs. Boyle and Sons.

John Haslem tells us that in the year following the closure of Nottingham Road, at the end of 1848:

"Mr. Samuel Boyle, having purchased the whole of the plant, had it transferred to the Staffordshire Potteries. The purchase included unfinished stock, models, moulds, raw material, benches, stools, in short, every article however trifling, the whole of which was sent by water, and filled more than twenty canal boats." (3)

This does not appear to be the complete picture. The introduction to the 1934-35 King Street factory sales catalogue contains an interesting statement:

".... but a group of employees (generally referred to as "old Derby hands") pooled their resources to transfer the bulk of the models, moulds, body and colour recipes and pattern books, together with the goodwill and trade marks, to the present china works in King Street. The old wheel of William Duesbury was included, and it remains to-day the most important momento of the birth of the china industry in this country."

Fred Williamson, of the Derby Museum and Art Gallery, wrote an article in *The Derbyshire Advertiser* in 1925, in which he states that Haslem's view of what items went to Samuel Boyle was "far too sweeping". He goes on to list the many appliances that were brought to King Street, from the old factory (4).

It is unlikely that the six workmen, having lost their jobs, would not have found some way of taking various things with them to their new job. In addition to the potter's wheel which is known to have been moved to King Street, evidence is provided in later chapters that recipes, patterns and moulds were also transferred.

Mrs. Diane Oddy and her husband are currently sorting and cataloguing those early Derby models and moulds that are now at the Spode factory, which found their way there via Boyle of Fenton. There is therefore confirmation that items from Nottingham Road went to both Boyle in the Potteries and some to King Street.

Larcombe, the penultimate proprietor at King Street, in handwritten notes, is the first person to suggest that the "old hands", who set up the new factory, paid for the equipment that they took with them. He says that "they purchased as much as they could afford".

THE SITE AND BUILDINGS

The sketch reproduced below which appeared in G. G. Thompson's Manuscript Notebook, has only recently come to light and shows a small part of the factory, including its two kilns. It is dated May, 1890, forty-one years after production commenced at King Street.

Part of the factory. Sketch dated May 1890.
Derby Local Studies Library.

In 1995 research covering the site and the buildings of the factory was carried out by Robin Blackwood and his findings were as follows:

Only one of the several buildings used by the Old Crown Derby China works still stands, the remainder having been demolished over the years. Armed with early maps of the area, of large enough scale to show clearly individual buildings, together with some old photographs, I obtained permission to wander round the site in an attempt to get my bearings and to establish what had been the original layout and later development of the factory buildings.

The first large-scale map of Derby in general circulation was produced in 1883, thirty-four years after production commenced in 1849. However, a special map had been produced in 1852 [1] for the Derby Board of Health in connection with sanitation and drainage and although this shows individual buildings on the factory site, it is not of large enough scale to reproduce here. Having been printed just three years after manufacture started, it has proved useful in establishing the buildings that existed in the early days of the factory. I have decided to place on record the results of my research and add these to what previous writers have said about the size and layout of the factory, in the belief that such research will become more difficult if the site is fully redeveloped at some future date.

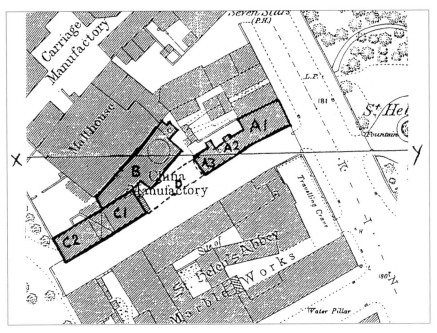

Fig. 1.

Map of factory site, 1883.
Records Office, Derbyshire County Council, Matlock.

Before visiting the site, it was helpful to be allowed to study the deeds and other relevant documents, now in the hands of Derbyshire County Council, in their Technical Services Department in Matlock.[2]

My perusal of these documents did not reveal anything startling, but confirmed that the various proprietors of the factory leased the premises from a succession of freeholders up to 1920, when William Larcombe and Francis Howard Paget, the proprietors at the time, purchased the freehold for the sum of £1050 from three sisters, Caroline, Eliza and Kate Sherwin of Eastbourne.

On the 1883 maps (Fig.1)[3] I have outlined with thick black lines those buildings which I believe made up the china manufactory at that time. The area is unfortunately spread over two maps which accounts for the unbroken horizontal line along my join which is marked XY. As the buildings fall into three convenient groups, I have marked them A, B and C and will deal with each in turn.

BLOCK A – The front section of this block (A1) which is the only building standing today, faces onto King Street. It is currently occupied by the Derby Mountain Centre, which is established not only in number 85 King Street, but also the adjoining numbers 87 and 89, the inside walls having been knocked down to make one large shop. It was in number 87, after the factory closure in 1935, that William Larcombe carried on a business selling and repairing porcelain. This remaining three storey building, along with the now demolished buildings A2 and A3 that were originally behind it, accounted for a working area of about 2183 square feet, the frontage onto King Street being only 18 feet. In a recently taken photograph (Fig.2) the dark brickwork above the left hand door denotes the right hand boundary of number 85. The signs reading "Old Crown Derby China Works" on the front and side of this building are still just discernible on close inspection when on the site.

Remains of the factory, facing onto King Street, 1995.
Private collection.

Fig. 2.

From an earlier work carried out by Hilda Moore [4] and from information gleaned by Anneke Bambery [5] and the author from the memories of a few living people who worked at, or visited the factory, it is believed that these block A buildings contained a small shop, fronting onto the road, with quality control inspection carried out at the rear. The upper floors contained the burnishing department, an area devoted to the riveting of china brought in for repair, a stock room for wares in the white, and accommodation for the manager on the top floor.

BLOCK B – Two kilns can be seen on the map in this area and these correspond with the two painted in Edwin Mosley's watercolour (Fig.3), [5] which shows part of the site. He would have had his back towards King Street and the factory on his right hand side when he painted this circa 1895. It is thought that the repairer's shop, where the separately moulded component parts of figures were joined together, was also housed in this area, which was of about 1030 square feet.

Part of the factory. From a watercolour by W. E. Mosley, c.1895.
Derby Museums and Art Gallery.

Fig. 3.

A small photograph – of too poor quality to reproduce – of the bottle kiln being demolished was published in 1935 [6] and below it the following caption, which calls for comment:

"**OLD CROWN DERBY OVEN**. A photograph showing the dismantling of the Old Crown Derby Oven (the bottle kiln) and marking the passing of the Old Crown Derby China Works, in King Street Derby, which started in 1750, and are now but a memory. The oven was erected in 1845."

For anyone unaware of the history of porcelain manufacture in Derby, it is a pity that the Nottingham Road factory gets no mention. This is perhaps understandable as the King Street factory used notepaper which stated "Established 1750." I was interested in the last sentence, as I have found no evidence that the site was used for porcelain manufacture prior to 1849 and I feel that the date of 1845 given for the erection of the oven is conjectural.

BLOCK C - This area, being at the farthest end and to the right hand side of the cobbled roadway leading in from the street, covered approximately 2085 square feet. It is shown on the map as two buildings with an archway between them. These two buildings, one of three storeys (C1), with an outside stairway, which can be seen on both the map and in Mosley's watercolour and the other of two storeys (C2), are remembered as the place where the Duesbury wheel was housed somewhere on the ground floor. Modelling and decorating was also carried out in this part of the factory, the latter in one large room on the first floor of the three-storey building.

During the eighty-five year life of the works a number of changes to the buildings were made. These variations and the approximate dates upon which they took place, are listed below. The infrequency of printing new maps prevents any closer dating of these alterations:

Between 1852 and 1883 – Construction of A3 +170 square feet.
Between 1852 and 1883 – Construction of C2 +948 square feet.
Between 1883 and 1900 – Demolition of A3 -170 square feet.
Between 1915 and 1935 – Construction of D +1568 square feet.

Of the above, the only building not shown on the 1883 map is D, which I have outlined with a broken black line. After 1919 Ordnance Survey was required to economise and from that date until 1938 no maps of the King Street area of Derby, which were of a scale sufficiently large to show individual buildings, were issued, so it is difficult to be precise about the date of the addition of this two-storey building. It had not been erected by 1914, but a photograph of some of the staff taken in the early 1930's shows them standing in front of it. It seems likely that it was constructed shortly after Larcombe and Paget had purchased the freehold in 1920 and it produced an additional working area of approximately 1568 square feet. I have not been able to establish what operations were carried out in this building during the last few years of the factory's existence. It is possible, perhaps, that some of the work performed in the older buildings may have been transferred to the more modern building.

I always find it difficult to visualize an area quoted in square feet unless I can equate it to something that I carry a picture of in my mind – such as a tennis court. In this case the total working space of 6696 square feet, when the factory was at its largest in its later years, is equivalent to little more than the area of two tennis courts. This confirms the generally held view that the operation carried out at King Street was on quite a small scale. This was borne out in a recent chat with Gwen Goodwin, who worked as the only burnisher just prior to the factory closure. She remembers working on her own in an upstairs room just behind the sales shop and that this was small and poky, being about the size of a small bedroom, which it probably had been at one time.

The reports of the number of workers employed vary. Haslem [7] wrote:"Including the six original partners there were at one time little short of twenty hands employed in different departments, all of whom if not brought up at the old factory, had formerly worked there. A less number of hands is at the present time engaged." - this being around 1876. Brayshaw Gilhespy[8] wrote that: "The numbers employed were never very large, about thirty to fifty at the most…"

John Twitchett[9] has recently revised downwards his original estimate of thirty-five as being the maximum number of hands employed and considers that this may well not have exceeded twenty at any one time.......

Whichever figure is taken, it is small compared with the full number reported to have worked at Nottingham Road [10] and as many as 400 at one time in the past at the present Royal Crown Derby factory in Osmaston Road.

Notes and References for these findings.
1. Surveyed by the Board of Ordnance. Facsimile held in the Records Office of Derbyshire County Council, Matlock.

2. I am grateful to Mr. Nelms of the Derbyshire County Council, Matlock, for making these papers available to me and for guiding me through them.

3. Maps reproduced by kind permission of Ordnance Survey, Southampton and copied with the help of the staff of the Local Studies Library, Derby.

4. Moore, Hilda. Articles in DPIS Newsletter, April 1987 and Antique Collecting, the journal of the Antique Collectors' Club, August 1983.

5. Anneke Bambery, The Senior Keeper of Fine Arts and Education, the Museum and Art Gallery, Derby, kindly made available to me notes of interviews carried out by her when preparing for the 1993 King Street exhibition and also several photographic slides.

6. Derby Advertiser, 28 June, 1935. Copy in Local Studies Library, Derby.

7. Haslem, John, *The Old Derby China Factory*, G. Bell & Sons, 1876, p.238.

8. Gilhespy, Brayshaw, *Royal Crown Derby China*, Charles Skilton, 1964, p.28.

9. Twitchett, John & Bailey, Betty, *Royal Crown Derby*, Antique Collectors' Club, 1988, p.13.

10. Haslem, John, *The Old Derby China Factory*, G. Bell & Sons, 1876, p.34.

Note: In the above references D. P. I. S. stands for Derby Porcelain International Society.

Early in 2002 the Derby Archaeological Society, whilst searching for the deeds of other buildings in the vicinity of the King Street factory, came across a set of plans submitted to the County Borough of Derby Sanitary Authority for an extension to the china factory.

These plans, one of which is shown below, are for the building D referred to in the above article. The plan shows that an old building was demolished in 1920, so the construction of the new building will have followed this and we know that it was completed by the early 1930s, as a group of workers was then photographed in front of it.

The plan shown is particularly useful in that it shows the operations planned to be carried out on both floors of the new building and for the first time shows three kilns, rather than the two depicted in Mosley's earlier watercolour of around 1895. The Saggars House was for kiln furniture and the Dipping House would have been used for the application of glaze.

As visitors were welcome at the factory, perhaps the Parlour was used as a reception room? On the first floor the Japanning room, next door to the Painting room would have been used by painters working on the Japanese style Imari decoration.

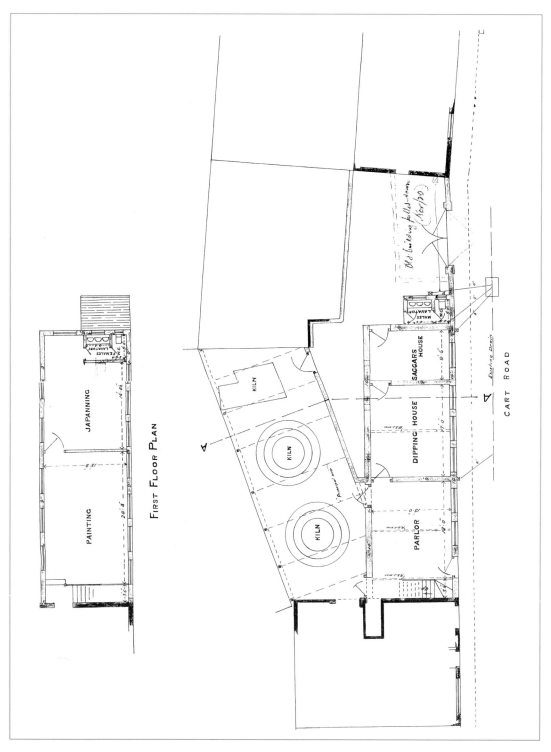

Plan of factory extension, c.1920.
Derby Archaeological Society.

34

RENT AND RATES

A study of the relevant Rates Books for the last half of the nineteenth century for the Parish of Saint Alkmund's has been made and details from the entries concerning the china manufactory are presented in the following chart:

Year	Gross Estimated Rental	Occupier	Owner
1850	£33	Mr. Locker	Mr. Sparkes
1860	£33	Samuel Sharp, Samuel Fearn & others	Mr. Sparkes
1865	£33	Stevenson & others	Mr. Sparkes & Joshua Heath/Hall
1870	£35	Sampson Hancock	Mr. Sparkes
1875	£40	Sampson Hancock	Mr. Sherwin
1880	£40	Sampson Hancock	Owner of the property left blank
1885	£40	Sampson Hancock	Mrs. Hobbs
1890	£35	Sampson Hancock	W. B. Sherwin
1895	£35	Sampson Hancock	W. B. Sherwin

There are several receipts concerned with the payment of rent by the King Street factory amongst the Royal Crown Derby Archives, an example of which, dated April 1872 is reproduced below:

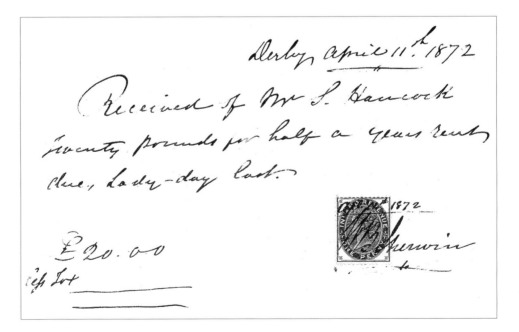

Receipt for payment of factory rent, 1872.
Royal Crown Derby Museum Archives.

FOUNDER PARTNERS, ALSO PROPRIETORS

The initial six partners were as follows:

Samuel Fearn	-	Potter
John Henson	-	Potter
Sampson Hancock	-	Decorator
James Hill	-	Decorator
William Locker	-	Warehouseman and clerk
Samuel Sharp	-	Potter

START-UP MONEY

A notebook, brought with him from Nottingham Road by William Locker, the first proprietor at King Street, contains the following record of the amount of money each of the founder partners put into the business.

	£		£
Fearn	10	Henson	8
Hancock	10	Hill	4
Locker	10	Sharp	2

The remainder of Locker's notebook contains mainly notes relating to the Nottingham Road works, covering recipes for gold, enamel colours and china body. Interestingly it also contains several remedies for illnesses (5).

Of the six founder partners, Fearn, Henson and Hill remained as workers. Locker, followed by Sharp and then Hancock headed up the firm. Sharp and Hancock were joined by George Stevenson, a draper, who was not a founder partner. John James Robinson, a grandson of Hancock, William Larcombe and Howard Paget also held managerial positions from 1895 onwards. Notes on all of the above follow, those on Sampson Hancock being more detailed, reflecting the important role that he and his family played in the world of ceramics.

WORKERS

Samuel Fearn
(Potter and China Manufacturer)

A founder partner of the King Street China Works, Samuel Fearn was born in Etwall, Derbyshire. The son of Charles and Ann Fearn, he was baptised there on 18 September 1808. On 25 October 1829 he married Elizabeth Band at All Saints Church, Derby.

Little is known of Samuel Fearn, except that he was apprenticed at Nottingham Road as a potter, where two more members of the Fearn family were employed. John Fearn, Samuel's older brother, was also baptised at Etwall on 10 May 1807, and his name appears in the marriage register of Saint Werburgh's Parish Church, Derby, on 7 April 1828, when he married Eliza Tomlinson. His occupation was given as "China Painter". A Robert Fearn, also a "China Painter", appears in the 1842 Glover's *Directory for Derby*.

Samuel Fearn is included in the 1832 list of employees then working at Nottingham Road. In the 1841 Census he is recorded as living in Green Street, Derby. He is aged 30, and his occupation is given as "potter, (born in Derbyshire)". He lived at that address with his wife

Elizah, an embroiderer, and their three sons, Robert, Edwin and Charles.

In the 1851 Census, his address is given as 22 Gisborne Street, Derby. He was living at this address with his wife Elizabeth, and sons, Robert Fearn, aged 21, painter, and Edwin, aged 19, apprentice painter. Whilst Robert probably worked at the King Street factory, son Edwin (1832-1901) is known to have worked there. The factory presented Edwin and his wife Sarah Ann Cooper with a tea service on the occasion of their marriage on 9 January 1881. A similar presentation was made to a member of the Hancock family (Harry Sampson Hancock's younger brother James) who married in 1899.

In Freebody's 1852 *Directory for Derby*, Samuel Fearn is listed as a china manufacturer, residing at 22 Gisborne Street. His occupation is again confirmed in the 1857 White's *Directory for Derby* as a china manufacturer, still residing at the same address.

John Henson
(Potter)

Born in 1823 in Derby, he was one of the last apprentice potters at Nottingham Road. He married twice, his first wife Ann being born in Dublin in 1823. Recorded as a labourer in the 1851 Census for Derby, John Henson and his wife Sarah, together with their one-year-old daughter Mary Ann, were lodging with brothers John and Joseph Eley at 48 Mundy Street.

John Henson and his wife, together with their one son and three daughters are recorded as living in Brick Street in the 1861 Census. By the time of the 1871 Census he was still residing at the same address, but with his second wife Mary, who had been born in Derby in 1838.

A founder partner at King Street, he died in 1873.

James Hill
(Decorator)

James Hill was born in 1791 and baptized on 2 March of that year at All Saints Parish Church in Derby, the son of Joseph Hill and Elizabeth Allin. The Parish Register for All Saints Church, Derby, records Joseph Hill, his father, as a "chinaman of this Parish" at the time of his marriage to Elizabeth Allin.

James Hill was apprenticed at Nottingham Road, to flower painting and gilding. Haslem tells us that Hill was wont to say that he "considered himself a gilder, and not a flower painter". Haslem was critical of Hill's flower painting and described it as "more conventional than natural". On the positive side Haslem states that Hill "was much respected for his inoffensive character and his quiet and amiable disposition" (6).

He married Mary Swindall on 22 February 1814 at All Saints Church, Derby. His name appears on the 1832 Nottingham Road List of Workers which records him as a flower painter. The 1840 Rates Books record James Hill owning and occupying a house in Parker Street. Probably related to John Hill, a china modeller who entered an exhibit in the Derby Mechanic's Institute Exhibition, in 1839, James Hill was known to model small animals with a penknife, and these he also exhibited. In Glover's *Directory for Derby* dated 1842 James Hill was residing at 26 Parker Street, and in the 1843 Directory he is recorded as a "China Painter, F. Fr." Glover's *Directory for Derby*, dated 1850 (taken 1849), gives his whereabouts as living in Parker Street, and he is recorded as a "china painter, F. Fr." These two abbreviations, F. Fr. are for Freeman and Freeholder, both Freemen and Freeholders were entitled to vote, a Freeman having rights and privileges within the town, and a Freeholder owning land or property.

The 1851 Census records that he was living at 43 Parker Street, Derby with his wife Mary. She was a silk winder aged 58 and he was a china painter aged 60.

Whilst working at the Nottingham Road factory the number 21 was attributed to James Hill by John Haslem.

Hill was a founder partner at King Street, where he worked for a short time. He died at his home in Parker Street on Tuesday, 15 April 1854.

An obituary notice published in the *Derby Reporter* on 20 April 1854, contained the following sentence:

"He was a meek and quiet spirit and was Deacon of the Baptist Meeting Chapel in St. Mary's Gate."

A further obituary notice which appeared on 3 May of that year in the *Derby Mercury* reads as follows:

"On Tuesday week, in Parker Street, Mr. Jas. Hill, in the 64th year of his age; an artist of considerable ability. The numerous specimens of flower painting produced by him at the china works in the town are characterized by an almost inimitable delicacy and beauty."

A different opinion of his work than that given by Haslem.

An illustration of his work can be found in Chapter Two.

PROPRIETORS

William Locker
(former chief clerk and warehouseman at Nottingham Road)

William Locker was baptized on 23 July 1797, at Blackfordby, Leics., the son of Samuel Locker. He began work at Nottingham Road in 1809 and the 1832 list of factory workers records him as one of two clerks. He rose to become chief clerk and warehouseman to Thomas Clarke.

He married Sarah Moorcroft by licence on 25 November 1826 at All Saints, Derby. The 1840 Rates Books record him as living at 26 Exeter Street, in a house owned by George Flood. The 1842 Glover's *Directory for Derby* records him as a "warehouse manager Fr.", residing at 26 Exeter Street. An entry in the *Derby Mercury* for 25 July 1849, suggests he married for a second time. It records William Locker, china manufacturer, married Miss E. Moorcroft of Derby, on 21 July 1849.

The circumstances leading up to the closure and sale of the Nottingham Road works quite clearly upset Locker and this is demonstrated in the following extract from a letter that he wrote to Haslem:

"I dare say that there are a number of things that I might think of, relating to the old works, if I could enter into that subject with good humour, but that I can never do as long as I live. Whenever I think of that place (which I was at forty years) I become sour and almost furious." (7).

William Locker became the first proprietor at King Street and used the mark, "Locker & Co. Late Bloor".

In the 1851 Census, William Locker is shown as living at 26 King Street, Derby, with his wife Elizabeth, daughters Sarah, Mary Jane, Charlotte, Selina and Emma, and son William, who was born in 1841. The address given suggests that as well as working there, perhaps he and his family were occupying the manager's accommodation at the works?

William Locker died on 10 January 1859 aged 62.

According to notes made by Fred Williamson, a former curator at Derby Museum and Art Gallery in the 1920s, the death of Locker apparently took some of the capital out of the business and his place as senior partner was taken by George Stevenson (8).

Following his death his surviving partners placed the following advertisement in the *Derby Mercury* on 26 January 1859.

CHINA WORKS, KING STREET, DERBY.

The surviving partners of the late William Locker beg to thank the Nobility, Gentry and Public for their support of the Firm hitherto, and hope by strict attention to business and the Manufacture of an Article of the best quality, to merit continued patronage.
Old Derby China can only be matched in shape and pattern at this Manufactory.
Outstanding Debts and Claims against the Firm to be sent to the Works.

George Stevenson
(former draper)

Although not absolutely certain, it is believed very likely that the George Stevenson concerned with the King Street factory was the person of the same name who was baptised at All Saints Church, on 29 November 1799, the son of George and Ann Stevenson.

George Stevenson, who was not a founder partner, entered the firm following Locker's death in 1859. He joined Samuel Sharp, one of the founder partners, and from c.1859 the firm traded as Stevenson, Sharp & Co. An explanation for Stevenson joining the business could be that he replaced the administrative skills of Locker. An advertisement placed in the *Derby and Chesterfield Reporter* in February 1825 recorded George Stevenson as a draper. Another advertisement which appeared in the *Derby Mercury* recorded his whereabouts as 68 St. Peter's Street, Derby, in 1849, and confirmed his occupation as being that of a draper.

From 1861 until 1866 he was the partner of Sampson Hancock, one of the founder partners, and the company traded as Stevenson & Hancock.

A copy of his Last Will and Testament reveals that his estate was realised at "under £600". He left everything to his wife and upon her death the residue was to be divided between his son, daughter and son-in-law. His will, dated 22 October 1866, signed one week prior to his death, desired that his share in the capital income and profits of the business of Derby China Manufactory be ascertained and realised as speedily as possible and he wished the sum realised from the china works together with £94.14/- due to him from Samuel Bolsover of Derby, be invested and the interest from the investment be paid to his wife.

The executors of his will were George Wilson Stevenson, his son, who was a Civil Engineer, of Westminster, and his son-in-law, Joseph Ward of 2 Gower Street, Derby. His will was proven on 18 November 1867.

Samuel Sharp
(Potter)

Samuel Sharp was born in 1821 in Derby, and was baptised at Saint Alkmund's Church on 20 April, the same year. The son of Richard Sharp and Hannah Bourn he was apprenticed at Nottingham Road as a potter.

In the 1851 Census for the Parish of Saint Alkmund's, Derby, he is recorded as living at 15 Gisborne Street. He was shown as being head of the household and has two occupations, being both a "Grocer and China Potter", aged 30. With him are his wife Eliza, aged 30, daughter Eliza aged 3, and son Thomas, aged 6 months.

His name appears in Freebody's *Directory for Derby* for the year 1852, when he was described as a "*China Manufacturer*" residing at 15 Gisborne Street.

The exact date of his departure from King Street is uncertain, but the date 1861 seems likely (9). A notice which appeared in the *Derby Mercury*, for 8 October 1862, sought claims against the estate of one Samuel Sharp, of Parker Street, shopkeeper, and it is thought this may well be the same Samuel Sharp who was involved with King Street.

He was a founder partner at King Street and in 1859 joined George Stevenson as co-proprietor and they styled themselves:

"Stevenson Sharp & Co. King Street, Derby".

Sampson Hancock
(Decorator)

Sampson Hancock, late nineteenth century. Private Collection.

Son of James Hancock and Margaret Beet, Sampson Hancock was born on 7 April 1817, in Worcester, and was baptized there on 4 May 1817, at Saint Swithin's Church. He was a grandson of John Hancock (1757-1847) whose apprenticeship deed records he had been apprenticed at the Nottingham Road factory to William Duesbury I on 29 September 1769 to *"learn the art of painting upon China or Porcelain or China Ware"*.

Sampson's father James, a china painter, had married Margaret Beet at Saint John the Baptist Church at Claines, on the outskirts of Worcester on 21 November 1814.

It has not been possible to establish where Sampson Hancock served his apprenticeship, except to say it was not at Derby. In all probability he may well have trained and worked at the Chamberlain's factory in Worcester, where his father was employed. One of the recipe books belonging to his father records that he (James) "entered Mr. Chamberlain's hous (sic) in 1825".

Sampson Hancock married Elizabeth Jefford in Burton upon Trent, Staffs., a town where his uncle George Hancock had been employed by Mr. Clarke at his china factory, on 29 January 1839. In the Marriage Register, Sampson's address was given as High Street, Burton upon Trent, which suggests he may have been employed in the town at that time. Both his own and his father's occupation were recorded as "Painter".

On 13 May, 1839, Sampson loaned a case of butterflies and insects caught near Derby, to the Derby Mechanics Institute for an exhibition held on that date, which suggests he was in Derby at that time. By the time of the birth of his first son John, on 25 July 1839, Sampson was living in Liversage Street, Derby. His occupation is recorded as a "China Painter" on John's birth certificate, which confirms he was working at the Nottingham Road factory.

Perhaps due to lack of work at the Nottingham Road factory, by the time of the 1841 Census which was taken in April, he is to be found in Staffordshire, living at Plot 62, Etruria, a house occupied by his grandfather John Hancock (1757-1847) and his second wife Ann Shenton and family. Whilst his grandfather worked as head of the enamelling department at the Wedgwood factory, Sampson is believed to have been employed at Spode. In an interview given in the *Yorkshire Weekly Post*, in 1894, he recalled that John Mountford "came" to work for Messrs. Copeland and Garrett, which implies that it was here where he was employed.

Sampson and Elizabeth's second child Fanny was baptised at Burton upon Trent in October 1841, suggesting that the family was still in Staffordshire some six months after the Census. Fanny married George Jabez Robinson in 1862, and it was their son John James Robinson who inherited the china works from Sampson in 1895.

By 1844, Sampson and family had returned to work at Derby. The couple's third child, William Henry, was baptised at Saint Alkmund's, Derby in March of that year, his burial, some six months later is also recorded. On both entries, Sampson's occupation is given as "china painter" residing in Erasmus Street.

In 1846 their fourth child Eliza was born. She married William Storer at Saint Alkmund's church on 1 July 1866. In the Parish Register her father Sampson's occupation is described as "China Manufacturer". Eliza died in 1891 prior to her parents, which explains why her children are referred to in Sampson's Will.

Some time around 1850 the family moved from Erasmus Street to 55 Nottingham Road. Rates Books for the Parish of Saint Alkmund's record the property as a house and shop. Slater and Freebody's *Directories for Derby* record Sampson Hancock as a "shopkeeper" living in Nottingham Road. However, in Glover's *Trade Directory* compiled in 1849 and published in 1850, he appears as a "grocer" living in Erasmus Street. This suggests he may also have kept a shop here, but a search of all the relevant Rates Books failed to reveal its whereabouts, although there is the possibility the shop referred to may have meant the family used the front room of the property to sell provisions. Confirmation of his two occupations is given in the 1851 Census where he is listed as both a "China Painter and Provisioner".

By 1858 he was the occupant of the New Britannia Inn on River Street. The 1861 Census records him living at 4 River Street, and his occupation is given as china painter. Drake's *Directory for Derby* for 1862 lists him as both "Victualler and China Manufacturer". When Sampson became landlord of the New Britannia Inn in 1858, Mrs. Bloor was the owner of the property, to whom he paid an annual estimated rental of £30, just £3 less than the rent paid for the Old Crown Derby China Works on King Street.

In the King Street archives are seven receipts covering interest paid twice yearly by Sampson to his brother-in- law Henry Jefford, of Burton upon Trent. An explanation for Sampson needing to borrow money may well lie in the fact that, as shown earlier in this chapter, George Stevenson's money was taken out of the business following his death.

On the death of Stevenson in 1866, Sampson was no longer in a partnership, but sole proprietor and perhaps without Stevenson's capital in the business, may well have found himself short of money.

The receipts show interest of £40 per annum being paid for the years 1870 and 1871, reducing to £20 in 1872. The only receipt to show a capital sum is dated 26 March 1875, when £370 is still owing.

By 1870, the family moved yet again, this time to Bridge Gate, to part of a large house known as St. Anne's, which Hancock rented from the executors of Mr. Wallis. The 1871 Census records Hancock as a China Manufacturer as does that for 1881. By 1890 Sampson had purchased the entire building, a thirteen bay former town house which had belonged to Lord Curzon of Kedleston Hall, fifth son of Lord Scarsdale. Its purchase suggests that the factory on King Street was flourishing at this time.

It has been recorded that:

> "Old Sampson Hancock lived at no. 18 Bridge Gate, the end house of a block of three storey houses opposite the C. Convent and the nearest house to St. Alkmund's Church. He kept cows on the fields between King Street and the River Derwent, and was very fond of these animals. He was also very fond of his beer which he took regularly in the Seven Stars and not too wisely. I am given to understand that he was given too much to drink one night and the right to use the old Derby trade marks and designation was obtained for the Osmaston Road factory from him" (10).

Note: The authors believe the address of 18 Bridge Gate to be inaccurate. Rates Books for the parish of St. Alkmund show Sampson Hancock as owner and occupier of 12 Bridge Gate, as do the memorial cards for both Sampson and his wife Elizabeth.

Sampson's wife Elizabeth died on 5 January 1892, and shortly after this date in July, Sampson had his Last Will and Testament drawn up. Referring to himself as "China Manufacturer of the Borough of Derby", two potters employed at the Old Crown Derby China Works witnessed the document, John Marshall of Saint Alkmund's Churchyard, and Henry Ellis of Queen Street. In 1893 a codicil was added and witnessed by Henry Jefford (Hancock's brother in law) and Benjamin Fearn. The china works were bequeathed to John James Robinson.

Never before suffering poor health, Sampson was ill for some six weeks prior to his death. He died on Friday, 15 November 1895. His funeral service was conducted at Saint Alkmund's

Parish Church on Monday, 18 November, following which he was interred at Plot 11731, at Nottingham Road cemetery, Derby.

The memorial cards for both Sampson and Elizabeth have been carefully preserved by a branch of the Hancock family for more than 100 years, and with their kind permission are reproduced here.

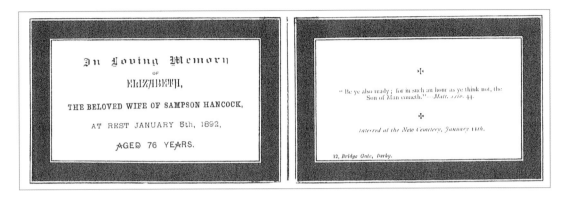

Sampson Hancock's Memorial Cards.
Private Collection.

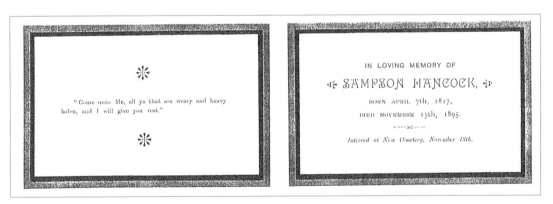

The following obituary notice appeared in the *Derby Biographer* dated 15 December 1895.

"DEATH OF MR. SAMPSON HANCOCK. – The funeral

took place on Friday morning of Mr. Sampson Hancock, the well-known potter, King Street. Mr. Hancock had been ailing for six weeks, suffering from heart problems complicated by dropsy and asthma, and it is a very worthy fact that up to the time he took to his bed he had never been laid up by illness for a single day of his life. He was attended up to his death by Dr. Copestake, and passed peacefully away. Although a member of a well-known Derby family, Mr. Hancock was born at Worcester in 1817, and had subsequently attained his 79th year. His grandfather John Hancock, better known as "The father of potters," was one of the first apprentices of William Duesbury more than 150 years ago,

43

and he attained the patriarchal age of 90. The family thus have an hereditary connection with the manufacture of porcelain, and the tradition was worthily maintained by Mr. Sampson Hancock. When Robert Bloor gave up the Nottingham Road Factory in 1848, Mr. Hancock in conjunction with a dozen fellow workmen, set up in business on their own account. It was a daring speculation, especially as at that time the taste for Derby china had undergone a slight depreciation in popular esteem. In Mr. Hancock – who by the way, was the last survivor of the little "syndicate" that started King Street works belongs the credit of having maintained unbroken the continuity of Crown Derby china manufacture and painting. He lived to see Crown Derby regain all its lost prestige and popularity, and to witness without pang the re-establishment of the Royal Crown Derby Porcelain Works on a modern basis on the Osmaston Road. The rivalry of this more ambitious concern did not drive the old gentleman out of the field, and he retained to the end many faithful aristocratic patrons. He employed from time to time some of the best modern china painters and some of his production in the Japanese are marvels of beauty and colours. They consist of the deep mazarin blue, red, green and gold, which have made Derby china familiar and famous all the world over."

A sale of his china collection from both his house and factory shop, together with a collection on loan to the Art Gallery, took place at The Mart on Monday, 23 December 1895. The cover of the sale brochure shown below, gives an indication of the collection formed by Hancock, in all 161 lots, some of which contained more than one item.

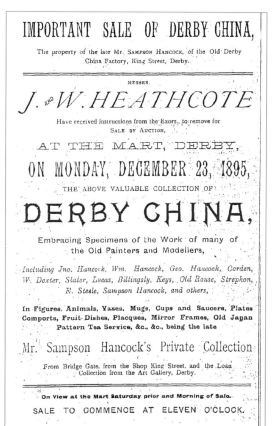

Notice of Sale of Sampson Hancock's china, 1895. Derby Museums and Art Gallery.

Probate of Sampson Hancock's will, with one codicil, was granted to John James Robinson and Edwin Haslam on 16 April 1896.

Illustrations of his work can be found in Chapter Two.

John James Robinson
(Potter)

John James Robinson was a grandson of Sampson Hancock.

Born in 1862 Robinson was trained as a potter at King Street, and inherited the china works from his grandfather following Hancock's death in 1895.

His mother Fanny, Sampson's eldest daughter, had married George Jabez Robinson, a miller, on 23 July 1862 at Saint Alkmund's Church, Derby. She died some time between 1862 and 1 November 1868, when his father George was married for a second time to Phoebe Ellen Roe. The couple had three children by the time of the next Census in 1871.

In the 1871 Census for the Parish of Saint Alkmund's, Derby, John James Robinson then aged 9, is to be found living with his grandparents Sampson Hancock and his wife Elizabeth at 3 Bridge Gate. In this Census his name is entered as "Jno. Jnr. Hancock (grandson)", perhaps suggesting that Sampson Hancock did not approve of his son-in-law George's second marriage. John's occupation at the early age of 9 was given as "potter". It appears he remained with his grandparents and was still living with them at the same address in Bridge Gate at the time of both the 1881 and 1891 Censuses. His occupation now had risen from "potter" to being an "ornamental potter".

When Sampson's wife Elizabeth died in January 1892, John James Robinson's name appears in the ledgers of the Nottingham Road Cemetery, Derby, as having purchased Plot 11731, a grave for two, at a cost of £1. 9/-6d. a few days prior to his grandmother's funeral. His address is given as being 12 Bridge Gate, the same address as his grandfather.

In July 1892 Sampson Hancock, describing himself *as "China Manufacturer of the Borough of Derby"*, bequeathed to John James Robinson in his Last Will and Testament his business, which included all the plant, tools and machinery, together with stock in made and patterns and other effects belonging to the same. However his stock of best finished china and book debts were to be divided equally between his son John Hancock for his own use, and the other half to be kept in trust by J. J. Robinson and Edwin Haslam (brass founder) for Sampson's Storer grandchildren. Some 18 months later a codicil was added to this Last Will and Testament in which John James Robinson was given the option to take the stock of best finished china, at a valuation to be made by two valuers appointed by himself and Edwin Haslam, the proceeds of which were to be divided between John Hancock and the Storer grandchildren.

A scrapbook belonging to Alice Amy Robinson, John James Robinson's daughter, which is now in private ownership, contains the following news clipping. It appeared in the Evening Standard and was dated April 1915:

OLD CROWN DERBY.
FAMOUS PORCELAIN BUSINESS TO BE SOLD.
"Evening Standard" Special.

The business of the Old Crown Derby China Works is stated to be for sale, owing to the death of the late proprietor, Mr. J. J. Robinson.

For 165 years the manufacture of Derby porcelain has been continued since the establishment of the industry by a Mr. Duesbury. The manufacture of small china objects, and two or three patterns of tea and dessert ware was specialised in by the firm. These were excellent of their kind, and were usually finished in the Japan red, blue, and gold, and finished with a touch of green.

The founder of the business was succeeded by his son, and in 1811 the firm was acquired by Mr. Robert Bloor. In 1848 the business, which, at that time, had been considerably extended, was disposed of, and the stock, patterns and everything moveable were taken over by a Staffordshire firm, and the original premises were demolished.

Firm Reconstructed.

Shortly afterwards, a man named Locker and two or three of Bloor's former workmen decided to re-start the business under the name of the Old Derby China Works. A small factory was secured, and an oven was set up, the manufacture of the original porcelain being proceeded with until about 1868, when the title "Old Crown Derby" was adopted. In due time the concern passed into the hands of Mr. S. Hancock, and then to his grandson, Mr. Robinson, who died a few weeks ago.

In the above article which appeared in a London newspaper, the reconstructed firm referred to was King Street, and as shown below William Larcombe was the next proprietor following Robinson's death.

William G.Larcombe

William Larcombe, lecturing in Derby, 1925.
Private Collection.

Larcombe was a Derby man born in 1872. He had run a business repairing china on Osmaston Road which was called the "China Hospital"(11). He is listed in both the 1903 and 1912 editions of Kelly's *Directory of Derbyshire*, as a "china riveter", living at 37 Green Lane, Derby.

In the later 1930s William Larcombe wrote several pages of notes, in which he recalls the setting up of the King Street factory and his time spent there, firstly as sole proprietor, and then jointly with Howard Paget. These notes are now in the possession of descendants of Larcombe's family, who have kindly agreed for them to be transcribed here:

> Now let us come to 1848 the year the factory now grown to a large establishment was closed down. Robert Bloor had died and his granddaughter was his heir and her husband having found everything in a bad way decided to sell everything (Mr. Clarke, Maltster) some of the old workmen seeing their livelihood disappearing formed a company and purchased as much as they could afford and having taken premises on King Street removed such plant and stock and moulds to these premises and continued the manufacture of china and it is due to these men that Derby can boast an unbroken record of china making to the present day.

Sharp, Henson	Hancock	Locker
Potters	Decorator	business

> These men also employed some others of their fellow work mates. Prince, Rouse, John Hancock Hopkinson, Winfield, Dudson (Pearson)
>   Flowerer
> Of these James Rouse came into some prominence for his beautiful flower painting and Sampson Hancock because he was the last survivor of the four partners mentioned and he I can remember very well, he died in 1896. He left the factory to his daughter who in turn left it to her son James Robinson who died in 1915 and it was in May of that year that I became possessed of it. I was always interested in it and spent many hours about the place. I have always from my school days worked among china and found it a continual occupation as I took over the lease which was extended to 7 years by the owner Miss Sherwin and an option to purchase was also inserted within the 7 years but at that time there was the Great War going on and as I expected to be called up I made an arrangement with a friend Mr. Paget who was a china collector and interested in the old factory and he took over a third share and became my partner in January 1917 he had been in the army and suffered from shell shock and was unfit for service again. In the autumn of 1917, I was called up but was pronounced as medically unfit for foreign service which was a disappointment and so had to be content on Home defence duty which was extremely boring.
> When the war finished we began pulling down dilapidated buildings and put up large light and airy workshops we exercised the option and purchased the premises, and had great hopes of the future.
> For 9 years we had our own showroom in the West end shopping centre of London and our American business increased but our rent was doubled and rates increased in proportion and in 1926 the coal strike made production impossible our china was spoiled by sulphur in such coal as we could purchase and the loss in wages and material was ruinous. Then came the great slump in America and our bank balance became an

overdraft, which worried me. Meanwhile my partner purchased a Brickyard in the South of England and it prospered exceedingly. It took all his time and attention and he went to live in London and kept in touch with our London showroom, eventually I asked him if he would release me of my liabilities and would give him my share in the china works and in 1933 he became the sole owner but in 1935 he sold everything to the Royal Works and so ended the King Street factory it is now dismantled kilns and ovens etc. demolished and used today for other purposes and the business and all materials belong to the Royal Crown Derby Porcelain Co. but there is a little shop next door where you can buy the old Derby designs and which you will not see elsewhere for they are specially done for me.

Note: The authors consider the statement concerning the china works being inherited by Sampson Hancock's daughter to be inaccurate. As can be seen from the entry concerning John James Robinson, Hancock's daughter Fanny had died prior to her father, which resulted in the china works being passed to John James Robinson.

Further thoughts, concerning the financial state of the business in the later years, are recorded in the following unsigned notes, dated 1964:

"Adjoining these premises was a small shop hat(sic) 87 King St. which belonged to Mr. Larcombe who dealt in antiques and old china, of which latter he had a most noteable collection. It appears that Larcombe was more interested in china collecting than in manufacturing, in that he attended sales all over the country buying for himself and on behalf of other collectors. Larcombe's co-partner Capt. Paget was for many years financing the factory from his brick business to the tune of £20-30 per week and ultimately London auditors were commissioned to look into the financial affairs of the company, when it was found that Larcombe's interest in the company had disappeared in the debt due to Howard Paget" (12).

Certain other information concerning Larcombe, which is not included in his notes, is worthy of mention. To finance the purchase of the lease of King Street, he borrowed £750 from William Henry Richardson, a Derby businessman. Richardson's ledger, recording the loan, survives in private ownership. A letter written by Larcombe to Richardson on 31 July 1915 explains that after being in possession a clear month, he had already fired "2 blue ovens" and one enamel kiln, although he had trouble with a second enamel kiln to which he had given too much fire, and that establishes that he was in possession of the factory by June 1915 (13).

Hilda Moore recalls that Larcombe's daughter Mrs. Hopkins, told her that her father "just loved beautiful china" and that he had a good collection, most of which had been dispersed over the years (14). The Accessions Register of the Derby Museums and Art Gallery shows that on 6 October 1935, W. Larcombe of Ferriby Brook, presented to the Museum an eighteenth century Derby porcelain biscuit group of "Nymphs awakening Cupid".

After leaving the factory early in 1933, he continued with his interest in china and in the later 1930s ran a business from the building next door to the factory, at No. 87 King Street. The following printed heading appears on a letter dated 26 March 1936 that he wrote to Alfred Goodey and it gives a clear picture of the business that he operated after leaving the King Street works. Alfred Goodey was a collector and antiquarian.

W. LARCOMBE, ANTIQUE AND MODERN CHINA ... REPAIRS A SPECIALITY.

RELIABLE WORK DONE ON THE PREMISES BY OUR OWN EXPERIENCED ASSIS-
TANTS, NO AGENTS ... EXCLUSIVE DESIGNS IN TEA AND COFFEE SETS, PRESEN-
TATION PIECES, WEDDING GIFTS ... Lectures upon – EARLY ENGLISH POTTERY.
OLD CROWN DERBY CHINA, EARLY ENGLISH PORCELAINE (sic). MANY INTER-
ESTING PERIOD EXHIBITS ... ANTIQUES AND REPAIRS ... Free Information and
Advice upon – ANTIQUE POTTERY, CHINA, GLASS, SILVER ETC. ... RARE AND FINE
PIECES PURCHASED."
This letter is held at The Derby Museum and Art Gallery.

William Larcombe died on 17 March 1940. John Twitchett records that he died on his way
to church at Breadsall on Palm Sunday, 1940, aged 68 (15). Descendants of the family suggest, if not Breadsall, it may have been Morley Church.

Francis Howard Paget

Howard Paget was born in 1886, his parents living at Elford Hall, near Tamworth (16). He
purchased the Dorking Brick Company and was a benefactor to the Middlesex Hospital,
donating his firm's bricks for the building of an extension. In 1917 he was taken into partnership at King Street by Larcombe. A shop that he owned in London was used as a showroom for the china factory (17).

By early 1933 Paget was in sole control and it was said of him,
" *as a connoisseur of Derby china, uses his collection as a guide and inspiration to the
present-day artists*" (18). A few years before the closure of the works, which is dealt with a
little later, Paget appointed Werner as Manager (19).

Because of his commitment to his Brick Company, he is said to have only visited the china
works once every week.

Following the sale of the factory to the present Royal Crown Derby Porcelain Company, in
Osmaston Road in 1935, Paget made two presentations to The British Museum in 1936,
including some fine examples of early Derby biscuit porcelain. He also bequeathed further
items on his death in 1945 (20).

THE NEW CHINA FACTORY

News of the advent of a new china factory in Derby appeared in the *Derby Reporter* in 1875:

A NEW CHINA FACTORY FOR DERBY.
We understand that a new China Manufactory is about to be erected in Derby. The leading
promoter of the enterprise is, we believe, a gentleman who was until lately one of the
managing directors and one of the largest shareholders in the Worcester Royal Porcelain
Company, and we hear that a company is to be formed to carry on the undertaking. A
piece of land in Litchurch, just beyond the Workhouse, has been purchased, and a forty-
horse power engine is being made by one of our local engineers for the new works. Many
people in Derby have lamented the close of the celebrated Derby China Factory, and the
dispersion of the workmen, moulds &c., in 1848 and will hope that the new enterprise
will rival the success which the energy and ability of the first Duesburys secured for the
manufacture of China in the later part of the last and beginning of the present century.

This announcement makes no mention of the King Street factory. Sampson Hancock, proud of "his" works, wrote a letter in reply, which is reproduced below. In this he politely reminds the Editor and the readers of his paper, of the role played by King Street in the manufacture of china in Derby and again stresses this point of continuity of production in the town.

THE DERBY CHINA MANUFACTURE.
TO THE EDITOR OF THE DERBY REPORTER.

Sir, - In briefly announcing the starting of a new China Factory in Derby in last week's issue, you mention the dispersion of the workmen, moulds, &c., of the old Derby China Factory, and lament that such a state of things did come to pass. Now anyone having the welfare of Derby at heart would naturally regret the collapse of any branch of industry that tends to be the commercial prosperity of the town; however, in this case, a slight misunderstanding has arisen, in this wise, that although the old premises and materials were disposed of, six of the workmen, including myself, formed a combination to carry on the old Derby China Works and trade in another part of the town with the same artistic, if not so extensive a success, is proof of which many of the Articles made previous to 1848, by the old firm have been sent to me to match, including three separate commands from the Queen, besides many of the most eminent collectors and admirers of antique china. As my grandfather served his time with the old firm, and I still carry on the business, it leads me in common fairness to regard our place as the old Derby China Factory because operations were never suspended.

I am yours respectfully,

SAMPSON HANCOCK.
King Street, Derby, Sept. 23, 1875.

As Hugh Gibson suggests, in his book *A Case of Fine China*, in this letter of Sampson's there is no hint of antagonism shown towards the setting up of a new china factory in Derby (21).

However, by mid-1894 his views would appear to have hardened a little. When interviewed for an article to be printed in the *Yorkshire Weekly Post*, he was asked the question, "*I expect that you have suffered a good deal from counterfeit ware masquerading as your own?*" Sampson replied, "*Yes, we have been and still are the victims of unprincipled makers.*"(22) Was he referring to the Royal Crown Derby factory, as it was turning out some of the same wares as his own works? It seems unlikely that he was thinking of fake marks, as so few of these have come to light.

The new factory on Osmaston Road, which started production in 1877, was to become the present day Royal Crown Derby Porcelain Company Limited.

FAILED TAKE OVER

Very little has been recorded about an attempted take over of the King Street works which took place in 1916. This was mounted by Royal Crown Derby, but failed (23).

KING STREET CLOSURE

After eighty-six years of manufacturing on the King Street site, recession in the china trade led Howard Paget to sell the concern to its larger rival, the Royal Crown Derby Porcelain Company, in 1935. The works were closed and with this came the end of the factory that had provided the link between Nottingham Road and Royal Crown Derby.

The price paid for King Street was £4,000, an approximate breakdown of this figure being (24):

Stock	£1280
Property	£1500
Bad Debts	£ 70
Trademarks & goodwill	£1280

Just prior to the closure, Sampson Hancock's grandson, Harry Sampson Hancock, wrote in the *Derbyshire Evening Times* on 21 February 1934, an article titled:

180 YEARS' TRADITION OF	AN INDUSTRY
DERBY CHINA	THAT HAS
"PRIDE AND ENVY OF	HELPED TO MAKE THE TOWN FAMOUS
THE CONNOISSEUR."	

Two paragraphs in this article sum up how Harry, as an artist working there, viewed King Street at that time:

> The works are still carried on under the tradition that has kept the name of Old Crown Derby China in the foremost places of the world for the last 180 years.
> The personnel of the works is changed as little as possible, and several of the hands have spent the whole of their lives in the making and decorating of the china which has been the pride and envy of the connoisseur for more than one and a half centuries.
> The wheel of William Duesbury still works to-day, and the hands of time have done little to mar or detract from the beauty of the old vase or cup that was thrown by the soft hands of the skilled craftsman on the potter's wheel. New processes have come to light, but the discerning eye still detects that smooth rhythm of shape that can only be contained from the apt hands of the potter.

These are surely words of which his grandfather Sampson would have approved. The final sentence of Harry's article reads:

> "The works are now being operated to their full capacity."

This statement, if accurate, does not reflect signs of the recession that was to play a part in the sale of the works in the following year.

AFTER CLOSURE

The lease of the buildings fronting King Street and those in the yard were purchased by Arthur Fox. He sold furniture, carpets and bedding and used the premises as a workshop and warehouse until 1954 when he sold the business as a going concern. Apart from the building facing the road, the rest were demolished in the early 1980s (25).

In 2001 it was rumoured that the site was to be redeveloped. This will be closely monitored.

THE PLAQUE

The brass plaque shown below was mounted on the outside wall, facing King Street. Having either fallen down, or been vandalised, it is no longer in position acting as a reminder to passers-by of the existence in the past of the Crown Derby China Factory. It was returned to the present Royal Crown Derby Company in 1997, and is now in their safe keeping.

Plaque on outside wall of the factory.
Royal Crown Derby Museum.

1. REFERENCES

(1) Bradbury, E., "The Story of Old Crown Derby China,"
reprinted from the *Yorkshire Weekly Post*, 12 May, 1894. Published by High Peak News, Buxton, 1894, p.10

(2) Wharf, F. & C., & Blackwood, R., "Across the Divide: From Nottingham Road to King Street." *Derby Porcelain International Society(DPIS) Newsletter*, June 1994.

(3) Haslem, J., *The Old Crown Derby China Factory*. G. Bell, 1876, p.30

(4) Williamson, F., of the Derby City Museum. An article, "Derby China - King Street Factory," published in *The Derbyshire Advertiser*, 13 February 1925. Ref. BA 738.2 (46159) Derby Local Studies Library.

(5) Commonplace and memorandum book of William Locker, c.1808-49. British Museum, Dept. of Medieval and Later Antiquities, Additional MS. 54574.

(6) Haslem, Op. Cit., pp. 124-5

(7) Haslem, Op. Cit., pp.166-8

(8) Williamson, Op. Cit.

(9) Bambery, A., & Blackwood, R., *The Factory at King Street, 1849-1935*. Derby Museums and Art Gallery, p.16

(10 & 12) An extract from ten pages of handwritten notes, dated May 1964, and now in a private collection. The source of these notes is not known, but both the owner and the authors consider that they were written by someone closely connected with the King Street factory – possibly a worker who had been employed there, and as such should be recorded.

(11) Bradley, H. G., "King Street Factory," *DPIS Newsletter*, May 1990

(13) Bambery & Blackwood Op. Cit., p.4

(14) Moore, Hilda M., "Porcelain Manufacture in King Street, Derby" an article in *Antique Collecting Magazine*, September 1983, published by the Antique Collectors' Club. Hilda Moore was an enthusiast of ceramics and in particular the King Street factory. In 1985, she wrote that she considered herself *"a Stalwart supporter and champion of the King Street factory."* She died in 1987.

(15) Twitchett, J., & Bailey, B., *Royal Crown Derby*. Antique Collectors' Club, 1988, p.231

(16) Twitchett. J., *DPIS Newsletter*. June, 1986, p.13

(17) Bradley, Op. Cit.

(18) King Street factory sales catalogue 1934-35, p.6

(19) Bradley, Op. Cit., p.48

(20) Dawson, A., "The F. Howard Paget Collection in the British Museum," *DPIS Newsletter*, January 1988.

(21) Gibson, H., *A Case of Fine China*. The Royal Crown Derby Porcelain Company Limited, 1993, p.38

(22) Bradbury, Op. Cit., p.15

(23) Twitchett & Bailey, Op. Cit., p.13

(24) Twitchett. Op. Cit., p.XVI

(25) Bambery, A., handwritten notes.

2. ARTISTS, MODELLERS AND OTHER MEMBERS OF THE WORK FORCE

Although a relatively small concern, the King Street factory appears to have had a very loyal work force. Many people employed there either worked at the Nottingham Road factory prior to its closure, or were descendants of former employees.

The output from this small factory stands as a tribute to the skills possessed by the employees. The modelling equalled some of the best pieces produced at Nottingham Road. The decorating, which showed all the accomplishment of the earlier factory, affirms the skills of the painters who at one time produced replacement pieces for dessert services used by the Royal Family. Unlike some other manufacturers, transfers were never used at King Street, all the enamelling being done freehand.

In 1881 Sampson Hancock recorded that he employed nine hands at King Street(1) . Haslem stated that the number was somewhat higher prior to 1876, and judging by the number of people employed at the china works for whom there are some form of records in existence such as census returns, parish registers and local directories, Haslem appears to have been correct. Arnold Machin recalled in an interview (2) that no more than thirty people were employed at the factory during the early part of the 1930s.

Perhaps the numbers dwindled following the founding of the present Royal Crown Derby Company in 1877, suggesting that some of the work force may have left to work for the new company, as was the case with James Rouse who left King Street in 1882.

There are no details of King Street employees in the surviving archives which are in the care of the present Royal Crown Derby Porcelain Company. The only book which gives any list of work force is Brock's Notebook which details personnel who worked for the present company in Osmaston Road, and which dates from the late nineteenth century.

Although not certain, it is believed that any artists, modellers and other members of the work force whose names appear in the 1851, 1861, and 1871 Census Returns for Derby, and whose occupations were connected with the china industry, were probably employed at King Street. This is especially so if the people concerned lived in either Saint Alkmund's or Saint Werburgh's Parish, both of which were situated close to the King Street factory.

It should be noted that in 1852 Freebody's *Directory for Derby*, a firm named John Lovegrove and Sons, of 32 Traffic Street, Derby, was listed as "China Manufacturer". Nothing is known about its size or what it produced, but it could have employed some local people.

Where proof has been found for any member of the work force, it has been included in the entry for each particular person; where there is none, but it is believed the person worked there, that too is recorded in the hope that it may help future researchers in their endeavours.

Opposite page top: A photograph, of the King Street workforce taken in the 1880s. Sampson Hancock is fifth from the left. Fourth from the left is John James Robinson, and sixth from the left is Harry Sampson Hancock.
Hancock family photograph album.

Opposite page bottom: A photograph of the King Street workforce, taken in the 1890s. From the left are: John Marshall, Harry Sampson Hancock, Sampson Hancock, John James Robinson, Edward Swainson. The other four persons are unknown.
Twitchett & Bailey, "Royal Crown Derby."

A small notebook which exists in the King Street Archives provides details of some of the prices paid to the artists for their finished work. Where legible, this has been transcribed and is included at the end of this chapter.

Above: A photograph of the workforce taken in the twentieth century.
Front row: Gwen Goodwin.
Middle row: (from left to right) Mrs. Minor, Florrie Cook, Jack Ratcliffe, Archie Gregson, Winnie Sayers, and an unknown person.
Back Row: Bill Hargreaves.
In the background, to the right is Mr. Henshall.
Private Collection.

Left; A photograph of the workforce taken in the twenthieth century. It is believed Gwen Goodwin is on the left of the picture and Florrie Cook on the right.
Private Collection.

RICHARD ABLOTT
China painter possibly employed at King Street

Amongst the last batch of apprentices at the Nottingham Road China Works, Richard Ablott is said to have been taught landscape painting along with Edwin Prince (1).

There are differing opinions as to whether Richard Ablott went immediately to the King Street works on the closure of the Nottingham Road factory, or whether he went to Staffordshire. Haslem records that he went to the Potteries (2), where he was employed by different manufactories, before joining Coalport, finally working for Ridgways during the mid 1870s. However another authority (3) states that he worked at King Street, prior to going to Coalport and later to Davenports.

His name does not appear on the 1851 Census for the town of Derby, suggesting that he had left the area at this time.

Similar discrepancies occur regarding his place of birth and while the authors have made an extensive search, they have not been able to resolve this question.

Of Richard Ablott, Haslem says:

> "After leaving Derby, Ablott was employed by different manufacturers, chiefly in the Staffordshire Potteries, and for a time at Coalport: he is now working for Messrs. Davenport. In the Derby Exhibition of 1870, Mr. Carter of Derby shewed a dessert-service which was made at Coalport, and painted with views in Derbyshire by Ablott, and he has since had services, numerous plates, and other pieces painted with rich and highly finished landscapes by the same artist."

Loving Cup

Description: A two-handled loving cup painted with a view of Matlock Tor in Derbyshire in one panel. The reverse panel depicts flowers and foliage.

Painter: Attributed in Royal Crown Derby Museum records to Richard Ablott, but unsigned.

Marks: Inscribed "Matlock High Tor" on base. Deep puce coloured crown over crossed swords and D, with two sets of three dots and initials S and H.

Measurements: Height 14cm.

Date: Uncertain, but probably nineteenth century.

Location: Royal Crown Derby Museum.

Notes: 1. The use of the S and H mark in puce, prior to c.1915, has not been previously recorded.

2. Gilding very rubbed.

MARY ATHERSTONE
Paintress

Entry No. 34, for 24 Exeter Street, Derby, in the 1851 Census for the Parish of Saint Alkmund's, records Mary Atherstone as a "China Paintress", aged 34, sharing a house with Mary Smith who was head of the household. It is not known what type of decorating she was engaged in.

BADDELEY
Fireman

Baddeley is a surname associated with the Nottingham Road china works. According to Fred Williamson (1), Baddeley went to the King Street establishment on the closure of the Nottingham Road works.

The 1832 List of Workers gives details of other members of the Baddeley family who were involved with the china industry at Nottingham Road, Louisa Baddeley was a burnisher, and Jane Baddeley a paintress.

A china packer by the name of Edward Baddeley is listed in the 1881 Census returns for Derby. Born in Hanley, Staffordshire, he was living at 33 Litchurch Street. The birthplace of Edward's sons suggests he was living in Worcester until 1878, and it is thought he may have been employed by the Derby Crown Porcelain Company in Osmaston Road which was founded in 1877.

MARY BAGULEY
China painter

Not a great deal is known about Mary Baguley, however details in the 1851 Census for the Parish of Saint Alkmund's, show her to be a "china painter" living at 6 Mansfield Road. Born in Coalport in 1805, Mary was sharing a house with Catherine Hesketh, a "china burnisher", also employed at King Street, and Catherine's sister Esther, a framework knitter.

There is a Mary Baguley listed as a paintress on Haslem's 1832 Nottingham Road list and it is thought this may be the same person. If it is, she probably went to the King Street factory on the closure of Nottingham Road.

Also included on the 1832 list were two more members of the Baguley family, George and Thomas, who were both employed as biscuit kilnmen.

ANNIE BAILEY
China Painter

Annie Bailey worked at King Street in the early 1900s when John James Robinson was proprietor of the factory. She is believed to have been apprenticed to china painting at the factory in 1898 (1).

Born in Breadsall, the daughter of a farmer, she painted flowers, fruit and landscapes, these often being views of historic buildings. She also decorated menu holders.

It is recorded that her style of painting was similar to that of Billingsley, in the way that she used a preliminary wash of neutral colour in order to obtain the colour of her leaves (2).

Arnold Machin recalled that he worked with her during the 1930s and the interview in which he mentions her can be found in this chapter under the entry for Arnold Machin.

A versatile artist, it is not known how long she remained at the factory, but examples of her work are occasionally seen, often bearing her initials.

Group of Tygs

Description: A group of three cylindrical tygs, each with a footrim and loop handles. The exterior of two tygs decorated with a green ground, the third having a blue ground. All have two reserves decorated with bouquets of flowers in enamel colours and one having an inscription in gilt.

Painter: Blue ground tyg: Annie E. Bailey. Two green ground tygs: Unattributed.

Marks: All three tygs are marked with red crown over crossed swords and D, with two sets of three dots and initials S and H. Blue ground tyg: Inscription in gilt *"William Haslam Hussey July 13th 1909."* Signed A.E.B. on base.
One green ground tyg: Inscription in gilt *"Kathleen Mary Hussey June 18th 1904."*
Other green tyg: Inscription in gilt *"Bessie Lake Hussey May 29th 1906."*

Measurements: Height 7cm.

Date: Circa 1905-1909.

Location: Private collection.

Exhibition: On display in "The Factory at King Street, 1849-1935" Exhibition held in 1993 at the Museum and Art Gallery, Derby. Catalogue numbers 149, 150, 151.

Notes: These tygs form a group of three christening mugs. The three Hussey children, two girls and a boy, were born into a Mickleover family. In adult life, one sister died and the brother William shot the other sister dead and then used his gun to kill himself. This information was supplied by the owner.

61

Tyg

Description:	A cylindrical tyg with three angular handles. The rim, base and handles are embellished with gilding. The panels between the handles are decorated in enamel colours with three different paintings: a fruit still-life, a view of Haddon Hall and a flower group.
Painter:	Annie E. Bailey.
Marks:	*Signatures*: "A .E. B." in painting of Haddon Hall. "A. E. Bailey" in painting of flowers and "A. E. B". in painting of fruit. Also, "A. E. B." in puce inside footrim. *Inscription*: "Haddon Hall " in puce on base. Puce crown over crossed swords and D, with two sets of three dots and initials S and H. Also in puce the crossed Ps of proprietor Paget and his wife.
Measurements:	Height 7cm.
Date:	Circa 1933-1935.
Location:	Derby Museums and Art Gallery. No. 1936-632.
Provenance:	Miss A. E. Bailey, Brook Cottage, Breadsall.
Exhibition:	On display in "The Factory at King Street, 1849-1935" Exhibition held in 1993 at The Museum and Art Gallery, Derby. Catalogue number 202.

Menu holders.

Description:	A boxed set of two menu holders each in the shape of an oval ring with modelled flowers and butterflies applied to the top surface.
Painter:	The painter is possibly Annie Bailey. Although unsigned, she was in the habit of painting the two sets of three dots in a particular way.
Marks:	On both, red crown over crossed swords and D, with two sets of three dots and initials S and H.
Measurements:	Length 9cm. Width 5.5cm.
Date:	Twentieth century.
Location:	Private collection.
Notes:	Minor chips and firing cracks.

THOMAS BANKS
Outside Modeller

Amongst the King Street Archives are eight receipts covering the dates 1872-1873, not all of which are legible. Of those that are, all of which are addressed to Mr. Hancock, the details are as follows:

December 7/72.
1 Shell   £0-15.0d.

On a separate receipt of the same date:
1 dog 1 Group   £1.13.0d.

April 12/73.
For Models Bought April 12/73 (of which there are no details).
This bill was settled on the 5ᵗʰ June, 1873.

On a separate receipt of the same date.
1 Figure and Dish   £2. 0. 0.
1 Large Bird and Dish   £1.10.0d
1 do do do   £1. 3. 0d.
1 do do Shell.   <u>£1. 0. 0d</u>.
Received on account £2.0.0. £5. 13. 0d.

August 8/73.
1 Bird   £0.16.0d.

The only discernible information acquired from the remaining receipts is for the dates and amounts paid, and are as follows:

September 20/73   £2.19.0d.
December 6/73   £3. 2. 0d.
Undated   £1.10.0d.

JAMES BARNETT
Modeller

A rather elusive member of the King Street work force to trace, James Barnett is known to have been employed as a modeller at some time prior to 1876. He was one of the modellers responsible for decorating looking glasses with raised flowers (1).

After a thorough search of all relevant material, the authors are satisfied that the James Barnett who appears in the 1881 Census, living at 49 Trafalgar Street, Stoke upon Trent, Staffordshire, is the James Barnett who was employed at King Street during the 1870s. He was born in Coalport and, when aged 33, was living with his wife Sarah, aged 28, and family. The couple had four children, the eldest James Barnett, aged 7 and his brother Edward aged 3, were both born in Derby. The birth of the couple's two daughters took place in Hanley. In the 1881 Census James Barnett's occupation is recorded as a "Potter Parian flower maker". Amongst the Haslem collection, item number 119 was a pair of small bisque baskets which were catalogued as having "modelled flowers by James Barnet".

Barnett's work was also exhibited at the Midland Fine Arts and Industrial Exhibition, held in Derby in 1870.

ANN BEESON
China painter

Believed to have been employed at King Street (1) Ann Beeson was born in 1867 in Derby. Aged 14 in the 1881 Census, and recorded as a "china painter", she was living at 23 Darley Lane with her parents, John and Harriet Beeson. Her father's occupation was shown as a bricklayer. John Beeson had been baptised at Saint Alkmund's Church, Derby, on 7 April 1828 but a search of the same parish registers failed to locate Ann's baptism.

JOHN BOOTH
China painter

Baptised on 20 June 1822 at Saint Alkmund's, Derby, John Booth was the son of Robert Booth and Letitia Sadler, who had married at Quarndon, Derbyshire, on 1 October 1816.

Possibly employed at King Street at the time of the factory's founding, although the authors have found no proof of this, John Booth is known to have worked there during the years 1861 until some time after 1881.

Rates Books for the Parish of Saint Alkmund's record on 20 February 1840, "Widow" Booth and her family occupied a house owned by John Walton in Duke Street. Her son John, who was employed at King Street, was still occupying the same house some forty years later in the 1881 Census. Although the owners of the property changed following his mother's death, John Booth remained the occupier according to the Rates Books for the Parish. The last entry where his name appears is dated 30 April 1895.

The 1851 Census for the Parish of Saint Alkmund's, Derby, records John Booth and his wife Mary, both aged 26, together with their three children, living in Duke Street with his widowed mother, Letitia, who was head of the household. Also at the same address was his older brother William, a joiner. John's occupation is given as "Journeyman/painter", suggesting that while John may have been employed at King Street at that time, caution must be exercised.

By the time of the 1861 Census for the same parish, the family still occupied the same house, number 4, Duke Street, with John Booth now head of the household. His mother had died at some time between 1851 and this date, when the couple had a further son. His occupation was recorded as "China Painter", and his age was given as 38, a discrepancy of two years. It appears he was no longer a journeyman.

He and his family remained at the same address in both the 1871 and the 1881 Censuses.

Although the numbers of the houses had changed, entries in both the 1880 and 1885 Rates Books for Saint Alkmund's Parish confirm he was still living in Duke Street.

His elder brother Robert was a potter, employed at King Street.

ROBERT BOOTH jnr
Potter

Robert Booth was baptised on 4 May 1820, the son of Robert Booth, and Letitia Sadler, and was the older brother of the china painter John Booth. Robert's name appears in Freebody's

1852 *Directory for Derby* when he was shown to be living at 31 Bradshaw Street. His occupation is given as "Potter".

Hilda Moore records that a Robert Booth was an enamel fireman, however it is not known if this is the same person or whether it was Robert Booth senior (1).

In the 1881 Census, Robert Booth junior appears to have left Derby.

LEWIS BRADLEY
Moulder in China

Recorded as a "Moulder in China" in the 1851 Census Returns, Lewis Bradley was born in Burton upon Trent, Staffordshire in 1830. A search of the parish registers has been made but to date no baptism for him has been found either in Staffordshire or in Derby. Living with the Bennett family at 2 Duffield Road, he is recorded as being a widower, aged 31.

According to Haslem (1) Lewis Bradley was a clever modeller who had been employed during the later Bloor period at Nottingham Road, and it is thought this may well be one and the same person.

SAMUEL BRASSINGTON
Figure Modeller

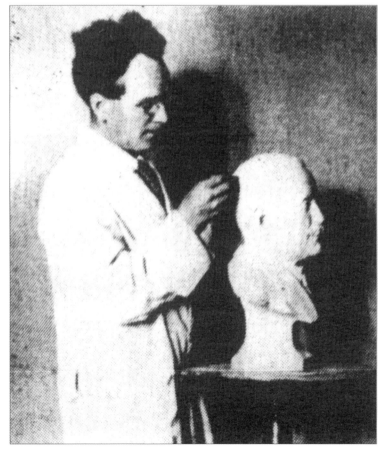

Samuel Brassington, modeller.
Private Collection.

Samuel's son Maurice Brassington wrote a brief history of his father's life story, which appeared in a Derby Porcelain International Society's Newsletter (1) and much of the information for Samuel Brassington has been taken from that source.

Born in Hulme, Manchester, on 4 June 1883 he began his career when aged thirteen with Parian makers Robinson & Leadbetter in 1896. There he was funded by Alderman Leadbeater to attend Stoke upon Trent School of Art, and later won several scholarships. Following the failure of the Robinson & Leadbeater concern, he worked as a caster at the Goss manufactory.

He married Elsie May Lawton in 1910 and the couple moved from Stoke upon Trent to Long Eaton where Samuel became an agent for the Prudential Assurance Company. Objecting to military service in 1916, he was imprisoned for a time, being released shortly before the end of the First World War, when he found employment as a watchman.

In 1919 he joined the Old Crown Derby China works as a figure modeller. He is well known for producing the bust of Edward Swainson, the modeller who worked at King Street from the early 1880s until his retirement in 1935.

In May 1921, when there was no coal available to fire the kiln owing to the miners' strike, Brassington left the china works and found employment with the Co-operative Insurance Company as an agent. He continued modelling for more than twenty years, having a studio at Derby School of Art until his retirement in May 1945.

He died on 6 February 1951.

JOSEPH BROUGHTON
Japan painter and Gilder

Joseph Broughton worked for the King Street factory from its inception, until a few days prior to his death in 1875.

Baptised 5 September 1804, at All Saints Church, Derby, he was the son of Thomas Broughton and Mary Jolly who had married at Saint Werburgh's Church, Derby on 27 December 1791.

He was apprenticed to gilding and painting at the Nottingham Road China factory in 1816, aged 11. According to Haslem his employment at Nottingham Road was broken by a few weeks when he was employed in the Staffordshire Potteries(1). On his return to Derby, he continued his employment at the Nottingham Road factory until its closure in 1848, a period of 32 years.

On 6 October 1829 he married Mary Cook at Saint Werburgh's, Derby.

In the 1840 Rates Books of 14 February, for the Saint Alkmund's Parish, he is recorded as living in a house in Nottingham Road which was owned by William Pool. The 1843 Glover's *Directory for Derby* also records him as living at the same address, his occupation being given as a "China Painter, and a Freeman".

Following the closure of the Nottingham Road works, Haslem (2) says of him:

"Afterwards and until within some ten days of his death, in July 1875, he was constantly employed at the small establishment in King Street.

Broughton remembered the numbers which most of the men who were employed at the factory in his time used in marking their work, as described elsewhere, and the writer is indebted to him for information on that and some other matters appertaining to the old works."

The 1851 Census records his address as 11 Nottingham Road, where he lived with his wife Mary, aged 40, who was also described as a china painter, and their seven children, Mary, Ann, Elizabeth, Joseph, William, Andrew, and Martha. In Freebody's *Directory for Derby*, published in 1852 he is recorded as a "china painter" living at 85 Nuns Street. Another source (3) recorded that he was:

> "constantly employed at Mr. Hancock's small establishment in King Street in this town, making altogether 60 years of working life. Employed constantly at King Street until within 10 days before his death he died in July, 1875."

A press cutting found in a file which belonged to Fred Williamson, a former curator of Derby City Museum and Art Gallery, and which has no source details, together with a probably inaccurate date of 1877 appears below (3).

> "DEATH OF AN OLD CHINA FACTORY HAND – Joseph Broughton, another relic of the old Derby China Manufactory, died on the 13th inst., shortly before completing his 72nd year. In 1816, when but eleven years of age, he began to work, and in due course served an apprenticeship to gilding and painting. With the exception of a short interval of two or three weeks; during which he worked in the Staffordshire potteries, he continued his employment at the Old Derby Factory until its close in 1848, a period of thirty-two years. Since that time he was constantly employed at Mr. Hancock's small establishment in King Street, in this town, making altogether little short of sixty years of a working life. Although of late he was a considerable sufferer he may be said to have died in harness as until within ten days of death he continued to work."

Whilst employed at the Nottingham Road factory Joseph Broughton used mark number 16 on pieces decorated by him. (4).

MARY BROUGHTON
China paintress

Formerly Mary Cook prior to her marriage to Joseph Broughton, her birth is recorded as "About 1808" at Saint Werburgh's Church, Derby. Her name appears in the 1851 Census as a " china paintress", living with her husband Joseph at 11 Nottingham Road, Derby. (See the entry for Joseph Broughton).

FRANK BUCKNALL
China painter

Born in 1876 in Dresden, Staffs, his parents lived at 22 Oak Street, Litchurch, Derby, at the time of the 1881 Census, his father then being employed as a tin plate worker.

In later life Frank lived at New House, Breadsall. Dying when relatively young, he was buried in Breadsall following his death on 1 August 1915, aged 39.

He is believed to have worked at King Street at the same time as Annie Bailey, but later went to the Osmaston Road factory where he was in charge of the pattern books from 1900-1914(1). He is also recorded by Hilda Moore as being employed at King Street(2).

ETHEL BURNS

It is recorded that Ethel Burns was employed at the King Street factory but nothing else is known about her time at the factory (1).

JAMES BUXTON
Possible China painter

Living at 15 King Street, in the 1881 Census with his widowed mother was James Buxton, son of Thomas Buxton and Sophia Heath, his parents having married at Duffield, Derby, on 31 July 1839. Described on the census as a "painter" it is thought possible he may have worked at King Street, being a cousin of Sampson Hancock's daughter-in-law Alice Buxton of Allestree. James had been baptised at Saint Edmund's Church, Allestree on 22 December 1839.

JOHN BUXTON
China painter

John Buxton worked at both Nottingham Road and King Street.

Baptised at St. Edmund's Church, Allestree, Derbyshire, on 3 January 1813, John was the first son, but second child of John Buxton and Ellen Hickling, who had married at Saint Michael's Church, Derby on 6 June 1810.

John Buxton's name appears on the 1832 Nottingham Road List, where he is recorded as a gilder.

Although no occupation for John is shown in the Parish Registers of Saint Alkmund's Church, Derby, at the time of his marriage to Ann Dallison on 26 December 1835, he is recorded as a "china painter" when the couple's son John's baptism took place at the same church on 26 May 1846, the family was living in Kedleston Street.

On 23 December 1871 his son Richard married Elizabeth Robinson. Living in Quorn Street, John's occupation is shown in the Parish Register for Saint Alkmund's as being a "china painter".

It appears that he transferred to King Street following the closure of the Nottingham Road factory, and remained there until his death, which occurred some time after 1871. He does not appear in the 1881 Census for the town of Derby.

HILDA CASTLEDINE
Paintress

At an exhibition of King Street wares held in Derby at the City Museum in October 1993, Hilda Castledine recalled that she had painted some of the exhibits and had signed some with an H, which she pointed out to members of the Derby Porcelain International Society who had attended the exhibition(1).

Believed to have been born some time around 1910, Hilda Castledine was employed as a paintress to decorate Imari wares, joining the works when she was aged 14, in 1924. She remained with the company until some time around 1935. She was recorded by Hilda Moore as a new worker who was employed with Ethel Burns in 1918-1919 (2).

FREDERICK CHIVERS
China painter

Born in 1881, he began his career at Worcester, from where he went to Coalport. He remained at Coalport from 1906-1926. His employment with Coalport was broken for a time when he was engaged in military service during the First World War, after which he returned to Coalport where he continued his career. The Coalport factory was taken over by Cauldon Potteries in 1924, and in 1926 they transferred manufacture to Staffordshire, which may have resulted in Chivers not transferring to the new company.

He was a well-known painter of fruit and his style of painting is easy to recognise. Although his impressionistic style of painting of certain subjects was somewhat unusual for King Street, he was employed at the factory between the years 1930-1935, and many signed pieces of his work exist. He is known to have painted flowers, fruit, butterflies and insects.

It is not known exactly what happened to Chivers following the closure of the King Street works in 1935. It is thought he may have left Derby and worked for a while for Paragon, possibly ending his career at Worcester, however John Twitchett records he worked as a shop cleaner in Derby and finished his life there, dying in 1965, aged 84 (1).

Plate

Description:	A dessert plate with gadroon rim and wide gilt border. The central panel is of fruit and foliage painted in enamel colours.
Painter:	F. H. Chivers.
Marks:	Signed "F. H. Chivers" near the border. Puce crown over crossed swords and D, with two sets of three dots and initials S and H.
Measurements:	Diameter 22cm.
Date:	1930-1935.
Location:	Royal Crown Derby Museum.

72

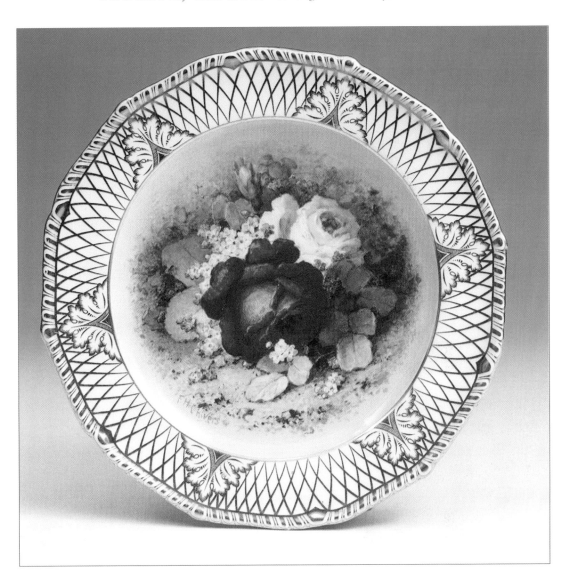

Plate

Description:	A dessert plate with gadroon rim, the border decorated with gilding. The centre panel of the plate decorated in enamel colours with a group of roses and forget-me-nots.
Painter:	F. H. Chivers.
Marks:	Signed "F. H. Chivers" in the painting. Puce crown over crossed swords and D, with two sets of three dots and initials S and H.
Measurements:	Diameter 22cm.
Date:	1930-1935
Location:	Private collection.

Coffee Can and Saucer

Description: Both can and saucer elaborately gilded. The can has a wishbone handle and two vignettes of flowers with a gilt outline.

Painter: F. H. Chivers.

Marks: Signed "F. H. Chivers" on both can and saucer. Puce crown over crossed swords and D, with two sets of three dots and initials S and H. Also in puce the crossed Ps mark of proprietor Paget and his wife.

Measurements: *Can:* Height 6cm.
Saucer: Diameter 14cm.

Date: Circa 1933-1935.

Location: In the collection of Dr. J. R. Freeman.

GEORGE COLLINSON
Potter possibly employed at King Street

The son of Thomas Collinson, George was recorded as a "Potter" at the time of his marriage to Mary Gillmore at Saint Alkmund's, Derby on 2 September 1860, when living in William Street, Derby.

FLORRIE COOK
Gilder

In an interview given at the time of the King Street Exhibition in 1993 at the Derby City Museum and Art Gallery, Florrie Cook recalled that she had been apprenticed at the Osmaston Road factory to learn gilding, having left school at the age of 14. As an apprentice she earned 6/3d. a week. Six months after commencing her apprenticeship she went onto piecework, decorating several different pieces, all of which fetched different prices. Whilst at the Royal Crown Derby Factory, she used gilder's number 4 which she applied in red enamel.

At the time of her apprenticeship she lived at Lock House, at Stenson Lock, and cycled to work daily, probably along the canal towpath.

Around 1934-1935 work at the Osmaston Road factory became scarce, which would have resulted in the lay off of some workers. King Street, however, had vacancies and Florrie joined their workforce when she was taken on as a gilder, working in the women's decorating room, alongside Annie E. Bailey, whom Florrie described as "a middle-aged, very nice, homely woman." She also recalled in the same interview: " the women's decorating shop was up some stairs on the first floor. The girls had to walk through the men's decorating room to get to their room."

Florrie only carried out the gilding on Imari patterns which varied at both the Derby factories.

Following the closure of the Old Crown Derby China Works, she returned to work at the Osmaston Road factory until April 1937 when she married Jack Ratcliffe, who had been employed as a painter at King Street.

JOSEPH COPE
China painter

Born in 1789, Joseph Cope is recorded in the 1871 Census as living in King Street, where his occupation is listed as that of a "china painter" (1).

MARY DAWES
China painter

Born in Derby in 1866 Mary Dawes was listed as a "China Painter" in the 1881 Census. Living with her parents Edward and Ruth at 28 Exeter Street, her father being a whitesmith, she was aged 15.

It has to be borne in mind that whilst Saint Alkmund's Parish was where the King Street factory was situated, there is the possibility that Mary may have worked at Osmaston Road, which was operating at this time, however the authors believe she worked at King Street.

According to Hilda Moore, Mary Dawes had been employed at King Street (1).

HENRY ELLIS snr
Moulder

According to Kelly's *Directory for Derby* for the year 1866, Henry Ellis was recorded as living at No.6, Court 2, Queen Street. His occupation was described as "China Moulder".

Head of the household in the 1871 Census for 6 Eagle & Child Lane, in the Parish of Saint Alkmund's, Henry Ellis was aged 61. The son of John and Lucy Ellis he was baptised in Rutland, on 27 April 1809. Henry's occupation is shown as Moulder and Pensioner, suggesting that he may have worked at King Street. Living with him are his wife Elizabeth, aged 56, born in Leicester, and sons James, a printer/compositor, and Henry, a "Potter in China". Both young men were aged 16. Also at the same address were two lodgers who were employed as framework knitters.

He died sometime between 1871 and 1881 when the later census shows his wife Elizabeth as being a widow

HENRY ELLIS jnr
China figure maker

Henry Ellis was born in 1855, the son of Henry Ellis snr and his wife Elizabeth. He and his older brother James were both baptised at Saint Alkmund's, Derby on 27 May 1855.

By the time of the 1871 Census, he is living with his father Henry Ellis at 6 Eagle & Child Lane, Derby, and his occupation is recorded as a "china potter". In the 1881 Census, under the name Harry Ellis, he is recorded as still living at the same address with his brother and widowed mother. However his occupation is now listed as a "china figure maker".

The 1891 census records him as a "China Potter", born in Derby. With him are his wife Alice and their daughter Martha, aged 8 months. Also at the same address is James Ellis, a printer, and Kezia Gregson, a general servant aged 15. The address is listed as a Greengrocer's Shop, suggesting that his wife may have managed the shop while he worked at King Street.

On 20 July 1892 when he witnessed the Last Will and Testament of Sampson Hancock, who had been sole proprietor at King Street for almost 30 years, Henry Ellis was described as a "Potter" living at 19 Queen Street, Derby.

BENJAMIN FEARN

Most probably a son of Samuel Fearn, although no baptism has been found for him, Benjamin was a witness on 6 October 1893 to a codicil which was added by Sampson Hancock to his Last Will and Testament. It is not known if he worked at King Street, or if so in what capacity. His name is included purely because of his association with Sampson Hancock.

There is recorded in the 1881 Census for Derby a Benjamin Fearn, living in North Street, Saint Alkmund's Parish, Derby, who was a watchmaker. A thorough search failed to reveal any other Benjamin Fearn who was involved with the china industry at this time.

EDWIN FEARN
China Painter

Son of founder partner Samuel Fearn and his wife Elizabeth Band, Edwin was baptised at Saint Werburgh's Church on 26 February 1832.

Probably apprenticed at King Street, he married Sarah Ann Cooper on 9 January 1881 his marriage certificate showing he was a "painter". On the occasion of their wedding they were presented with a tea service made at the King Street factory (1). The giving of a tea service to its employees appears to have been standard practice, a similar presentation being made to a member of the Hancock family as a wedding present.

In the 1851 Census for the Parish of Saint Alkmund's, Derby, Edwin was living with his parents at 22 Gisborne Street. He was aged 19 and was recorded as an "Apprentice Painter" (2).

There is no mention of an Edwin Fearn who was a china painter in the 1881 Census for Derby.

He died in 1901.

ROBERT FEARN
Possible China Painter

Aged 21 when the 1851 Census for Derby was taken, Robert was recorded as a "Painter", living with his father Samuel Fearn at 22 Gisborne Street. Born in Derby, there is the possibility that he worked at the King Street factory. His father was recorded as a "Porcelain Manufacturer" in the same census.

SAMUEL FEARN
Potter

A founder partner of the King Street factory, his details are dealt with under Proprietors in Chapter One.

BENJAMIN FORD
China maker

Baptised on 29 April 1799, at Saint Alkmund's, Derby, the son of James Ford and his wife Elizabeth, Benjamin Ford was employed at the King Street china works as a China Maker.

The 1871 Census for the Parish of Saint Alkmund's, Derby, records Benjamin Ford, 74, a china maker, living at 33 Mundy Lane, with his son James, a spar worker, and daughter Ann.

A spar worker was concerned with working with marble and fluorospar such as Blue John.

THOMAS A. GADSBY
China Painter

The son of Harriet Gadsby and stepson of her husband George Heaton, who was a monumental mason, Thomas was employed at King Street as a china painter. Born in Derby, in 1865, he was aged 16 in the 1881 Census for the Parish of Saint Werburgh's. Listed as a "China Painter" the family address was 41 Normanton Road.

The Gadsby family had connections with the earlier Nottingham Road factory where William Gadsby (1760-1845) had entered into an agreement with William Duesbury dated 2 September 1772, for four years as a modeller. He was recorded as being a modeller of flowers (1).

GWEN GOODWIN
Burnisher

Gwen Goodwin was a burnisher who had served a five year apprenticeship at Royal Crown Derby from 1927-1932. When interviewed, she explained that some time around 1932 she obtained a job at King Street as a burnisher. She recalled it was a much better job than the one she had at Osmaston Road because at King Street there was no piecework and no short time, as there had been at Royal Crown Derby. She worked on her own in a room on the second floor of the building fronting onto King Street(1).

A photograph taken in the 1930s showing Gwen Goodwin and some of her fellow workers at King Street appears at the beginning of this chapter.

ALBERT GREGORY
Possible China Painter

A fine flower painter, there is the possibility that Albert Gregory may have worked at King Street in the early 1930s. Arnold Machin, mentioned later in this chapter, recalled working with Gregory at King Street during the years 1930-1932 (1).

Gregory was apprenticed at Mintons at the end of the nineteenth century, and some Minton porcelain can be found bearing his script signature. On leaving Mintons, he was employed at the Derby factory in Osmaston Road, where Litherland recognised his talent and, prior to 1900, sent him to Art School. Known as the Gregory Rose, his paintings are regarded in much the same way as Billingsley's and Pegg's were at the earlier factory (2).

Having left his employment as a porcelain painter, he travelled to America, and although it is not known how long he remained there, he returned to Derby some years later.

It has been suggested that Albert Gregory may have worked as an outside decorator, painting blanks supplied by both Osmaston Road and King Street.

Although Albert Gregory belonged to a large family, he remained a bachelor, and towards the end of his life became something of a recluse (3).

GREGSON
Ovenman

No-one with this surname connected with the china industry was discovered in the 1851 Census for Derby.

Very little is known concerning the ovenman employed at King Street with the surname Gregson. However, the 1881 Census for Derby reveals persons with that surname who are believed to have been connected with the china trade who were employed by the present day company in Osmaston Road.

ARCHIE GREGSON
Possible Modeller

No details of Archie Gregson are known except that he may be a descendant of the ovenman employed by the factory with the same surname. Archie Gregson's name appears on a caption to a photograph taken of the workforce of the King Street factory in the 1930s, where he is described as belonging to the modelling room.

ENOCH GRIFFITHS
China potter

Born in 1842 in Newcastle under Lyme, Staffs, Enoch Griffiths appears as a lodger living in Bath Lane, Derby, in the 1871 Census, where his occupation is given as "China Potter".

His name does not appear in the 1881 Census for Derby, suggesting he had found employment elsewhere.

SARAH GUDLAD
Potter's daughter

Sarah Gudlad's name appears in the 1861 Census for Derby, where she is listed as a "Potter's daughter". Living with her uncle Johnathon Ward and his wife Mary, at 10 Mansfield Road, it is not known if Sarah or her father had any connections with King Street. A search of the relevant Census returns did not reveal her father's whereabouts.

ALBERT HADDOCK
Gilder

Albert Haddock, gilder, at work at Royal Crown Derby.
Twitchett & Bailey, "Royal Crown Derby."

Albert Haddock was born in 1888, and was the most important gilder employed at King Street.

It is recorded that he began his career in 1902 under the tuition of George Hemstock (1) whom the authors believe never worked at King Street but who was employed at the Osmaston Road factory. In 1912 Haddock began to work for Mintons. Following the First World War, he returned to Derby and found employment with King Street, where he remained until the factory's closure in 1935. Following the closure, he transferred to the Osmaston Road factory. Whilst there he is recorded as giving tuition to the male apprentices, John McLaughlin being apprenticed to him in 1957.

He is said to have completed unfinished decorated pieces, completing both painting and gilding for his own pleasure (2).

An obituary notice which appeared in the *Derby Evening Telegraph* on 9 June 1969 gives details of his career:

ALBERT HADDOCK.
Death of a fine old craftsman.

Mr. Albert Haddock of 123 Bower Street, Derby, former chief gilder at the Royal Crown Derby Factory Osmaston Road, died suddenly at his home aged 80.

Mr. Haddock was best known for his work on the Queen's Vase presented to her as a Coronation gift. He joined the company in 1902 at the age of 14 and went to the gilding shop where the chief gilder Hemstock carefully trained the young boy.

At 3s.6d. a week.

In those days apprentices earned 3s.6d. per week rising to 5s. in the second year.

Mr. Haddock progressed in remarkable fashion and gilded baskets of flowers decorated by Gregory and spent two years completing a service for Judge Parry.*

In 1912 Mr. Haddock was attracted by Mintons of Stoke on Trent, but joined the Army in 1914. After serving in the Cavalry and later in the 6th Battalion of the Warwickshires, he returned to the Derby factory.

Since that time until his retirement in 1967 Mr. Haddock decorated a fascinating variety of Derby china. The elaborate caskets which are presented to Freemen of Derby and plaques used for presentation by the Football Association and numerous commissions from governments and rulers throughout the world were among his much admired work.

He was particularly proud of the gilding he did on the Queen's vase. This wonderful piece was presented by the British Pottery Manufacturers Federation to the Queen as a Coronation gift. It was made by Royal Crown Derby and other members of the Fine China Association.

During his long and brilliant career Mr. Haddock always took an interest in the welfare of his fellow workers. Following the tradition of true craftsmen he passed on his skills and knowledge to the younger generation.

He leaves a widow who was once a "scrutineer" at the Derby factory and a son and a daughter.

* Note: The authors believe this refers to the Judge Garry Service.

Figure of Madame Vestris

Description: She wears a bodice and knee length skirt and stands on a circular base. Her right hand is clenched ready to take hold of a broom and her left arm is behind her back, with provision for a further broom. Decorated in enamel colours and gilding.

Painter/Gilder: Possibly Albert Haddock.

Marks: Red crown over crossed swords and D, with two sets of three dots and initials S and H. Also initialled "AH" in red.

Measurements: Height 15.5cm.

Date: Circa 1918-1935.

Location: Private collection.

Provenance: The Albert Haddock collection.

Notes: 1. This figure is believed to represent the actress Madame Vestris who, dressed as a Bavarian peasant, sang "Buy a Broom" on the London Stage in 1826.

2. As there is only little gilding on this figure, perhaps Albert Haddock, principally a gilder, also applied the enamel decoration.

81

MARY HANCOCK
China painter

Employed at King Street as a china painter, Mary Hancock is recorded in the 1861 Census as living in Mansfield Road, sharing a house with Catherine Hesketh, a china gilder employed at the factory. Born in Madeley, Shropshire, she was a widow aged 57.

Formerly Mary Ann Baguley, her marriage to George Hancock (the son of John Hancock 1777-1840), had taken place at Saint Alkmund's Church, Derby, on 11 March 1833. The marriage was witnessed by the groom's uncle George Hancock, who like his brother John had been employed as a china painter at the earlier Nottingham Road factory.

SAMPSON HANCOCK
China painter and Founder partner

One of the founder partners and sole proprietor for almost 30 years, his detailed history is dealt with in Chapter One.

Signed pieces by him are rarely found, but a plate decorated in Imari and bearing his signature is shown on p.84. In addition to his painting carried out on china, other examples of his work as an artist are also shown. Several members of the Hancock family have kindly agreed that those pieces by him may be reproduced, being family heirlooms, which have been passed down the generations.

Sampson Hancock, painter and founder partner.
Private Collection.

Framed Sketch

Description:	A pencil sketch of a child on the floor, distressed by spilt milk and four playful dogs.
Painter:	Unsigned and handed down in the Hancock family. Believed to have been drawn by Sampson Hancock.
Marks:	Unmarked.
Measurements:	Picture size: 24cm. x 17cm.
Date:	Nineteenth century.
Location:	Private collection.
Provenance:	Hancock family.
Notes:	On the original mount the wording "Mr. Hancock whill (sic) frame."

Plate

Description:	A plate with gadroon rim, the whole of the upper surface decorated in enamel colours in the "Old Japan" Imari pattern. On the reverse, two trailing stems of leaves painted in underglaze blue.
Painter:	Sampson Hancock.
Marks:	Signed in red on reverse: "S. Hancock". Red crown over crossed swords and D, with two sets of three dots and initials S and H.
Measurements:	Diameter 22cm.
Date:	Circa 1861-1895.
Location:	Royal Crown Derby Museum.
Literature:	Twitchett and Bailey, *Royal Crown Derby*, Antique Collectors' Club, 1988, p.23.
Exhibition:	On display in "The Factory at King Street, 1849-1935" Exhibition held in 1993 at The Museum and Art Gallery, Derby. Catalogue number 98.

Plaque

Description: A circular plaque, decorated in enamel colours with a summer
                        landscape. The view is believed to be of Fountains Abbey. In the
                        foreground are two figures.

Painter: Believed to be Sampson Hancock.

Marks: Unmarked.

Measurements: Diameter 16cm.

Date: Nineteenth century.

Location: Private collection.

Provenance: Hancock family.

Oil painting

Description:	A still life oil painting of various fruits, on a dark background.
Painter:	Believed to be Sampson Hancock.
Marks:	Unmarked.
Measurements:	39cm. x 28.5cm.
Date:	Nineteenth century.
Location:	Private collection.
Provenance:	Hancock family.

Oil Painting

Description:	A rectangular oil painting depicting fruit and flowers.
Painter:	Sampson Hancock.
Marks:	Signed "S. Hancock" in the bottom right of the picture.
Measurements:	34cm. x 22.5cm.
Date:	Nineteenth century.
Location:	Private collection.
Provenance:	Hancock family.

Watercolour

Description:	A watercolour on paper depicting garden flowers and leaves.
Painter:	Sampson Hancock.
Marks:	Signed in painting, "S. Hancock, Derby".
Measurements:	Within the oval mount: 17cm. x 12.25cm.
Date:	Later nineteenth century.
Location:	Private collection.
Notes:	A conservationist has treated the paper and removed the foxing.

Wooden Bowl

Description: An oval wooden bowl, the well painted in oils, depicting a house on an estuary in the foreground, and a windmill on the opposite bank.

Painter: Unsigned. This piece has been handed down in the Hancock family and is believed to have been painted by Sampson Hancock.

Measurements: Length 27.5cm.
Width 25.5cm.

Date: Nineteenth century.

Location: Private collection.

Provenance: Hancock family.

Comport

Description:	A comport, with scalloped rim and raised gilding, the centre well decorated in enamel colours with a specimen tulip, on a white ground.
Painter:	Believed to be Sampson Hancock.
Marks:	Unmarked.
Measurements:	Top diameter 25cm. Height 12cm.
Date:	Later nineteenth century.
Location:	Private collection.
Provenance:	Hancock family.

SAMPSON HENRY HANCOCK later to be known as
HARRY SAMPSON HANCOCK
China painter

The photograph, at the beginning of this chapter, taken during the 1880s by the factory gates shows Harry Sampson Hancock as a young man. He is third from the right, standing next to his grandfather Sampson Hancock, who is fifth from the left. On the other side of Sampson Hancock is John James Robinson, Harry's elder cousin.

Grandson of founder partner and proprietor Sampson Hancock, Harry Sampson Hancock was one of the foremost china painters at King Street. He painted flowers, landscapes and birds, examples of the latter being somewhat scarce. Pieces by him are highly sought after. He began and ended his career at the King Street factory, which spanned more than 40 years.

Born in September 1870, he was the first son of John Hancock and Alice Buxton of Allestree, and his birth is registered as Sampson Henry Hancock. In the 1871 Census he was living with his parents at 33a Bath Street, Derby, where he is recorded as Sampson H. Hancock, aged 7 months. His father John Hancock was a boiler maker who was employed on the ever-growing railways. A search of the relevant Rates Books for 1875 suggests the family had moved away from Derby by this date, to live at 8 Edward Street, Leicester, where they remained,

The birth of James Hancock in 1876, the great grandfather of one of the authors, confirms the family's whereabouts as being in Leicester, as does the 1881 Census, for the Parish of Saint Margaret's, in which Sampson Henry Hancock is to be found living with his parents and is recorded as being a "scholar". At some time after that date, and most likely prior to 1887, it is believed he moved to Derby. In that year he painted a porcelain plaque on which was written a dedication for his father's 48th birthday in July. Whilst the front of the plaque is signed S. H. Hancock, the reverse bears the initials HSH suggesting that perhaps in order to prevent confusion with his grandfather of the same name, Sampson Henry Hancock had changed the order of his Christian names and was now working at King Street.

It has been recorded that he lived with his grandparents Sampson and Elizabeth Hancock in Bridge Gate, Derby, along with his cousin John James Robinson. At no time whilst carrying out research into her family's history has Cherryl Head been able to find any material which substantiates this statement. Neither Hancock family hearsay confirms he resided with his grandparents, nor does the 1891 Census return for Bridge Gate, where Sampson Hancock lived with his wife Elizabeth and grandchildren Frances and Lucy Storer and John James Robinson.

Although a very elusive member of the workforce to trace, he was a very talented china painter who frequently signed his work. His signature, which is always neatly executed, is often found on the reverse of the piece. It is also thought he was an accomplished gilder. Believed to have been taught to paint by his grandfather Sampson Hancock, he became a very versatile artist. Landscapes by him are often copies of those produced at the earlier factory at Nottingham Road, and it is usual for the view to be identified by him on the reverse of the piece in script handwriting. His flower painting is very intricate and detailed, as are his bird studies.

A handwritten document dated 1964, which lacks any author, and which is in a private collection has the following entry:

"Harry Hancock was the last at Derby of a long line of ceramic artists of this name. His mark on china was two parallel marks on the back of the piece thus // and he was by the way an equally good a gilder as a painter. His painting is distinguished by its immense depth and brilliancy of colour, quite unlike any of the other artists. His fellow artists such as Annie Alice? Bailey were always trying to get him to teach them the secret of his brilliant colouring and he would never divulge his secrets, which were undoubtedly family secrets handed down from father to son and no doubt died with Harry Hancock" (1).

A page from Hilda Castledine's autograph album was painted in watercolour by HSH and depicted her initials in flowers. She recalled that when she was employed at King Street, Harry Sampson Hancock was a senior decorator.

He remained unmarried and died of stomach cancer in Derby Royal Infirmary in April 1934. Mrs. Eileen King, whose grandfather James was a younger brother of Harry, used to accompany her grandfather on his many trips to see his older brother whilst he was in Derby Royal Infirmary in 1934. She recalled that Harry used to moisten his paintbrushes with his tongue and it was thought this had caused Harry's illness.

His apprentice pieces are still treasured by members of the Hancock family and are included in this section so that the reader may see how with practice, his ability progressed and greatly improved over the years.

Plate

Description:	A plate painted in enamel colours, the outer rim decorated with garlands of roses. The centre panel has a collection of summer flowers on a marble plinth.
Painter:	Sampson Henry Hancock (later Harry Sampson Hancock).
Marks:	Signed S. H. Hancock on reverse. The plate bears no factory mark.
Measurements:	Diameter 20.5cm.
Date:	Later nineteenth century.
Location:	Private collection.
Provenance:	Hancock family.
Notes:	A pansy covers what appears to be a firing crack.

Bowl

Description:	A circular bowl, the rim decorated with a dark green line and a border of butterflies and flowers. Two lines of green encircle the centre well of the bowl which is painted in enamel colours with shells on a plinth.
Painter:	Sampson Henry Hancock (later Harry Sampson Hancock).
Marks:	Signed "S. H. Hancock" in the painting and on the reverse in the centre in script writing "S. H. Hancock". The bowl bears no S and H mark.
Measurements:	Diameter 21cm. Height 3cm.
Date:	Late nineteenth century.
Location:	Private collection.
Provenance:	Hancock family.

Circular Plaque

Description:	A circular plaque, painted in enamel colours with a variety of garden flowers and butterflies. A single border of puce enamel is applied to the rim.
Painter:	Sampson Henry Hancock (later Harry Sampson Hancock).
Marks:	Signed "S. H. Hancock" on the reverse. The initials S. H. H. appear in the bottom right hand corner amidst the flowers. Originally blue mark, but overpainted in red with crown over crossed swords and D, with two sets of three dots and initials S and H.
Measurements:	Diameter 19cm.
Date:	Late nineteenth century.
Location:	Private collection.
Provenance:	Hancock family.

Plaque

Description:　　　　A rectangular plaque, painted in enamel colours with a landscape view of what is believed to be Salisbury Cathedral.

Painter:　　　　Believed to be Sampson Henry Hancock
(later Harry Sampson Hancock).

Marks:　　　　Unmarked.

Measurements:　　　　20cm. x 15cm.

Date:　　　　Probably late nineteenth century.

Location:　　　　Private collection.

Provenance:　　　　Hancock family.

Notes:　　　　This piece is believed to be one of S. H .H.'s apprentice pieces.

Plaque

Description: A rectangular plaque, decorated in enamel colours. The centre painted with a winter landscape, encircled by summer flowers.

Painter: Sampson Henry Hancock (later Harry Sampson Hancock).

Marks: Signed in the painting " S. H. Hancock. 1887".
On the reverse the inscription:

"Presented by H. S. H. To his Father On his 48th Birthday 1887".

The plaque bears no factory mark.

Measurements without frame:
Height 23.5cm.
Width 15.5cm.

Date: 1887.

Location: Private collection.

Provenance: Hancock family.

Notes: 1. The plaque was given to James Hancock by his elder brother Harry Sampson Hancock, to be kept in trust for James' granddaughter Eileen Hancock, who received it from her grandfather in 1953. She in turn passed it on to her daughter Cherryl Head in 1997.

2. The frame was added in 1953 to protect the edges of the plaque.

Plate

Description:	A dessert plate with gadroon rim and green ground border with raised gilding. The central panel is painted in enamel colours with a bowl of garden flowers placed on a table.
Painter:	Harry Sampson Hancock.
Marks:	Signed "H. S. Hancock" on reverse in puce. Puce crown over crossed swords and D, with two sets of three dots and initials S and H.
Measurements:	Diameter 22cm.
Date:	Circa 1915-1934.
Location:	Royal Crown Derby Museum.

Plate

Description:	A dessert plate with wide gilt border. The centre panel painted in enamel colours with three passion flowers and leaves.
Painter:	Harry Sampson Hancock.
Marks:	Signed "H. S. Hancock" on reverse in puce. Puce crown over crossed swords and D, with two sets of three dots and initials S and H. Impressed "Derby" on reverse.
Measurements:	Diameter 21.5cm.
Date:	Circa 1915-1934.
Location:	Private collection.

Plate

Description: A dessert plate with gadroon rim and green border embellished with gilding. The centre panel is decorated with garden flowers in enamel colours.

Painter: Harry Sampson Hancock.

Marks: Signed in puce on reverse "H. S. Hancock". Puce crown over crossed swords and D, with two sets of three dots and initials S and H.

Measurements: Diameter 21.5cm.

Date: Circa 1915-1934.

Location: Private collection.

Provenance: Previously in the collection at Popplewick Hall.

Plate

Description: A dessert plate with gadroon rim. Within the wide gilt border are three cartouches painted with flowers. The central panel painted in enamel colours with a hollyhock, butterflies and a ladybird.

Painter: Harry Sampson Hancock.

Marks: Signed "H. S. Hancock" and inscribed "Hollyhock" in puce on the reverse. Puce crown over crossed swords and D, with two sets of three dots and initials S and H.

Measurements: Diameter 22cm.

Date: Circa 1915-1934.

Location: In the collection of Mr. G. Orme.

Bread and Butter Plate

Description: A bread and butter plate decorated with raised gilding and a
                  central spray of roses in enamel colours.

Painter: Harry Sampson Hancock.

Marks: Signed on the base in puce "H. S. Hancock". Puce crown over
                 crossed swords and D, with two sets of three dots and initials S
                 and H.

Measurements: 25.5cm. x 21.5cm.

Date: Circa 1915-1934.

Location: Derby Museums and Art Gallery.   No. 1971-424/1.

Plate

Description:	A cabinet plate with a green ground, three reserve panels around the border, and a central circular panel. The three border panels are painted in enamel colours with flower groups and the centre panel with a view of Derby. Raised gilding decorates the area around the panels.
Painter:	Harry Sampson Hancock.
Marks:	Signed in puce on reverse "H. S. Hancock". Inscription in puce on reverse "Derby from Burton Rd". Puce crown over crossed swords and D, with two sets of three dots and initials S and H.
Measurements:	Diameter 20.5cm.
Date:	Circa 1915-1934.
Location:	Derby Museums and Art Gallery. No. 1973-929.
Exhibition:	On display in "The Factory at King Street, 1849-1935" Exhibition held in 1993 at The Museum and Art Gallery, Derby. Catalogue number 154.

Dish

Description:	An oval dish with one handle, gilt border and panels of flowers interspersed with butterflies in enamel colours.
Painter:	Harry Sampson Hancock.
Marks:	Signed "H. S. Hancock" against a flower stem. Red crown over crossed swords and D, two sets of three dots and initials S and H. Also the mark of two crossed parallel lines in red, and two parallel lines in red at the rim.
Measurements:	22.5cm. x 20.5cm.
Date:	Twentieth century.
Location:	On loan to Royal Crown Derby Museum.
Notes:	One crack.

Dish

Description: A lozenge-shaped dessert dish with a green ground border, the border and gadroon rim embellished with gilding. In the centre, a view of Morley Church yard, near Derby. Painted in enamel colours. On the reverse the border is decorated with gilt scrolls.

Painter: Harry Sampson Hancock.

Marks: Signed in red on the reverse: "H. S. Hancock". Inscription in gilt: "Presented to Miss Boden by the Parishioners of Morley, as a token of affection and esteem, 1883-1917". Red crown over crossed swords and D, with two sets of three dots and initials S and H. Also in red, the initials "WL" which form the monogram of proprietor William Larcombe.

Measurements: Length 27.5cm.
Width 20.5cm.

Date: Circa 1915-1917.

Location: In the collection of Sheila Williams.

Literature: Twitchett and Bailey, *Royal Crown Derby*, Antique Collectors' Club, 1988, p.18.

Notes: 1. The dish is said to be one of a pair.
2. The present owner recalls that Miss Boden was the sister of the Vicar at Morley Church.

Plate

Description:	The entire decoration on this dessert plate is gilt, some of which is raised. The unusual central panel depicts ducks swimming on a lake.
Painter:	Harry Sampson Hancock.
Marks:	Signed "H. S. Hancock" on the reverse in puce. Puce crown over crossed swords and D, with two sets of three dots and initials S and H.
Measurements:	Diameter 21.5cm.
Date:	Circa 1915-1934.
Location:	Royal Crown Derby Museum.

106

Plate

Description:	A dessert plate with gadroon rim and the border decorated in flat and raised gilding. In the centre of the dish is a scene painted in enamel colours depicting a peacock standing on a tree stump, in parkland.
Painter:	Harry Sampson Hancock.
Marks:	Signed "H. S. Hancock" in puce on reverse. Puce crown over crossed swords and D, with two sets of three dots and initials S and H.
Measurements:	Diameter 21.5cm.
Date:	Circa 1915-1934.
Location:	Private collection.
Exhibition:	On display in "The Factory at King Street, 1849-1935" Exhibition held in 1993 at The Museum and Art Gallery, Derby. Catalogue number 61.

Coffee Cup and Saucer

Description:	A cup of tapering form decorated in enamel colours with a central landscape scene of the arch leading to Repton College, Derbyshire and depicting a boy bowling a hoop, with a lady and gentleman in the foreground. The saucer has a gilt beaded edge, with inner gilt band entwined with gilt foliate scrolls. Central, painted in enamel colours, is a scene of Ashford Mill, Derbyshire, with a forest in the background and brook and weir in the foreground.
Painter:	Harry Sampson Hancock.
Marks:	Both cup and saucer signed "H. S. Hancock" on the reverse in puce. Puce crown over crossed swords and D, two sets of three dots and initials S and H. The saucer is impressed "MES". Cup inscribed on reverse, "School Arch, Repton, Derbyshire". Saucer inscribed on reverse, "Old Mill, Ashford, Derbyshire".
Measurements:	*Cup*: Height 6.25cm. *Saucer*: Diameter 14cm.
Date:	Circa 1915-1934.
Location:	In the collection of Mr. G. Orme.

Coffee Cup

Description:	A cup of tapering form with a straight sided and sharply angled handle in gilt. The white ground has a gilt band at the rim and footrim and a band of stylised gilt foliage encircling the body. An oval panel is enamelled with a view of Littleover Hollow, Derbyshire.
Painter:	Harry Sampson Hancock.
Marks:	Inscribed on the base in puce, "Littleover Hollow, Derbyshire". Signed on base in puce, "H. S. Hancock". Puce crown over crossed swords and D, with two sets of three dots and initials S and H.
Measurements:	Height 6.5cm.
Date:	Circa 1915-1934
Location:	In the collection of Dr. J. R. Freeman.
Exhibition:	On display in "The Factory at King Street, 1849-1935" Exhibition held in 1993 at The Museum and Art Gallery, Derby. Catalogue number 32.
Notes:	1. This is part of a large service decorated with local views by Harry Sampson Hancock. 2. Littleover Hollow was a popular subject and painted by other Derby artists.

Pin Tray

Description:	A pin tray with gilt rim and green border. The central panel outlined in raised gilding depicts The Long Bridge, Derby.
Painter:	Harry Sampson Hancock.
Marks:	Signed "H. S. Hancock" on reverse. Puce crown over crossed swords and D, with two sets of three dots and initials S and H. Also inscribed "Derby 1850" in puce.
Measurements:	Length 14.5cm. Width 9cm.
Date:	Circa 1915-1934.
Location:	Private collection.
Notes:	Some firing cracks and crazing.

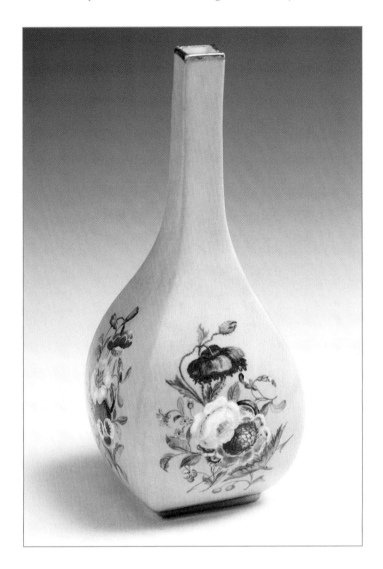

Vase

Description:	A four-sided vase, with tapered square neck. The green ground painted with enamelled flowers and a single rose.
Painter:	Attributed in Royal Crown Derby Museum records to Harry Sampson Hancock, but unsigned.
Marks:	Red crown over crossed swords and D, with two sets of three dots and initials S and H. Also the mark of two parallel lines in red.
Measurements:	Height 18cm.
Date:	Twentieth century.
Location:	On loan to Royal Crown Derby Museum.
Notes:	Slightly misshapen.

Bottle and Stopper

Description:	A large bottle and stopper with all over decoration in enamel colours of flowers, exotic birds, butterflies and insects.
Painter:	Harry Sampson Hancock.
Marks:	Signed "H. S. Hancock" on base in puce. Puce crown over crossed swords and D, two sets of three dots and initials S and H. Also in puce the initials "WL" which form the monogram of proprietor William Larcombe. The zeppelin mark of gilt moon and black zeppelin is also painted on the base.
Measurements:	Height 41cm.
Date:	31 January 1916.
Location:	Royal Crown Derby Museum.
Notes:	Some kiln blacks at neck.

Watercolour

Description:	A watercolour depicting roses and a colourful vase resting on a tabletop.
Painter:	Harry Sampson Hancock.
Marks:	Signed "H. S. Hancock, 1899".
Measurements:	24cm. x 16cm.
Date:	1899.
Location:	In the collection of Dr. J. R. Freeman.
Notes:	The frame maker's label on reverse reads: "Fine Art of Oakham Ltd. Harry Sampson Hancock. Roses and vase on a ledge."

Plaque

Description: A small circular plaque decorated in enamel colours with five pink roses, buds and leaves.

Painter: Harry Sampson Hancock.

Marks: Signed "H. S. Hancock" in puce on reverse. Puce crown over crossed swords and D, with two sets of three dots and initials S and H.

Measurements: Diameter 7.75cm.

Date: Circa 1915-1934.

Location: Private collection.

WILLIAM HANCOCK
China painter

William's father John Hancock (1777-1840) had been employed at the Nottingham Road factory from 1820 until his death in 1840. On his arrival at Nottingham Road, from Staffordshire, he was employed as a colour maker and groundlayer.

When John Hancock arrived at the Nottingham Road factory from Staffordshire, several members of his family accompanied him. His eldest son John, who had been born in Penkhull in 1804, and his second son, George, who had been baptised in Hanley in 1810, worked with their father. George was later to marry Mary Ann Bagguley at Saint Alkmund's Church, Derby, on the 11 March 1833. John's third son, James, also worked at the Nottingham Road factory, but it is thought he may have joined his father at a slightly later date. James later married Elizabeth Slater on 15 December 1834, at Saint Alkmund's Church, Derby. It was this James Hancock, who on the closure of the Nottingham Road works went to Mr. Samuel Boyle's manufactory in Staffordshire, and later became the proprietor of the Diglis Colour Works in Worcester, a company which provided his cousin Sampson Hancock with colours and items for use at King Street.

It is also thought that four of John's (1777) daughters, Elizabeth, Mellisant, Charlotte and Martha accompanied their father to Derby. It is not known if John's (1777) first wife Sarah Walker, whom he had married on 19 May 1799 at Norton in the Moors, Staffordshire, was deceased by the time of his arrival in Derby, the last child whose birth is recorded to the couple being Sarah in 1818.

John Hancock (1777), a widower, married for a second time to Sarah Sowter of Quarndon, on 22 July 1827. It was their son William who was baptized on 8 June 1828 at Saint Alkmund's, Derby, who was later to work at King Street.

Half brother to those children of John (1777) mentioned above, William was one of the last apprentices to be trained at the Nottingham Road China Works, and was apprenticed to china painting.

Following the closure of the Nottingham Road works, William remained in Derby and went to work for the King Street factory. His marriage to Ellen Oldbury the daughter of Edward Oldbury, and Mary Moors, on 25 December 1849, at Saint Alkmund's, Derby, confirms William's occupation of "China Painter" in the Parish Register.

The 1851 Census for Saint Alkmund's Parish reveals him living at 153 Nottingham Road, with his wife Ellen, both aged 22, with their six-month-old son, John. His widowed mother Sarah (formerly Sowter) is also with them. His occupation is again confirmed as being a "china painter". By the time of the 1861 Census for the same parish, the family has moved to 8 Bridge Gate. William, still recorded as a "china painter", and his wife now have four children, John aged 10, Mary aged 7, Edward aged 5, and Sarah aged 3.

At some time after this date, and possibly before 1871, William and his family left Derby. When Haslem wrote his book, "The Old Derby China Factory", he recorded:

> "William, the youngest son of the second John Hancock was one of the last lot of apprentices at the old Derby works, as his grandfather had been one of the earliest. He possesses no small portion of the family talent, being a clever painter and gilder, and excelling as a pattern designer. He is now superintending the enamelling department of the Brown Hill Pottery, at Tunstall, near Burslem".

By the time of the 1881 Census for Stoke upon Trent he is to be found living at 38 Wharf Street, Burslem, with his wife Ellen, their unmarried son Edward and grandson. Both William and Edward are listed as "Potter's gilders".

SARAH HARDING (nee Winfield/Wingfield)
China painter

Daughter of John Winfield and his wife Mary, Sarah was baptised at Saint Alkmund's Church, Derby on 14 January 1808, where on 18 April 1840 she married Thomas Harding. Mary Wingfield and Sarah Wingfield are recorded on the 1832 List for Nottingham Road, Mary being a burnisher and Sarah a paintress. Her father John is also recorded under the section titled Kilnmen, where he was a glaze dipper. Her older brother John, who worked at King Street, also appears on the 1832 list.

Entry No. 92 for 18 Erasmus Street, records Sarah Harding, aged 40, as a china painter living with her husband Thomas, a silkmaker in the 1851 Census.

It appears Sarah remained at the china works for more than 30 years, her name appearing in subsequent census returns. Still recorded as a "china painter" in the 1881 Census, she was occupying a house in the Parish of Saint Werburgh's at 159 Abbey Street with her husband Thomas, who was a warehouseman and 10 years her junior. At the same address were two of the couple's nephews and Sarah's brother James Winfield who was recorded as a "painter".

WILLIAM HARGREAVES
China painter

William Hargreaves was working at the King Street factory in the 1930s. He painted flowers, birds and dogs and his pieces are often marked with his initials W.H.

A photograph of him appears at the beginning of this chapter.

Pin Tray

Description:	A rectangular pin tray with gilt scroll border. A terrier is painted in the main panel in enamel colours.
Painter:	William Hargreaves.
Marks:	Initialled "W. H" in main panel. On reverse monogram M in Puce crown over crossed swords and D, with initials S and H. Two sets of three dots are missing.
Measurements:	Length 9cm. Width 7.25cm.
Date:	1930-1935.
Location:	Royal Crown Derby Museum.

JOHN HENSON
Potter

One of the founder partners, John Henson's details can be found in Chapter One, under the section devoted to Proprietors.

HENSHALL

A person with the surname Henshall is believed to have worked at King Street, prior to working for the present day Royal Crown Derby factory in Osmaston Road. It is not known in what capacity he was employed (1).

CATHERINE HESKETH
China burnisher

Born in 1800 in Little Chester, she appears in the 1851 Census Returns for the Parish of Saint Alkmund's as a "China Burnisher". At that time she was living in Mansfield Road at an address occupied by Mary Bagaley, a china painter.

In 1861 she was still living in Mansfield Road, in Saint Alkmund's Parish, with Mary Hancock, a china painter, mentioned earlier.

JAMES HILL
China painter

One of the founder partners of the King Street factory, his details are recorded in Chapter One.

Hill used the number 21 at Nottingham Road.

Watercolour

Description:	A circular view of lovers, in regency dress, walking in a vale of trees.
Painter:	James Hill.
Marks:	Inscription on reverse "In Lovers walk, Matlock, Derbyshire". A piece of paper attached to the reverse bears the inscription "James Hill" in pencil.
Measurements:	Diameter 15.5cm.
Date:	Nineteenth century.
Location:	In the collection of Dr. J. R. Freeman.
Exhibition:	On display in "The Factory at King Street, 1849-1935" Exhibition held in 1993 at The Museum and Art Gallery, Derby. Catalogue number 207.

WILLIAM HOPKINSON
China potter/figure maker

Edward Hopkinson, whose name appears on the 1832 list, had been apprenticed to William Smith at the Nottingham Road factory to learn the art of gilding. Edward's eldest son, William, was also apprenticed at the Nottingham Road works but was trained to be a china potter figure maker (1).

Born in 1808 in Derby, William appears in the 1832 List as a figure maker, and called an ornamental repairer, along with several other members of the family. Edward Hopkinson, senior and junior, and Richard Hopkinson, all of whom were gilders, and Sarah Hopkinson, a burnisher, were also employed at Nottingham Road.

When the Nottingham Road works closed, William Hopkinson went along with the small group of men to King Street when the factory was founded (2). Haslem in his book, "The Old Crown Derby China Factory" records:

"He was until lately, so employed for Mr. Hancock at the works in King Street, Derby, and the writer is indebted to him for some of the information contained in this work."

His name appeared in the 1871 Census for the town of Derby when he was living in Garden Street.

Because of the information given by Haslem regarding William Hopkinson, it is thought he may still have been employed at the King Street factory up until some time around 1876.

WILLIAM HOPKINSON
Outside Modeller

Amongst the King Street Archives are three invoices, all addressed to Mr. Hancock, from W. Hopkinson, of 3 Burlington Gardens, Burlington Road, Fulham, London, which cover the period 1871 to 1872.

The first, dated 31 January 1871 was for:

Models of Shakespere(sic) and Milton   £2. 0. 0d.

The second invoice, dated 18 December 1871, asking that payment be made by postal order, payable at Fulham Post Office, lists:

To Clay Presses of Ewer⁵.
1 Brick Box.
2 figures of Sweep and Copper sir.
1 Boy and Swan.
1 Man same stance.

£1. 0. 0d.

1 Bust of Flora.
2 Cupid B? for approval

10. 0d.

The third invoice, dated 12 January 1872, for £1-10/-is for providing Presses in Clay, and bears William Hopkinson's signature.

120

GEORGE JESSOP
China painter

Born in 1882, opinions vary as to the exact date of George Jessop's apprenticeship at Royal Crown Derby. The authors believe it was at some time around the turn of the twentieth century.

In 1914 he left the Osmaston Road concern and went to work in a munitions factory in Coventry for the majority of the First World War, returning to Royal Crown Derby in 1918. Leaving the Osmaston Road factory in 1927, he was employed as a sign writer for the LMS Railway at their Carriage and Wagon works, where he remained for three years (1).

He became a painter at King Street in 1930 and, following the factory's closure in 1935, returned once again to Royal Crown Derby, in Osmaston Road, where he remained until his retirement in 1939.

He was a very fine flower painter, his work being of the highest quality, although some of his pieces can look a little rushed.

Brock's MSS notebook, has an entry dated 15 May 1925, which records a Mrs. Mary Jessop on a list of girl and women gilders employed at Royal Crown Derby (2).

George Jessop, painter.
Twitchett & Bailey, "Royal Crown Derby."

Plate

Description: A dessert plate with lemon colouring to the gadroon rim. The border is painted with single flower heads of garden flowers and foliage. The well has a central single flower and sprays of mixed flowers close to the border.

Painter: George Jessop.

Marks: Signed "G. Jessop" on border .Puce crown over crossed swords and D, with two sets of three dots and initials S and H. Also in puce the crossed Ps mark of proprietor Paget and his wife.

Measurements: Diameter 22cm.

Date: Circa 1933-1935.

Location: In the collection of Dr. J. R. Freeman.

Altar Vase

Description: One of two altar vases decorated with a variety of flowers on both white and yellow grounds. The vase stands on four shaped feet.

Painter: G. Jessop.

Marks: Signed "G. Jessop" on body of the vase. Puce crown over crossed swords and D, with two sets of three dots and initials S and H. Also in puce, the crossed Ps mark of proprietor Paget and his wife.

Measurements: Height 19cm.

Date: Circa 1933-1935.

Location: On loan to Royal Crown Derby Museum.

Notes: Heavily crazed.

Watercolour

Description: A watercolour depicting a spray of lilac against a background of stylised grey clouds.

Painter: George Jessop.

Marks: Signed "G. Jessop" in the painting.

Measurements: 16cm. square.

Date: Twentieth century.

Location: In the collection of Dr. J. R. Freeman.

Exhibition: On display in "The Factory at King Street, 1849-1935" Exhibition held in 1993 at The Museum and Art Gallery, Derby. Catalogue number 143.

Jug

Description:	A bulbous shaped jug, with a band of gilt foliate scrolls at the neck. Decorated in enamel colours with mixed flowers.
Painter:	George Jessop.
Marks:	Signed "G. Jessop" in black in the painting. Puce crown over crossed swords and D, with two sets of three dots and initials S and H. Also in puce the crossed Ps mark of proprietor Paget and his wife.
Measurements:	Height 12.5cm.
Date:	Circa 1933-1935.
Location:	In the collection of Mr. G. Orme.

HERBERT JEWITT
Apprentice potter

The son of Llewellynn Jewitt, the art historian, Herbert was born on 20 January 1850. Apprenticed by his father Llewellynn to Sampson Hancock in 1866 he trained under John Mountford and is reported to have made small animals and figures. He did not remain at King Street long as it was his life's ambition to become a sailor. Following an accident at sea, he died on board HMS Shackamaxon in 1869.

His father's diary (1), for the year 1866, contained the following entries:

20th January, 1866	My dear boy Herbert's birthday – he is sixteen to-day.
February 12th 1866	Took Herbert to the Derby China Works to see about his going there to learn the trade. He seems to like the idea, and I hope we shall come to terms.
April 2nd 1866	Llewellynns* birthday. He is eighteen today. How time flies! Herbert gone for the first time to the Derby China Works on trial to learn to be a potter. I hope he likes it.
August 22nd	Herbert apprenticed to Joseph Heap and Sons for 4 years to learn everything so as to be able to take command of a vessel.

* Herbert's brother.

IRIS JOHNSTON
Possible china painter

Living at 19 Grove Place with her widowed mother Mary Johnston, who was an unemployed dress maker, Iris was aged 16 in the 1881 Census for the Parish of Saint Alkmund's. She was born in Derby in 1865, and her occupation is given as a "China Painter". A few doors along the same street was Elizabeth C. Powell, who was recorded as a burnisher at the china factory.

Hilda Moore records that she was employed at King Street (1).

W. JONES
China painter

Employed at King Street in the early part of the twentieth century, examples of his work bearing the dates 1905 and 1906 have been seen, and it is thought he remained with the firm for a period of more than ten years. Examples of his work are scarce.

He often painted landscapes which featured birds, and although well-painted some of the poses adopted can look rather awkward. His flower painting was nevertheless very good.

In his book *Royal Crown Derby*, John Twitchett states Jones was active at King Street during the first quarter of the twentieth century (1).

Plate

Description: A dessert plate with a gadroon rim and border of raised gilding. The central panel depicts two pheasants leaving a wooded area, all painted in enamel colours.

Painter: W. Jones.

Marks: Signed "W. Jones 06". close to one pheasant. Red crown over crossed swords and D, with two sets of three dots and initials S and H.

Measurements: Diameter 22cm.

Date: Circa 1906.

Location: On loan to Royal Crown Derby Museum.

Notes: Badly cracked.

Plate

Description:	A dessert plate with gadroon rim. The border is decorated in enamel colours with wildfowl and a further four, in flight, are painted in the central panel.
Painter:	W. Jones.
Marks:	Signed "W. Jones" in the painting. Red crown over crossed swords and D, with two sets of three dots and initials S and H.
Measurements:	Diameter 22cm.
Date:	Twentieth century.
Location:	Royal Crown Derby Museum.
Notes:	Badly cracked and also crazed.

ELSIE LARCOMBE
Possible china burnisher

Elsie Larcombe was the daughter of proprietor William Larcombe. Although it is not known in what year she was born, she married Herbert Reginald Hopkins in 1947, in Matlock.

Hilda Moore has recorded that Elsie Larcombe occasionally worked at the factory (1), however a nephew of Herbert Hopkins believes that his favourite Aunt Elsie was not employed at the china works, but probably tried her hand at burnishing when accompanying her father to the premises when she was a young lady.

An undated obituary notice records her death:

Mrs. Elsie Hopkins
    The death of Mrs. Elsie Hopkins occurred at her home 5 Ecclesbourne Close, Duffield, on October 19. Born in Whitecross Street, Derby, she was the daughter of Mr. W. Larcombe who owned the old China Works in King Street, Derby. She subsequently lived in Morley for many years where she was a founder member of the W. I. and Drama Group, was church organist for a time and a Sunday School teacher at Morley and Breadsall churches.

She was married in 1947 at Matlock Bath Church, her husband being gardener to four succeeding Bishops of Derby. The couple moved to Turnditch with the late Bishop Allen and spent about twelve years in the parish.

Mrs. Hopkins particularly enjoyed living in the village where she made many friends and took part in community activities. She also attended All Saints' Church, Turnditch and Green Bank Chapel.

The service and cremation took place at Markeaton October 25, at which the prayers were led by the present Bishop of Derby, the Rt. Rev. Cyril Bowles.

Donations were for the P.D.S.A. at Mrs. Hopkins' request.

*Elsie Larcombe, photographed
with her parents.
Private Collection.*

WILLIAM LARCOMBE
Proprietor

Details of William Larcombe can be found in Chapter One, under the section devoted to Founder Partners and Proprietors.

LEONARD LEAD jnr
Possible china painter

There is a possibility that Leonard Lead was employed at the King Street factory for a short time when the small firm commenced production in 1849, and for that reason his details are included here.

Although Haslem records that on the closure of the Nottingham Road factory, Lead began painting spar ornaments for local firms (1), the 1851 Census for Derby records his occupation as still being that of a china painter, suggesting that he may have been employed by King Street for a short time when the factory began production.

Haslem states that Leonard Lead worked at Pinxton and was probably a native of that place (2). Major Tapp, in his handwritten notebooks, which are on microfilm at Derby Local Studies Library, shows him to be born in Pinxton in 1786 and records he was apprenticed at the china works there on 15 April 1797(3).

The son of Leonard Lead snr, who had been a charcoal burner at the Nottingham Road factory, and who had found employment at Pinxton as a woodcutter, Leonard Lead jun, married twice. Shown to be a "china painter and widower" in the Parish Registers, his second marriage to Ann Vernon at All Saints Church, Derby, took place on 23 June 1822. The couple went on to have numerous children. Their son John was baptised on 4 January 1825 when his father's occupation of "China Painter" is confirmed in the Saint Alkmund's Parish Registers, as is the couple's address of Lodge Lane. John was later to be apprenticed to Lead himself to learn the art of china painting(4). When the couple's daughter Frances was baptised at the same church on 7 September 1829 the family had moved and were living in Chester Place.

The 1832 Nottingham Road List records Leonard Lead sen as a flower painter together with his son Leonard Lead jnr whose name appears amongst the gilders.

The 1840s Rates Books confirm he was still occupying a house at 5 Chester Place, Derby, which was owned by William Horsley. He is also recorded in the Poll Books from 1841 to 1848 as Leonard Lead of Chester Place(5).

By the time of the 1851 Census, the family was living still in the Parish of Saint Alkmund's, but at 5 Arthur Street, a house formerly occupied by John Lead, a china painter, who had worked at the Nottingham Road factory. Leonard Lead jnr was shown as a "China Painter", born in Staffordshire, and aged 59. His wife Ann was 49 and with the couple were three of their children, Henry, Oswald and Alfred, as well as their daughter-in-law Eliza.

Perhaps it was some time after this date that Leonard Lead became involved with painting spar ornaments as Haslem mentioned (6).

The 1852 Freebody's *Directory for Derby* lists Leonard Lead as a "flower painter" which possibly suggests he may have been decorating spar ornaments rather than china at this date.

Haslem says of Leonard Lead jnr:

"He removed to Derby early in the present century, and was employed at the old works for more than forty years; his work, therefore, is oftener to be met with on the Derby China, which was produced during its later days, than that of any other flower painter.

As a flower painter Lead possessed considerable merit; his colour, though rather florid, is rich and varied. After the close of the old works, and until near the close of his life, he was employed in painting Derbyshire spar ornaments in varnish colours, a style of work which will not prove so durable as that which he has left on Derby china."

After a lifetime of painting, Leonard Lead died in December 1869 in Leicester, at the home of one of his three sons all of whom had moved there with their families and were working in the printing industry.

Whilst decorating at the Nottingham Road factory, plate pattern number 393, and cup and saucer pattern number 770 were attributed to him (7).

WILLIAM LOCKER
Proprietor

Details of William Locker can be found in Chapter One under the section devoted to Founder Partners and Proprietors.

An article written by Hilda Moore, following an interview with Locker's great great granddaughter, appeared in a Derby Porcelain International Society Newsletter, and stated that William Locker was known to have painted flowers, fruit and insects. Perhaps, although primarily a proprietor at the factory, this statement may suggest that when business demanded it, he was also a painter.

WILLIAM LOVEGROVE snr
Possible China painter

It is believed that William Lovegrove senior may have been employed at King Street, however when making this statement caution is needed. Born in Derby in 1796, William Lovegrove senior was apprenticed at the Nottingham Road china factory under William Smith, where he trained to become a gilder.

His name appears in the 1852 Freebody's *Directory for Derby*, when he is recorded as a china painter, living at 12 Albion Place, Derby.

He died in Derby in 1873.

William Lovegrove junior, the youngest son of William above, was apprenticed at the Nottingham Road works to learn the art of gilding, becoming a good flower and bird painter (1).

The Lovegrove family had a long association with the Derby China industry. A John Lovegrove had been involved with Hopkinson and Kirkland in the Cockpit Hill works. Several members of the Lovegrove family appear on the 1832 Nottingham Road List, Elizabeth Lovegrove being shown as a burnisher, whilst John and James Lovegrove were gilders.

William Senior may have been employed at King Street, but there are several other members of the Lovegrove family employed in their own businesses which are involved in the china industry. John Lovegrove and Sons were listed as China Manufacturers of 32 Traffic Street, Derby, in the 1852 Freebody's *Directory for Derby*. A further entry in the same directory lists Lovegrove and Son, china and glass dealers of 22 Sidalls Lane, Derby. Shown at the same address of 22 Sidalls Lane, is a William Lovegrove who is also a china and glass dealer.

In the Saint Peter's Parish Registers for Derby, there are two entries concerning William Lovegrove, a china painter. Son of John, who was also a china painter, William married

Emma Thorpe, at Saint Peter's on 29 November 1849, when his occupation was recorded as a "china painter". His name appears in the same Parish Registers on 12 August 1868, at the time of his second marriage to Sarah Taylor. Still recorded as son of John, "china painter", William's occupation was also given as being a "china painter".

JOSEPH LOWE
Apprentice

Joseph Lowe was baptised on 11 September 1836 at Saint Edmund's Church, Allestree, on the outskirts of Derby.

The son of Thomas Lowe and his wife Ursula Warner, Joseph's name appears in the 1851 Census for the Parish of Saint Alkmund's. Occupying a house at 29 Nottingham Road, Chadeston Hill (sic)*, are Thomas Lowe, his father, a brewer's labourer, his wife and several children. Born in Derby, Joseph was aged 14 and his occupation was recorded as "Apprentice to China Manufactory". Unfortunately it does not record whether Joseph was training to be an artist or potter. There is mention of the Lowe family in the 1832 Nottingham Road List, where a George Lowe is recorded as a china painter, perhaps suggesting Joseph was talented in that direction.

According to the Parish Rates Books, Joseph's parents had occupied the house owned by Mrs. Blood since the 14 February 1840.

*Note: The authors believe the area referred to is Chaddesden.

ARNOLD MACHIN. O.B.E. R.A.
China painter

Two photographs of Arnold Machin, painter. Private Collection.

Born in 1911 Arnold Machin was apprenticed at Mintons. In an interview with Brayshaw Gilhespy, Arnold Machin explained that up until the 1930s employment for artists had been easy to find in the Potteries.

In 1930 he joined the King Street factory where he mostly painted flowers, and remained there for two years, leaving in 1932, the year of the slump. He also stated that he enjoyed Albert Gregory's painting whilst working at Mintons with him, and was again able to work with him at King Street. He is also known to have painted fish, and is thought to have painted some sporting scenes.

He recalled in the same interview that he enjoyed his painting at King Street because he admired the work of his fellow artists, in particular Annie Bailey's flower painting (1).

When he left the small china works he turned his hand to sculpting, finally becoming a member of the Royal Academy.

Plate

Description:	A dessert plate with gadroon rim and wide gilt border, within which are three reserve panels with seashells depicted in gilding. The centre painted with an underwater scene of fish and seaweed in enamel colours, in an impressionistic style.
Painter:	Arnold Machin.
Marks:	Signed "A. Machin". Puce crown over crossed swords and D, with two sets of three dots and initials S and H. Also in puce the crossed Ps mark of proprietor Paget and his wife. Inscribed close to the footrim, the named fish "Haddock". Also inscribed on reverse in gilt "Henry Blogg from Mr. and Mrs. Paget, 1934".
Measurements:	Diameter 22cm.
Date:	Circa 1934.
Location:	On loan to Royal Crown Derby Museum.
Literature:	Illustrated in the booklet "The Factory at King Street 1849-1935", by A. Bambery and R. Blackwood, Derby Museums and Art Gallery, October 1993, plate iv.
Notes:	1. This plate is part of a dessert service.
	2. The Royal Crown Derby Museum records show that Henry Blogg was Coxswain of the Cromer Lifeboat.

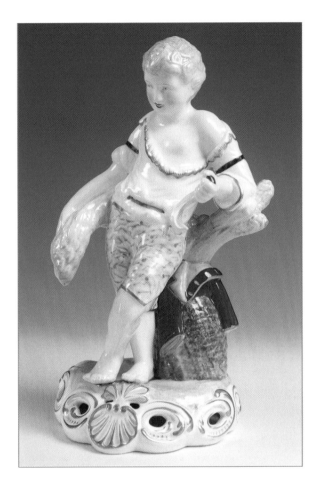

Figure of Summer

Description: A male figure representing Summer from the Four Seasons. He is holding a sickle in his left hand and a sheaf of corn in the other. He is wearing a pale yellow shirt and mauve trousers. His jacket is draped over a tree stump, against which he is leaning. The figure stands on a pierced shell base. The whole decorated in enamel colours and gilding.

Painter: Probably Arnold Machin.

Marks: Puce crown over crossed swords and D, with two sets of three dots and initials S and H. Also the monogram "AM" in puce.

Measurements: Height 22cm.

Date: 1930s.

Location: Private collection.

Notes: It seems likely that the monogram is that of Arnold Machin. It has previously been recorded on another figure decorated by him, but on plates he usually signs his name in full.

JOHN MARSHALL
Potter

Born in 1859, John Marshall was recorded as a "Potter", living at 3 Saint Alkmund's Church-yard, Derby, on 20 July 1892, when he was a witness to Sampson Hancock's Last Will and Testament.

In the 1881 Census he is shown as living with his mother Mary who is aged 45. She is not shown as a widow, suggesting that her husband is working elsewhere. John, their son, is aged 22 and is listed as "Potter in China Works". At the same address is John's brother George aged 16, and an unemployed china painter.

A potter by the name of Mr. Marshall, who had worked in his early years with Edward Swainson, has been recorded by Hilda Moore, and it is thought this may well be to whom she was referring (1).

WILLIAM MARSHALL
Potter

It is thought William Marshall may have worked at King Street as a potter. Hilda Moore suggested that he may have been employed at the factory.

OLIVE MEAKIN
Gilder

Nothing more is known of Olive Meakin except that she was a gilder employed at King Street (1).

MRS. MINOR
Inspectoress

She is recorded as being employed at the factory. During an interview she recalled she had been employed at the Royal Crown Derby Porcelain Company in Osmaston Road, but left following a supervisor's query regarding some china she had rejected. She took a similar post at King Street, working in a room at the back of the building, which she described as the sales shop, which was next to the large entrance gates.

She did however order butter and cream once a week from the dairy in St. Helen's Street, for Mrs. Paget to take home with her, following her husband's weekly visit to the King Street factory (1).

A photograph of her appears at the beginning of this chapter.

JOHN MORRIS
Outside Modeller
5 Regent Street, Old Hall Terrace,
Hanley, The Potteries.

Amongst the King Street Archives are eight invoices from John Morris, which cover the period 1871 to 1875. Some of the invoices are undated and fail to give details of the purchases made, however, the majority give an insight into this outside modeller's ware. All addressed to Mr. Hancock, the invoices are as follows:

April 14/71	£.	s.	d.
2 Cupid Candlesticks	2	10	0
1 Extinguisher		10	0
	3	0	0
Feb. 12 1873			
To Modelling 1 Donkey & Cock	3	10	0
31/8/74			
1 Dog		12	0

Jan 7/75
Received from Mr. S. Hancock
the sum of Seven Pounds two.

May 20/75			
To Modelling Sheaf group	5	0	0
Children & Basket	5	10	0

May 21/75
Received from Mr. Hancock
the sum of five pounds.
Undated invoice.
Bought of John Morris

1 basket	1	5	0
First Group	2	7	0
Second Group	2	2	0
Received on account	1	10	0
Remainder	4	4	0

There is one further undated invoice which records that Sampson Hancock paid J. Morris the sum of 2 guineas.

ESTHER MOSCROP/MOSCROFT (nee GOADSBY)
China painter

Esther Moscrop returned to china painting following her husband's death.

Born in 1803, no baptism has been found for Esther Goadsby. She married John Moscrop on 6 April 1833 at Saint Alkmund's Church, Derby.

Her name appeared on the 1832 list for Nottingham Road, where she was shown to be a "china painter". She appears as a housewife in the 1851 Census for Derby, however, by the time of the 1861 Census for the Parish of Saint Alkmund's, she has become a widow and her occupation is listed as a "china painter." At the same address with her is her unmarried daughter Mary, aged 27. (See the entry for John Moscrop/Moscroft for more details).

JOHN MOSCROP/MOSCROFT
China painter

John Moscrop worked at both the Nottingham Road and King Street factories.

Born in 1790, John Moscrop married Esther Goadsby on 6 April 1833 at Saint Alkmund's

Church, Derby.

Whilst at the Nottingham Road factory, he used gilder's number 18. In the 1843 Glover's *Directory for Derby*, he is shown as living in Erasmus Street, and is listed as a "China Painter".

The 1851 Census for the Parish of Saint Alkmund's, Derby gives his whereabouts as 16 Erasmus Street, a house owned and occupied by himself. Aged 61, he is listed as a "China Painter", born in Derbyshire. With him is his wife Esther (with no occupation), aged 48, and their son William, a shoemaker, aged 16. John died at some time between this date and 1861, when his wife Esther's whereabouts are given at 105 Erasmus Street, Derby. Her surname appears as Moscroft. Now a widow, she is aged 58. Interestingly her occupation has become that of a china painter, perhaps suggesting she took her husband's place at the factory and returned to her former occupation.

Although John Moscrop was attributed with using No. 18 at the Nottingham Road factory, no King Street porcelain bearing that number together with the S and H mark will be found as the introduction of this new mark occurred after his death in 1861. There is however the possibility that there are King Street pieces decorated by Moscrop which bear the old red Nottingham Road mark of crown, crossed batons and script D, together with his number.

MISS E. H. MOSLEY
China painter

Miss Mosley was an aunt of Colonel Mosley of Calke Abbey, Derbyshire, although very little is known of her. She is said to have lived at Thornhill and is recorded as being employed at the King Street factory (1).

WILLIAM EDWIN MOSLEY
China painter

Although the year of his birth is not known, William Edwin Mosley was apprenticed at the Osmaston Road factory in 1893. There is a difference of opinion as to when exactly he joined the workforce at King Street, however it is believed it was at the beginning of the twentieth century.

He is thought to have gone to Australia in 1932, following which he returned to King Street in 1934. After the takeover in 1935 he returned to the factory in Osmaston Road where he was previously apprenticed.

William Mosley, painter.
Twitchett & Bailey, "Royal Crown Derby."

He was one of the leading artists at King Street and worked alongside Harry Sampson Hancock. A senior decorator at the factory, Mosley was described by Hilda Castledine who had worked at King Street, as "a very quiet and kind person". She also described him as "One of nature's gentlemen" (1).

Handwritten notes in a private collection, dated 1964, make reference to William Mosley thus:

"Whenever Mr. Mosley's china painting was praised to him, his invariable comment was "It's had a good firing," thus acknowledging that the final result was in the hands of the ones in charge of the firing of the kiln. Such was the modesty of the man, which was typical of him.
The above information was recounted to the writer by Miss Evelyn Sadler who with her sister Miss Amy Sadler carried on business of china dealers at no. 87 King Street. Having taken over the business from Mr. Larcombe when he gave up on his retirement" (2).

Miss Ward, whose father had been a close friend of Mosley for over fifty years, recalled of him in an interview with Brayshaw Gilhespy: (3).

"As with all true artists, his painting on china was not only his work, but a joy, and if, as it has been said, genius is an infinite capacity for taking pains, he indeed deserves to be known as one. His work was always meticulous; whatever the subject or piece of china he was embellishing, every detail was executed so painstakingly, with such delicate exactness, that I feel he would not mind being called a craftsman, as well as an artist, as were the Old Masters in the past.

"His work on Crown Derby china is appreciated by collectors the world over, but it is not generally known that he was a water-colourist of rare distinction, his work reminiscent of Birket Foster. His work on china was exquisite, and those who have treasured his signed pieces will find them valuable in the future.

"He looked for the beauty in life always, and was both a student and lover of nature, and this, again and again, was apparent in his painting. It was from this love of nature that his great aptitude for painting flowers, birds and countryside stemmed. The finer and more difficult, the more he enjoyed the work. His work was characterised by accuracy in every detail. This accuracy is clearly seen in a portrait he painted of my Champion Tumbler pigeon. This has been seen by many pigeon judges, and the general opinion is that they have never seen a more life like portrait. He would often ask me to take to his home the pigeons we reared. He studied them very carefully, would place them on his table, and, so gentle himself he could make a friend of all animals, they posed for him for hours; his patience was inexhaustible.

"His garden was a bird sanctuary; he encouraged all feathered creatures, and took delight in transferring their beautiful plumage on to china. He studied and painted all kinds of birds on china, once rearing by hand a pair of wagtails so that he could make numerous sketches, but he always returned to his favourite models, his brilliantly plumed parrot and our softly coloured pigeons.

"He would go out into the hills and dales of Derbyshire, patiently studying the country-side and watching the wildlife around him, and return to paint on plaques and plates, vases and bowls, the beautiful scenes he had memorised. He delighted, too in painting the great country houses of Derbyshire, capturing for us their stateliness and mellow beauty.

"My father's friendship with him lasted over fifty years, and both keen naturalists, they would for hours discuss the detail on some piece of china, ensuring every detail to be correct. He fished a little on occasion; he and my father frequently visited our fishing on the River Dove, and he once gave my father a cigarette box, with a leaping trout painted on the lid, which was perfect in every detail.

"His Derbyshire scenes have a peaceful beauty and give a feeling of tranquillity amidst the stresses of modern life, and for a Derby artist, painting on Derby china what could be more appropriate? Beautiful as his bird and countryside painting is, I feel his speciality was the painting of flowers on china. In my collection I have brooches, rings and miniatures, on china, with my monogram painted in rosebuds; even tiny thimbles, monogrammed with the smallest and most perfect rosebuds. In fact, he was something of a miniaturist, and many of the beautiful pieces by him show this in their perfection of detail; done on so small a scale, one wonders how anyone could have the skill to paint them with the naked eye.

"His use of rosebuds for decoration reminds me that on the 28th February, 1922, on the occasion of the Princess Mary's marriage, he painted and sent to Her Royal Highness, a beautiful miniature of a peacock with Harewood House in the background, and her monogram on the reverse side in tiny exquisite rosebuds every petal perfect. It was one of his treasured memories that Her Royal Highness accepted and graciously acknowledged the gift, for like all Englishmen, he was always honoured when any of his work was for the Royal Family. He painted a pair of Derby Dwarfs for Her Majesty Queen Elizabeth, and one of the last things he painted was a christening mug for Prince Charles.

"His christening mugs were always lovely, and make beautiful possessions ....

"He has painted many famous pieces. It always seems amazing to me that the work of this quiet retiring man should grace the rooms of palaces and mansions all over the world. My tribute to Mr. Mosley is to a fine artist and a great gentleman."

He was a very versatile artist, his work occasionally being signed in full. His signature is also often seen on Royal Crown Derby Dwarfs, which were produced at the Osmaston Road factory.

He was living in Garden Street at the time of his death in 1954.

Figure of Spring

Description: A female figure representing Spring from the Four Seasons. She is wearing a pink coat, with yellow lining, over a pale green bodice and floral decorated white skirt. She holds a garland of mixed flowers in each hand. The figure stands on a pierced scroll base. The whole decorated in enamel colours and gilding.

Painter: W. E. Mosley.

Marks: Initialled "W. E. M." on base. Puce crown over crossed swords and D, with two sets of three dots and initials S and H.

Measurements: Height 21cm.

Date: Circa 1915-1935.

Location: Private collection.

Notes: This is the second recording by the authors of Mosley decorating a figure.

Plate

Description:	A plate with gadroon rim, the border decorated with gilding and an armorial crest in enamel colours. In the centre panel a group of gloxinias in enamel colours.
Painter:	W. E. Mosley.
Marks:	Signed "W. E. Mosley" in the painting. Puce crown over crossed swords and D, with two sets of three dots and initials S and H.
Measurements:	Diameter 22cm.
Date:	Circa 1915-1935.
Location:	Private collection.
Literature:	Illustrated on the front cover of the booklet "The Factory at King Street 1849-1935" by A. Bambery and R. Blackwood, Derby Museums and Art Gallery, October 1993.
Exhibition:	On display in "The Factory at King Street, 1849-1935" Exhibition held in 1993 at The Museum and Art Gallery, Derby. Catalogue number 133.
Notes:	1. The crest possibly belongs to the Hunter family of Norfolk, but no authority has been found.
	2. Plate is crazed.

Plate

Description:	A plate with gadroon rim, the border decorated with gilding and an armorial crest in enamel colours. In the centre panel, a group of dahlias.
Painter:	W. E. Mosley.
Marks:	Signed "W. E. Mosley" in the painting. Puce crown over crossed swords and D, with two sets of three dots and initials S and H.
Measurements:	Diameter 22cm.
Date:	Circa 1915-1935.
Location:	Private collection.
Notes:	1. The crest possibly belongs to the Hunter family of Norfolk, but no authority has been found.
	2. Plate is crazed.

Dish

Description:	A shallow lobe shaped dish, with rococo handle and "C" scrolls picked out in gilt. The centre painted with an enamelled group of flowers, fruit and insects.
Painter:	W. E. Mosley.
Marks:	Signed "W. E. M." in the painting. Red crown over crossed swords and D, with two sets of three dots and initials S and H.
Measurements:	22cm. x 19.5cm.
Date:	Twentieth century.
Location:	In the collection of Dr. J. R. Freeman.
Exhibition:	On display in "The Factory at King Street, 1849-1935" Exhibition held in 1993 at The Museum and Art Gallery, Derby. Catalogue number 17.

Dish

Description:	A lozenge shaped dish with gadroon edge. In the centre a still life of flowers and fruit in enamel colours. The border is undecorated and there is no gilding.
Painter:	W. E. Mosley.
Marks:	Signed "W. E. Mosley" in the painting. Red crown over crossed swords and D, with two sets of three dots and initials S and H.
Measurements:	27.5cm. x 21cm.
Date:	Twentieth century.
Location:	Private collection.
Exhibition:	On display in "The Factory at King Street, 1849-1935" Exhibition held in 1993 at the Museum and Art Gallery, Derby. Catalogue number 45.
Notes:	1. Although factory marked, it is likely that work on this dish ceased, when some roughness, which is present in the body, was noticed and the gilding was therefore not applied.
	2. Some crazing.

Saucer Dish

Description: A saucer dish with narrow gilt border and swags of mixed flowers in enamel colours, similar to pattern 320 used at Nottingham Road. The centre panel decorated in enamel colours with a land-scape depicting a group of children overlooking a river.

Painter: W. E. Mosley.

Marks: Signed "W. E. Mosley" in puce on the reverse and inscribed in puce "Chepstow Castle". Puce crown over crossed swords and D, with two sets of three dots and initials S and H. Also in puce the initials "WL" which form the monogram of proprietor William Larcombe.

Measurements: Diameter 20.5cm.

Date: Circa 1915-1917.

Location: Private collection.

Notes: Dish is crazed.

Dish

Description:	Lozenge shaped dish with gadroon rim and wide gilt border. The centre panel decorated in enamel colours with a landscape view of Derby, depicting the churches of Saint Alkmund's and Saint Mary's in the background, the bridge over the river Derwent and the Bridge Chapel , Derby, on the far bank.
Painter:	W. E. Mosley.
Marks:	Signed in painting "W. E. Mosley". Inscribed on reverse, "St. Mary's Bridge" in puce. Inscribed above footrim, "W. St.A.St.J." in gilt, over the Welsh Dragon in enamel colours, followed by "Mercia L. of I. 1936." in gilt. Puce crown over crossed swords and D, with two sets of three dots and initials S and H.
Measurements:	27.5cm. x 20.5cm.
Date:	1930s.
Location:	Private collection.

Coffee Can and Saucer

Description:
Cylindrical can with wishbone handle and a circular saucer. Each decorated in enamel colours with a circular landscape scene within a gilt band. The border of the saucer and the exterior of the cup decorated in enamels and gilt with floral swags and grey seaweed.

Painter:
W. E. Mosley.

Marks:
Can and Saucer: Puce crown over crossed swords and D, with two sets of three dots and initials S and H. Also the initials "WLP" which form the monogram of proprietors William Larcombe and Howard Paget.
Can: Inscribed "Iona. W. E. Mosley", near footrim in puce.
Saucer: Inscribed "Nidpath Castle. W. E. Mosley", near footrim in puce.

Measurements:
Cup: Height 6.5cm.
Saucer: Diameter 14cm.

Date:
Circa 1917-1933.

Location:
Private collection.

Literature:
S. Reyburn, *Antiques Trade Gazette*, 11 April 1992, "Auction Reports ", p.14, an account of a sale at Par in Cornwall. A King Street part tea and coffee set was sold for the sum of over £4,600. The set was subsequently split up, and this is part of it.

Exhibition:
On display in "The Factory at King Street, 1849-1935" Exhibition held in 1993 at The Museum and Art Gallery, Derby. Catalogue number 69.

Notes:
The pattern on this can and saucer is in imitation of the earlier Nottingham Road pattern number 320.

Plaque

Description:	An unusually small circular plaque, decorated in enamel colours with a spray of mixed flowers.
Painter:	W. E. Mosley.
Marks:	Puce crown over crossed swords and D, with two sets of three dots and initials S and H. Also the mark of two crossed parallel lines and the initials "W.E.M" in puce.
Measurements:	Diameter 2.5cm.
Date:	Circa 1915-1935.
Location:	In the collection of Mr. and Mrs. H. Cordwent.

Watercolour

Description: A watercolour of two exotic birds, one perched on a branch and the other standing on one leg.

Painter: W. E. Mosley.

Measurements: 27cm. x 22cm.

Date: Twentieth century.

Location: In the collection of Dr. J. R. Freeman.

Literature: A similar bird, also painted by H. S. Hancock on a large bottle, is illustrated in Twitchett and Bailey, *Royal Crown Derby*, Antique Collectors' Club, 1988, plates 11a and b.

Exhibition: On display in "The Factory at King Street 1849-1935" Exhibition held in 1993 at The Museum and Art Gallery, Derby. Catalogue number 142.

Notes: This is unsigned, but was found in a folder of paintings by W. E. Mosley.

Watercolour

Description:	A watercolour of a country scene depicting a lake with a king-fisher, framed by silver birch trees, in the foreground. Cattle crossing a bridge and buildings in the middle ground and wooded country in the background.
Painter:	W. E. Mosley.
Marks:	Signed "W. E. Mosley" in the painting.
Measurements:	24.5cm. x 16.8cm.
Date:	Twentieth century.
Location:	In the collection of Dr. J. R. Freeman.
Exhibition:	On display in "The Factory at King Street, 1849-1935" Exhibition held in 1993 at The Museum and Art Gallery, Derby. Catalogue number 141.

WILLIAM MOSLEY snr
Possible Modeller

William Mosley senior may have been employed at King Street, however, no proof for this statement has yet been found.

JOHN MOUNTFORD
Potter & inventor of the Parian Body

A very important man in the world of ceramics, and whilst trying to re-create the recipe for Old Derby biscuit figures, John Mountford invented the Parian body when working for Alderman William Copeland in Stoke. The merit of his discovery was claimed in 1851 by Thomas Battam, Copeland's manager, but Mountford wrote a letter to the Staffordshire Advertiser which proved his right to be the real inventor (1).

Born in 1816, he was the youngest son of Thomas Mountford, who had been employed as an enamel kiln fireman at the Nottingham Road factory, and whose name appears on the 1832 List. Born in Staffordshire, his father Thomas also appears in the Glover's *Directory for Derby* dated 1843 where he is recorded as a Freeholder, "working at the china works". The family was then living in Erasmus Street, a street where many families associated with the china trade dwelled.

Apprenticed at the Nottingham Road China Works, John Mountford

John Mountford, potter and inventor of the Parian Body.
Derby Local Studies Library.

remained there until its closure in 1848 when he left to work as a figure maker for William Copeland.

He recalled in an interview that he returned to Derby and began work at the King Street factory around April 1866 and remained there into his old age (2).

Sampson Hancock, the sole proprietor of King Street from 1866 until his death in 1895, recalled of Mountford, who was one year older than himself in an interview which was published on Saturday, 12 May 1894 by Edward Bradbury "Strephon", of the *Yorkshire Weekly Post*:

"If you had paid me a visit a few days ago, you might have seen John Mountford, whom I employed. He was apprenticed at the Old Works, in Derby, but he left early in life, and came to Messrs. Copeland and Garrett's at Stoke on Trent, to start the figure trade there. While in their employ he brought out the composition known to the trade as Parian, or imitation marble, which has done more to increase that branch of the potter's art than anything invented in the present century. The name of this man will be recorded in time to come among those of famous potters, and he is the oldest potter from the original works. I regret to say that he is now suffering from a paralytic seizure."

ISAAC NEWTON
China turner

Isaac Newton was born in 1802. His baptism, which took place when he was an adult, occurred on 20 February 1820, at Saint Alkmund's Church, Derby.

His father George Newton had married Hannah Hesketh at the same church on 25 September 1797, and had been employed at the Nottingham Road manufactory, and in 1843 in the Derby Directory for that year, was living in Bath Street when his occupation was described as "working at the china factory".

In the 1840 Rates Books Isaac Newton, who was later to work at King Street, is recorded as occupying a property at 12 City Road, Derby, a house which was being administered by Street's executors, the latter being a family who had several members involved with boat and barge building in Derby.

The 1851 Census for Derby has only one entry for the name Isaac Newton. Taken in the Parish of Saint Alkmund's, Isaac Newton was a labourer living in City Road. He was aged 48. His age when taken with the year of his birth suggests that this may be the Isaac Newton employed at King Street.

He is recorded in the Census Returns for Saint Alkmund's Parish for the years 1871 and 1881 as living at 33 City Road, Derby. Described as a "China Turner" in the 1881 Census, he is now a widower, living with him are his unmarried daughter Eliza who was a silk reeler aged 33, and granddaughter Mary Newton, aged 19, a cigar maker.

It is thought most probable that he transferred with the small band of men to King Street following the closure of the Nottingham Road factory in 1848.

Recorded in the marriage register of Saint Alkmund's Church, Derby, was a china thrower with the surname Newton. The entry appears for the date 31 August 1827, however there is no Christian name given (1).

DORIS LOUISE PACEY, later to become MRS. MORRIS
Painter

Doris Pacey, later to become Mrs. Morris, was born in Derby in 1903. She attended the School of Art, Technical College, Derby and on 3 September 1918 was awarded a second class award in freehand drawing, and drawing of plant form, in the East Midland Educational Union.

In 1918, she joined the King Street factory where she was taught by William Mosley. When she first started decorating, items such as Toby jugs, Mother Gamp extinguishers and thimbles were done by her. She also painted wild flowers and witches Japan pattern.

In an interview with Hilda Moore she recalled that on one occasion she broke the hand from a Mother Gamp, and that Mr. Hancock had tried to repair it for her, only to find that when the piece was fired the hand came away in the kiln. Mr. Larcombe who did the dipping came upstairs and said to her, "Doris be sure your sins will find you out." She also recalled that when she was a young worker, William Mosley had been very kind to her and that she often went for tea with him and his wife at their flat in Friargate and later to their house in Duffield Road (1).

Her daughter remembered that her mother lived in Rutland Street, Derby, and cycled daily to work.

Aged 27 or 28, Doris went to India where she was employed as a nanny. It was here she met her husband Mr. Morris who was a member of the Indian Army. Approximately four years later she and her husband returned to Derby and settled in Rutland Street, with the first of their four daughters.

After returning to Derby, Doris decorated Christmas cards, often bearing her signature, which retailed at the Central Educational bookshop in Derby for 2/6d. and for which she was paid 1/- each.

She later painted watercolour inserts for brooches.

One of her daughters recalled that she continued painting watercolours up until her death, and occasionally decorated place settings in watercolours for family weddings. Her daughter also recalled being taken to William Mosley's house in Duffield Road, and recalled Mosley had two parrots in the house. He was "always very thin and always wore plus-fours. He was very kind – a gentleman"(2).

Doris died in 1991.

F. HOWARD PAGET
Proprietor

A proprietor of the King Street factory, an account of his involvement can be found in Chapter One.

ELIZABETH PARWICH
Burnisher

Recorded in the 1861 Census for the Parish of Saint Alkmund's, Miss Elizabeth Parwich was living at Court No. 2, Bridge Gate. Her occupation was given as "Burnisher".

ALICE PATES
China painter

Very little is known of Alice Pates, except that she was recorded as a flower paintress, working at King Street. She is said to have worked at a table with Annie Bailey (1).

ELIZABETH C. POWELL
Possible china burnisher

Living at 24 Grove Place in the Parish of Saint Alkmund's, Derby, Elizabeth's name appears in the 1881 Census. It is thought she may have been employed at King Street.

The daughter of George H. Powell, an Iron Foundry Cupola Minder and his wife Sarah, Elizabeth was born in Mansfield, Notts. Her occupation is given as a "Burnisher at the China Factory".

EDWIN PRINCE
China painter

Edwin Prince was baptised on 6 November 1825 at Saint Alkmund's Parish Church, Derby, the son of Paul Prince and his wife Sarah Kerry, who had married at the same church on 17 May 1813. One of the last apprentices at the Nottingham Road factory, Edwin specialised in painting landscapes.

It has been recorded that Edwin Prince never actually worked at the King Street factory, but during the 1880s decorated blanks supplied by Sampson Hancock, which he returned from Norfolk to the china works for firing, and which bore the King Street mark(1). An alternative suggestion is that these pieces were fired locally in Norfolk. However, in his notes covering the life of the factory, which are transcribed in Chapter One, proprietor Larcombe states that Prince was employed at King Street.

There are many theories as to where and when Prince was employed. One authority records that following the closure of the Nottingham Road works, Prince worked in London for a time before being employed at Wales' Glass manufactory in Newcastle upon Tyne between the years c.1855 and 1875, suggesting that his pieces provided for King Street would date from around 1880, whilst others believe that when the Nottingham Road factory closed in 1848, Prince moved to King Street, from where in 1855 he went to work at Newcastle upon Tyne as a painter on glass, producing ecclesiastical windows (2). For many years he produced work for leading figures such as Pugin.

There is no mention of Edwin Prince in the 1851 Census for the town of Derby.

Of Edwin Prince, Haslem (3) says:

"On the closure of the old Derby works Prince, for a short time, worked in London, and for more than the last twenty years has been engaged at glass painting at Messrs. Wales's establishment, Newcastle-upon-Tyne. Others of the old Derby apprentices found employment at the same establishment. Prince's landscapes, on Derby China, may be known by the prevalence of warm brown tints, which are used in finishing. A pair of large bottle-shaped vases, painted by Prince, with landscapes all round, were shewn in the Nottingham Exhibition in 1872, in which this characteristic was apparent. They were the property of Mr. Sulley, of Nottingham, and had been originally purchased at the manufactory by the late Mr. Horsley, of Pye Bridge, Derbyshire. Prince painted several views on china plaques, of various sizes, of the Nunnery which was erected on, and covered the whole of the site formerly occupied by Duesbury's early china works, on the Nottingham Road."

Although establishing his whereabouts is somewhat difficult during the earlier years, Edwin Prince retired to Norfolk. By the time of the 1881 Census for the county he was living with his sister Sarah Payne at Londs in Overstrand. Sarah was a widow and Edwin a widower. Edwin was shown to be a retired glass painter aged 55. Perhaps painting blanks for Sampson Hancock was influenced by the fact that one of his neighbours was Edward Seago, the famous Norfolk artist. Examples of Edwin Prince's watercolours have been recorded by the authors at auctions in Norfolk, perhaps suggesting that not only did he paint for the King Street factory at that time, but also supplemented his income with other forms of artwork.

Edwin Prince remained in Norfolk for the rest of his life, dying in Overstrand in January 1896, a few weeks after the death of Sampson Hancock.

An obituary, taken from *Painters and the Derby China Works* by J. Murdoch & J. Twitchett (4), which was published in 1896, is shown overleaf:

DEATH OF A DERBY ARTIST – THE DEATH IS ANNOUNCED OF Mr. Edwin Prince, of Overstrand, Cromer, which took place on Thursday evening. The deceased was the last of the old school of china painters, employed at the old Crown Porcelain Works, Nottingham Road, and excelled particularly in landscape work. At the break up of the old factory in 1848, he went to Newcastle-on-Tyne, where he was employed for many years as a painter on glass for ecclesiastical windows. His work had a national reputation, and he executed many commissions for the Pugins. In his retirement at Overstrand he occupied his leisure in landscape painting on china for his old friend Mr. Sampson Hancock of King Street, Derby and it is a somewhat remarkable coincidence that these two links with the past should be broken within a few weeks of each other. No-one who has seen specimens of Mr. Prince's work could fail to admire the extreme delicacy of its shading and the faultless character of his perspective, in which he stood almost without a rival. Mr. Prince was a member of the old Derby family, and one of his brothers occupies a responsible position at Messrs. Haslam Union Iron Factory. At the time of his death, which was caused by bronchitis, he was in his 70th year.

Prince's initials often appear on landscapes by him, and his signature and S and H mark on the reverse are usually accompanied by the additional initials JW which it is believed refer to the gilder John Winfield. Items decorated by Prince were nearly always flatware.

It is not known if Edwin's younger brother Henry and their father Paul Prince worked at King Street. In the 1851 Census for the Parish of Saint Alkmund's Derby, they are both recorded as model makers, and may have been employed at the china works.

Plate

Description:	A dessert plate with gadroon rim and wide gilt border. The central landscape is of High Tor, Matlock.
Painter:	Edwin Prince.
Marks:	Signed "E. Prince" in the painting. Red crown over crossed swords and D, with two sets of three dots and initials S and H. Also initials " JW" in red.
Measurements:	Diameter 22cm.
Date:	Circa 1880-1896.
Location:	Royal Crown Derby Museum.
Notes:	Several cracks.

Plate

Description:	A plate with gilt border and touches of pink enamel. The centre panel decorated in enamel colours with a landscape depicting a ruined castle with sheep in the foreground.
Painter:	Edwin Prince.
Marks:	Signed "E. Prince" in the painting, also inscribed in the painting "Remains of Castle Dinas Bren or Bron". Red crown over crossed swords and D, with two sets of three dots and initials S and H.
Measurements:	Diameter 20cm.
Date:	Circa 1880-1896.
Location:	Private collection.

Plate

Description:	A dessert plate of daisy shape, with wide embossed border. The central panel is painted in enamel colours with a landscape view of Rhuddlan Castle by moonlight.
Painter:	Edwin Prince.
Marks:	Signed "E. Prince", with inscription "Rhuddlan Castle" in the painting. Red crown over crossed swords and D, with two sets of three dots and initials S and H. Also on the base a full S and H mark is impressed above the painted one and in script "J.W. 12".
Measurements:	Diameter 22cm.
Date:	Circa 1880-1896.
Location:	In the collection of Mr. G. Orme.
Provenance:	Kent collection, No. 7.
Literature:	Twitchett and Bailey, *Royal Crown Derby*, Antique Collectors' Club, 1988, p, 23.

Dish

Description:	A small dish with scalloped rim, and cut-out loop handle and wide gilt border. The central panel is painted in enamel colours with a landscape view of Raglan(d) Castle, with cattle in the foreground.
Painter:	Edwin Prince.
Marks:	Signed "E.Prince" with inscription "Raglan(d) Castle" in the painting. Red crown over crossed swords and D, with two sets of three dots and initials S and H. Also on the base, the script "JW12".
Measurements:	21cm. x 19.5cm.
Date:	Circa 1880-1896.
Location:	In the collection of Mr. G. Orme.

Saucer

Description: A circular saucer with spiral fluted border decorated with a complex pattern of flowering foliage in gilt, in a wide border around the rim. In the centre is an enamelled landscape view of Netherby Hall with an expanse of water in the foreground.

Painter: Edwin Prince.

Marks: Signed "E. Prince" in painting. Red crown over crossed swords and D, with two sets of three dots and initials S and H. Also on the base in script "J.W.12" and "Netherby Hall". Impressed in the base "Derby".

Measurements: Diameter 14cm.

Date: Circa 1880-1896.

Location: In the collection of Dr. J. R. Freeman.

Exhibition: On display in "The Factory at King Street, 1849-1935" Exhibition held in 1993 at The Museum and Art Gallery, Derby. Catalogue number 20.

Mug

Description:	A cylindrical christening mug with a handle having an angular top. On one side of the exterior a monogram and date encircled by garlands, all executed in gilding. On the other side, a view of Haddon Hall in enamel colours.
Painter:	Edwin Prince.
Marks:	Signed "E. Prince." with inscription " Haddon Hall" in the landscape view. Monogram "E.W.T." and date "1892" on exterior. Worker's mark "J.W. 12" on base, near rim, in red. Red crown over crossed swords and D, with two sets of three dots and initials S and H.
Measurements:	Height 12cm. Diameter 13cm.
Date:	1892.
Location:	Derby Museums and Art Gallery. No. 1984-250.
Exhibition:	On display in "The Factory at King Street, 1849-1935" Exhibition held in 1993 at The Museum and Art Gallery, Derby. Catalogue number 188.
Notes:	The Museum's accession register states that this mug was made for the christening of Edgar W. Tacchella.

162

Pair of Vases

Description:	A pair of small vases, with covers, decorated in Islamic style in enamels and lavishly gilt.
Painter:	Attributed in Royal Crown Derby Museum records to Edwin Prince, but unsigned.
Marks:	On bodies only, red crown over crossed swords and D, with two sets of three dots and initials S and H. Also the initials "J.W." on both bodies.
Measurements:	Height 12.5cm.
Date:	Late nineteenth century.
Location:	Royal Crown Derby Museum.
Notes:	Several areas of restoration.

JACK RATCLIFFE
China painter

Born in 1910, Jack Ratcliffe first worked for Mintons, before coming to King Street, having been laid off during a slack period. His wife Florrie Cooke recalled in an interview that he and two other young men had come to King Street to work at the same time in the early 1930s. Jack remained at the factory until the takeover in 1935. It is recorded that he worked with Chivers, Mosley, Machin, Haddock, Hancock and Hargreaves (1). He was employed as a flower painter.

When he arrived in Derby he began courting Florrie and rented a caravan at Stenson Lock to be near her, returning home to Stoke at weekends. Having foresaken the caravan he then lived in Edward Street, prior to his marriage to Florrie in April 1937, when the couple lived at 33 Friar Avenue*.

On the closure of the King Street works in 1935, Jack went to work at Rolls Royce (2), where he remained until 1971.

Jack Ratcliffe, painter.
Twitchett & Bailey, "Royal Crown Derby."

Many pieces decorated by Jack Ratcliffe are signed with his initials JR. A signed tea service, bearing the Pug and Peg mark, decorated by him and in a private collection, shows that not only was he a traditional flower painter, he also produced some pieces which had a very art deco style, which was slightly unusual for King Street. Landscapes by him on King Street china are rare.

Painting only for pleasure in his later years he was well known as a watercolour artist, occasionally painting commissions.

He died in 1976.

*Note: The authors are unsure if the Friar Avenue referred to was in Derby.

Milk Jug

Description:	A milk jug of swelling body shape with sparrow beak spout and loop handle, with gilt rim top and bottom. Part of a tea service, the jug is decorated with a large single pansy and trailing forget-me-nots in enamel colours.
Painter:	Jack Ratcliffe.
Marks:	Inscribed initials "JR" in red. Red crown over crossed swords and D, with two sets of three dots and initials S and H. Also in red the crossed P's of proprietor Paget and his wife.
Measurements:	Height 8.75cm
Date:	1933-1935.
Location:	Private collection

Gypsy Cauldron

Description:	An ornamental piece in the form of a gypsy cooking pot, with a bellied body, three short conical feet and two fixed small angular handles. Decorated with flowers in enamel colours and gilding.
Painter:	Jack Ratcliffe.
Marks:	Signed "J. H. Ratcliffe", in the painting. Red crown over crossed swords and D, with two sets of three dots and initials S and H. Also initials "J.R".
Measurements:	Height 5.5cm.
Date:	1930-1935.
Location:	Private collection.
Literature:	A similar cauldron, but with applied flowers, illustrated in factory sales catalogue, 1934-5, number 61.
Exhibition:	On display in "The Factory at King Street, 1849-1935" Exhibition held in 1993 at The Museum and Art Gallery, Derby. Catalogue number 130.
Notes:	Some crazing.

LIZZIE RAYWORTH
Burnisher

Born in Barnsley, Yorkshire, in 1871, Lizzie was the step-daughter of William Rayworth jnr, china painter, and his wife Margaret Rayworth, formerly Hatton, a china gilder. Aged 20 in the 1891 Census for the Parish of Saint Alkmund's, Derby, Lizzie was occupying a house with her parents in Bridge Gate. (See the entry for William Rayworth). In the 1891 Census she is not recorded as being unemployed which may suggest she worked at King Street in some capacity.

MARGARET RAYWORTH
Gilder

The wife of William Rayworth jnr Margaret was born in Stone, Staffordshire c.1851. In 1881 she and her husband were employed in the china trade in Staffordshire (see entry for William Rayworth jnr.). Formerly Margaret Hatton, a widow, she appears as Margaret Rayworth living at 2 Bridge Gate, an address she shared with her husband and family, in the 1891 Census for Derby. Her occupation was shown as a gilder. Not recorded as unemployed in the 1891 Census she may have been employed as a gilder at King Street.

WILLIAM RAYWORTH snr
China painter.

It has not yet been possible to establish personal details of William Rayworth senior, although an extensive search has been carried out.

Two pieces by William Rayworth were featured in the 1993 King Street Exhibition at the Derby City Museum and Art Gallery. One was dated 1853 but bore no S and H mark, and the second, a signed plaque, dated 7 October 1868, bears the S and H mark confirming he was employed by Sampson Hancock at that time.

He died in 1880 and is known to have painted both flowers and landscapes.

Plaque

Description:	A framed plaque, depicting a bunch of mixed garden flowers and leaves, painted on a rectangular shaped sheet of opaque glass.
Painter:	W. Rayworth.
Marks:	Signed "W. Rayworth" in painting.
Measurements:	16cm. x 12cm.
Date:	Late nineteenth century.
Location:	Private collection.
Notes:	One of many known pieces painted on opaque glass and signed by W. Rayworth, but produced outside the King Street factory.

Plaque

Description: A framed plaque, handpainted with a portrait of a milkmaid, in enamel colours on porcelain. Trees and landscape in the back ground.

Painter: William Rayworth.

Marks: Signed "W. Rayworth. Derby Oct. 7 1868". Red crown over crossed swords and D, with two sets of three dots and initials S and H.

Measurements: 20.5cm. x 15cm.

Date: 1868.

Location: Derby Museums and Art Gallery. No. 1988-329.

Exhibition: On display in "The Factory at King Street, 1849-1935" Exhibition held in 1993 at the Museum and Art Gallery, Derby. Catalogue number 195.

Notes: William Rayworth painted many subjects on opaque glass. His painting on King Street china is rare, this plaque being one of only two known marked pieces, the other being a vase dated 1873.

WILLIAM RAYWORTH jnr

Possible china painter

In 1881 William Rayworth jnr was living at 26 Middle John Street, Stoke upon Trent, when he was described as a "China Painter". With him at the same address were his wife Margaret (this was her second marriage), who was a china gilder, father-in-law Thomas Heath aged 62, who was a "Potter's slipmaker", brother-in-law Thomas Heath junior and Lizzie Hatton his stepdaughter.

Born in Derby, c.1852, William Rayworth and his family appear in the 1891 Census for Saint Alkmund's as occupying No. 2 Bridge Gate. The property was part of St. Anne's Terrace, which was owned by Sampson Hancock, proprietor of the King Street factory, for which William Rayworth and his wife Lizzie were paying a rental of £10 per annum.

William was recorded as a "china painter", and had been born in Derby. His wife Margaret, aged 40, and born in Longton, Staffs., is recorded as a china gilder. Their eldest daughter Lizzie, aged 20, who was born in Barnsley, Yorkshire, is shown to be a china burnisher.

It is believed that both he and his wife decorated glass panels, and more examples of his fruit and flower painting produced in this way exist than his work on porcelain bearing the S and H mark. Up until a few years ago it was possible to see examples of his work on opaline glass in almost every public house in Derby. It is thought these glass pictures were a means of paying for his beer.

MR. REDFERN

Gilder

Very little is known concerning Mr. Redfern, except that he is said to have worked at the King Street factory as a gilder during the 1920s.

Doris Pacey recalled that she worked at a table opposite to Mr. Redfern, the gilder (1).

In the late eighteenth and early nineteenth century the Redfern family married into the Longdon, Cooper, and Goadsby families, all of whom had connections with the china industry.

JOSEPH BARLOW ROBINSON

Outside modeller

"DERBY CHINA:- The new Cavendish Mirror Frame is designed geometrical with leaf and bead mouldings, the centre forming an oval. On the raised part of the frame are introduced festoons of flowers modelled with great delicacy, and coloured to imitate nature, the other portions being so richly coloured and gilt. This beautiful specimen of Derby China has been produced at the Derby China Works, and it was designed by Mr. J. B. Robinson, sculptor of Derby."

This advertisement appeared in the *Derby Mercury* on 23 October 1867, confirming that King Street continued in the tradition of the Nottingham Road China Works in having eminent sculptors provide them with models.

The newspaper advertisement helps to establish Joseph Barlow Robinson's connection with porcelain manufacture. Barlow's interest in porcelain was recorded by Haslem who stated that he owned some interesting pieces by him. Haslem had also borrowed letters written by William Pegg which belonged to Joseph Barlow Robinson, which illustrates that the man had an interest in historical matters to do with porcelain.

Born in 1821, in, South Wingfield, Derbyshire, when aged 21, Joseph Barlow Robinson worked in the Sculpture Department of the Houses of Parliament, where he remained for five years.

Robinson's Medieval Carving Works was founded by him in Derby in 1852. This venture was swiftly followed by the Midland Sculpture and Monument Works, a company which exhibited at the 1870 Midland Counties Exhibition of Works of Art and Industrial Products, which was held in Derby. Renowned throughout the country, his company produced numerous ornate wooden carvings of fountains, statues, pulpits and headstones as well as armorial designs.

The mirror frame, which is illustrated here, measures 33cm. long x 26cm. wide. In glazed white, it is marked with the blue S and H mark.

JOHN JAMES ROBINSON
  Proprietor and potter

A grandson of Sampson Hancock, he inherited the china works upon the death of his grandfather in 1895. For more details see Chapter One under the section covering Proprietors.

ALFRED ROOME
  China maker

Hilda Moore records that Alfred was living in Parker Street at the time of the 1871 Census, when his occupation was listed as china maker. His name does not appear in the 1881 Census for Derby. The only Alfred Roome listed may have been his son who was a stocking maker.

JAMES ROUSE. snr
China painter

James Rouse was employed by Sampson Hancock at the King Street factory for seven years. His employment commenced in 1875 and ceased in October 1882.

The son of William Rouse and Sarah Hallam, James was baptised at Saint Alkmund's Church, Derby, on 27 February 1803, and was apprenticed to Robert Bloor at the Nottingham Road factory c.1815. His occupation of "china painter" is confirmed in the Marriage Register of Saint Werburgh's, Derby, at the time of his marriage to Sarah Allsop on 23 September 1823, when he was living in London Road.

The couple had several children, and the baptism of their son Charles at St. Peter's Church, Derby, on 18 January 1830, suggests James Rouse was still employed in Derby. At some time after this date he left and went to the Potteries before settling at the Coalport factory. His name is included on a broadsheet concerned with the porcelain trade

James Rouse, Snr., painter.
Twitchett & Bailey, "Royal Crown Derby."

which was published in Ironbridge in 1833, helping to confirm his whereabouts at that time (1). In 1837 his son James was born in Ironbridge.

John Haslem (2), at the time of writing *The Old Derby China Factory* in 1876, said of Rouse:

"James Rouse was apprenticed at Derby where he learned flower painting. He left the factory before 1830 and for a time worked in the Potteries, and afterwards for many years at Coalport, chiefly painting flowers, and occasionally figure subjects. He painted portraits in oil and on china also. He is now in Birmingham, employed in painting small enamels on metal, such as figures, flowers, animals & c., for jewellery and goldsmiths' work."

Godden records that whilst at Coalport James Rouse snr, in addition to his usual floral decoration, had painted pieces decorated with figures and cupids, as well as portrait miniatures on porcelain (3). The 1859 wages list for the factory shows that James senior earned £2-14-0d per week, whilst his son James earned 2gns. Shortly after this date, having remained in Coalport for almost thirty years, he left and was employed in Birmingham, where he was engaged in decorating enamelled jewellery.

The 1881 Census for Derby confirms his second wife Elizabeth was born in Shirley Heath, Warwickshire, and that the couple's unmarried daughter Emily's birthplace had been Birmingham. Aged 21, Emily's birth in 1860 suggests James Rouse was in Birmingham at this time. It is also thought he worked for Ridgways in the Potteries before returning to Derby in 1875 to work for Sampson Hancock at his china manufactory in King Street.

The same Census confirms his whereabouts as being 44 Fleet Street, Litchurch, Derby, where he lived with his wife Elizabeth and their daughter Emily. Shown to be a "China painter", aged 68, he was either unsure of his age, or wished to be younger, in view of the fact his wife was 21 years his junior.

In an interview given with Edward Bradbury of the *Yorkshire Weekly Post*, published on 12 May 1894, Sampson Hancock said of James Rouse:

> "In 1875 I engaged Mr. James Rouse, who died in February 1888, at the ripe age of eighty-five years, having continued to within a few years of his decease to practise as a china painter, an art he learnt at the Old Derby China Factory over seventy years before. He left Derby for the Potteries, and worked also at Coalport, and in coming to me in King Street he returned to his native place and to employment the direct offshoot of the original Old Derby Factory, on the Nottingham Road. To me, for the ensuing seven years, he proved a valuable workman, for, being so good a general hand, he was able to paint all kinds of subjects that were required. I have still a few examples of his work remaining, in his various styles, such as flowers, figures, birds, landscapes &c., which illustrate his manner and show that his reputation was not over-rated."

The sale catalogue of the W. W. Winter Collection, which took place on 27 June 1884, at the Athenaeum Rooms, Derby, at 11 o'clock, contained the following entry:

> "The lots 120 to 126 were painted by Rouse, Sen., when working, some years ago, for the Old China Works, Duffield Road and were bought up by Mr. Winter on account of their increasing value. Since Mr. Rouse assisted in painting the celebrated "Gladstone Service," his work has been in great demand and is becoming very scarce.
> James Rouse, Snr., the Veteran Flower Painter, was apprenticed at the Old Works and remained there until 1830, he worked in the same room with Pegg the Quaker, Robertson, Cotton, Corden, and others, and at night, together with other boys, often met at the house of Pegg for instruction in Flower Painting. He returned to Derby some years ago and painted for Mr. S. Hancock, of the Old Derby Works, when the above lots were executed. Although over 82 years of age, he is still painting with his accustomed vigour at the Crown Derby Porcelain Works, Osmaston Road, where he recently took part in painting the celebrated Gladstone Dessert Service."

One of the most accomplished painters ever employed by King Street, all his work commands great respect. Signed pieces by him are extremely sought after. Watercolours by him are seldom seen.

He died in February 1888.

Plate

Description:	A cabinet plate with a pierced, gilt trellis work border, and within the border three panels painted in enamel colours with bouquets of flowers. In the centre is a landscape scene depicting a gun dog and dead game.
Painter:	James Rouse senior.
Marks:	Signed near the footrim "J. Rouse Sen." Red crown over crossed swords and D, with two sets of three dots and initials S and H.
Measurements:	Diameter 23.5cm.
Date:	1875-1882.
Location:	Royal Crown Derby Museum.
Exhibition:	On display in "The Factory at King Street, 1849-1935" Exhibition held in 1993 at The Museum and Art Gallery, Derby. Catalogue number 100.

Plate

Description: A cabinet plate with gadroon rim and blue ground border embellished with gilt acanthus scrolls. In the centre is a scene of a barefoot woman and child crossing a stream. The woman carries a basket of straw on her back.

Painter: James Rouse senior.

Marks: Signed "J. Rouse" in the painting. Red crown over crossed swords and D, with two sets of three dots and initials S and H.

Measurements: Diameter 22cm.

Date: 1875-1882.

Location: Derby Museums and Art Gallery. No. 1993-113.

Exhibition: On display in "The Factory at King Street, 1849-1935" Exhibition held in 1993 at The Museum and Art Gallery, Derby. Catalogue number 213.

Vase

Description:	A vase of similar form to the Kedleston shape. There are two panels painted with flowers in enamel colours on a turquoise ground.
Painter:	Attributed in Royal Crown Derby Museum records to James Rouse senior, but unsigned.
Marks:	Underglaze blue, incomplete crown over crossed swords and D, with two sets of three dots and initials S and H.
Measurements:	Height 31.5cm.
Date:	Later nineteenth century.
Location:	Royal Crown Derby Museum.
Notes:	The turquoise ground colour has not taken well.

Plaque

Description:	An oval plaque decorated in enamel colours with mixed flowers within a moulded gilt border, this having two bows.
Painter:	James Rouse senior.
Marks:	Signed "J. Rouse" in the painting. Red crown over crossed swords and D, with two sets of three dots and initials S and H.
Measurements:	14.25cm. x 12.5cm.
Date:	1875-1882.
Location:	Private collection.
Notes:	1. This plaque was turned out in the white (blue mark), perhaps for use by amateur painters at home.
	2. There is no means of displaying this plaque, other than by hanging it.

Watercolour

Description:	A watercolour depicting fruit and flowers in a basket on a marble slab.
Painter:	James Rouse senior.
Marks:	Signed "J. Rouse" in the painting.
Measurements:	15cm. x 12cm.
Date:	Later nineteenth century (before February 1888).
Location:	In the collection of Dr. J. R. Freeman.
Exhibition:	On display in "The Factory at King Street, 1849-1935" Exhibition held in 1993 at The Museum and Art Gallery, Derby. Catalogue number 144.

THOMAS ROUSE
China potter

Recorded as a "China Potter" in the 1851 Census for the Parish of Saint Alkmund's, Derby, Thomas Rouse was living with his wife and four children at 10 King Street. It is highly probable that he went to the King Street factory when the Nottingham Road China Works closed.

Hilda Moore also records he was living in King Street at the time of the 1851 Census (1).

There is an Edward Rouse who was a potter at Nottingham Road who is mentioned on the 1832 list.

JANE RUTLAND
Employed at China Manufactory

Born in Derby in 1830, Jane is believed to be the daughter of James Rutland and Sarah Cotton. Living with her brother James, aged 12, and sister Ann, aged 19, she occupied a house with her widowed mother Sarah at the time of the 1851 Census. The family's address was 57 Nottingham Road in the Parish of Saint Alkmund's, and one of their next door neighbours was Sampson Hancock one of the founder partners of the china works. Jane was aged 21 and shown as being employed at the china manufactory. It is not known in what capacity she was employed.

If she is the daughter of James Rutland and Sarah Cotton, her parents were married at Saint Michael's church on 22 May 1820.

There were several members of the Rutland family whose names appear on the 1832 Nottingham Road List. Thomas Rutland snr and William Rutland were both gilders, and an M. Rutland was listed as a burnisher.

AMY AND EVA SADLER
Burnishers and china repairers

Very little is known of the personal life of both Amy and Eva Sadler, however an interview given by Mr. Colwyn Evans which recalls them can be found in Chapter Seven.

In another interview(1) given by Elsie Larcombe , the daughter of proprietor William Larcombe, she recalled that the Misses Sadler, Amy and Eva, were responsible for the burnishing, and that they also repaired china that had been brought into the shop, repairs often performed by riveting, which was a very skilled occupation.

Handwritten notes which are in a private collection and which are dated 1964 record that:

"Miss Evelyn Sadler, who with her sister Miss Amy Sadler carried on business of china dealers at no. 87 King St. having taken over the business from Mr. Larcombe who had given up on his retirement. The Misses Sadler worked first for Mr. Larcombe first at a shop in Green Street and then at no. 87 King Street.
Miss Evelyn Sadler's death occurred in April 1964 at the age of 74 years, her sister having predeceased her in 1962" (2).

F. SCHOFIELD
   China painter

Worked at the King Street factory at the time of its acquisition by Royal Crown Derby. He has been recorded as a painter of landscapes and flowers (1).

Menu Holder

Description:	A menu holder in the shape of an oval ring with modelled flowers and butterflies in enamel colours applied to the top surface.
Painter:	F. Schofield.
Marks:	Initialled "F. S." on base. Red crown over crossed swords and D, with two sets of three dots and initials S and H. Also in red, the crossed Ps mark of proprietor Paget and his wife.
Measurements:	Length 9cm. Width 5.5cm.
Date:	Circa 1933-1935.
Location:	In the collection of Mr. G. Orme.
Literature:	Illustrated in factory sales catalogue, 1934-35, number 82.

SHARDLOW

Very little is known of Shardlow except when he began working at the factory, possibly in the 1930s.

In an interview with Hilda Moore he recalled he was first put to work lighting fires and digging out the saggar clay from the pit in the yard. At times this had been a very messy occupation, particularly when the pit was half full of water. He said that there were three men on the clay side, Gregson, Shaw and Shaw jnr (1).

SAMUEL SHARP
Founder partner and potter

One of the founder partners of the china works, Samuel Sharp's details can be referred to in Chapter One.

SHAW snr
Caster

No dates are known for Shaw's employment as a caster, but it is thought most probable the date was during the late nineteenth century and possibly into the twentieth century.

SHAW jnr
Pedal boy

Son of the caster Shaw, he was employed as a pedal boy, which involved turning the potter's wheel. According to Shardlow, a member of the King Street workforce, Shaw had risen to become a caster when aged 16 (1).

The Shaw family are related to the Hancock family through Sampson Hancock's son John's marriage to Alice Buxton of Allestree, which might explain the Shaws' involvement with the china works.

Handwritten notes, dated May 1964 and now in private ownership, record that following Larcombe's leaving the factory:

> "the factory was carried on for a short-time by two different managers, but with indifferent success. The last of these was I think a man named Shaw who removed the exquisite gold scales in the mahogany cabinet which had belonged to the first Duesbury for his wife to keep her jewellery in and I wonder what has become of them" (2).

H. SHUFFLEBOTTOM
Potter

Described by Haslem (1) as: "an artist-workman of no mean ability", personal details of him are extremely difficult to trace. Probably a native of Staffordshire, where the surname has numerous members connected with the china industry, Shufflebottom was recorded by Haslem as having been employed at King Street, together with the fact that he had died by 1876.

A Catalogue of China belonging to John Haslem, refers to Shufflebottom in the following way:

"Looking glass frames, baskets, and other ornamental ware, decorated with raised flowers, in the style of the baskets (Catalogue entry 119) are in great demand; and, at different times, clever artistic workmen have been employed at this establishment (King Street) who excelled at this kind of work, among them Shufflebottom, Stephan, Barnet, &c."

In the 1851 Census for Derby there were two members of the family recorded, but neither was employed in the china trade.

A thorough search of the 1881 Census has been made, which suggests that the statement by Haslem is accurate. There are only two people with the same surname mentioned and they have no connection with the china trade.

H. Shufflebottom, modeller. Self portrait, with his dog Jock. On a china plaque, circa 1850. G. Orme Collection.

WILLIAM SLATER
China maker

Recorded by Hilda Moore as being a china maker, born in 1818 at Church Broughton, Derbyshire. Living in Darley Lane, with his wife and daughter in 1861 at the time of the census (1), he died in Derby in 1864.

WILLIAM SLATER
China painter

In the Freebody's *Directory for Derby* which was published in 1852, a William Slater who was a china painter is recorded as living in Nuns Street, Derby.

ANN STANLEY
Possible china painter

Her name has been recorded as being employed at King Street (1), when staying at an address in St. James Street, in the town in 1861.

Her name does not appear in the 1851 Census for the Parish of Saint Alkmund's, Derby.

HORATIO STEELE
China painter

The second son of the famous Derby painter Thomas Steele, Horatio's birth is recorded as 6 December 1807 at Burslem, the son of Thomas Steele and his wife Susannah who had married circa 1806 in Burslem.

Of Horatio Steele, Haslem says:

"Three of Steele's sons, Edwin, Horatio and Thomas, were apprenticed at the Derby Works, and they all inherited much of their father's talent. Edwin and Horatio were both clever flower painters."

A clever flower painter, Horatio painted a dessert service which was got up at Derby for the Queen in 1841 and 42(1). The following extract from Haslem records details of the Queen's service.

A dessert set for Her Majesty was made in 1841-42, and was one of the last orders of importance executed at the old Derby works. A number of patterns were made on the occasion, which were designed and executed by Joseph Slater, William Lucas, and one or two others. Several of these pattern plates are in the writer's possession, and they are for the quality of the ware, good tastes, and excellent workmanship, among the finest examples of the Bloor period, indeed several of them would do credit to the best manufactories of the present day. The pattern chosen for the Queen's service was a border of chrome-green, with six small panels in the border, in which were painted birds, insects, and small groups of flowers, the greater part of them being the work of Horatio Steele. The ground between the panels was gilded in embossed gold, and chased, in the style of Sevres. The comports were eight inches in height, supported by intertwined cornucopias. There were a number of mounted plates (assiettes montées) some with two, the largest with three tiers of plates, and on the top a vessel to hold flowers, altogether thirty inches in height. These, together with the comports and the ice-pails, were modelled from designs made expressly for the service, and the height of the pieces was determined by instructions from the Queen's confectioner and table-dresser, to suit the particular purposes for which they were required.

The firing of the twisted cornucopias caused considerable difficulty in manufacturing the comports, and many of them were split or otherwise spoiled before the proper manner of burning them was discovered.

On two occasions since the close of the old works the losses by breakage of this service have been made up by the new firm in King Street, Derby, in a satisfactory manner, and some matching has also been since done at Coalport, but the fruit dishes were made with different feet, on account of the difficulty in firing the cornucopia mounts above described (2).

Horatio Steele remained at the Nottingham Road works until its closure in 1848. He was still living in Derby in 1850 which suggests he possibly found employment at King Street during the early years.

"For a number of years after its commencement the King Street Works produced a good deal of ware turned out in the style of the later old Derby patterns, and a great deal of matching was from time to time done, the most important being, on several occasions, the making up of losses by breakage of the dessert service made for Her Majesty in 1842" (3).

Perhaps it had been Horatio Steele who had decorated the King Street replacements. In the Haslem Collection was the famous "Thistle Dish" by William Pegg, The Quaker, which Haslem records he purchased from Horatio in Derby in 1850. The following was said of the dish which appears in Haslem's Catalogue of China as entry no. 41:

"The Comport was always kept at the Old Works as a study for the flower painters, and was highly prized by them. On the dissolution of the Factory in 1848, it fell into the possession of Horatio Steele, one of the flower painters, from whom I bought it in Derby for four shillings, Jan. 1st, 1850. The same day I called and showed it to Pegg in his little huckster's shop on the Nottingham Road. As soon as he saw it, he began in his quiet manner to relate that how more than fifty years before he had gathered the original of that thistle, a Lady Thistle it was called, while taking a walk on Nun's Green one Whitson holiday"(4).

In the 1850s, Sampson Hancock, Quaker Pegg and Horatio Steele and the Rutland family were all living within a few doors of each other on Nottingham Road, Derby.

It is thought that since Horatio would have been in his forties at this time, he would have needed to be employed in some capacity, possibly at the china works.

The 1851 Census for the Parish of Saint Alkmund's, Derby, gives details of Horatio and his family. Living in Siddals Lane, he is recorded as a china painter, aged 43, having been born in Longport, Staffordshire. With him is his Derby-born wife Mary, and daughter Susanna who was a dressmaker.

Hilda Moore also records him as being in Derby at the time of the 1851 Census (5). At some time after this date he left Derby, dying in the Potteries in 1874.

WILLIAM STEPHAN
Modeller

A descendant of the famous modeller Pierre Stephan who had been employed by William Duesbury 1 at the Nottingham Road factory in the late 1700s, William Stephan was employed at King Street as a modeller.

Baptised on 8 April 1821 at Saint Leonard's, Broseley, Shropshire, William Stephan was the second of three sons born to Peter Stephan and his wife Sarah Shenton, who had married at the same church on 4 July 1818. William's elder brother Peter, and younger brother John, were also born in Shropshire whilst their father Peter was employed as a modeller at the Coalport factory.

William's father Peter, was the son of Pierre Stephan (1), the famous Derby modeller, and had been born in Shelton, Staffordshire, in 1796. Peter is thought to have arrived in Shropshire in the early 1800s and the first record of his whereabouts was in 1818 at the time of his marriage. When the couple's first son Peter was born in Broseley in 1819, Peter's snr's occupation was described as a "china modeller", the family living in Jackfield at the time. When William's baptism was recorded some two years later in 1821, the spelling of the family surname had changed from Strephan to Stephan. Some six months following the birth of the couple's last son John, Peter's wife Sarah Shenton died (2).

At a later date Peter remarried and is believed to have remained in Shropshire for the rest of his life. Described as a "China modeller" aged 75, he appeared in the 1871 Census for Shropshire, living with his wife Susannah aged 70. Described in the 1851 Census as an "Artist Modeller" and later in the 1861 Census as a "Modeller of China – Artist" he died at some time between the 1871 Census and the next one in 1881.

It is not known when William Stephan, who was employed at King Street, arrived in Derby.

His name appears with that of his father as living at Lloyd's Head in the 1841 Census. Peter, William's father was referred to as a "Modeller" whilst his son William was recorded as a "Chinaman", a term which meant that he was connected with the china trade, in any sort of capacity.

It is most likely that he learnt his trade under the tuition of his father, William Stephan. Of William, Haslem says:

> "A grandson worked for several years at the present Derby factory for Mr. Hancock who exhibited at his stall in the Derby Exhibition in 1870, some large vases and other ornaments, profusely covered with flowers in biscuit, in which kind of modelling Stephan greatly excelled. Lady Crewe, of Calke Abbey, near Derby, became the purchaser of several of the best examples."

By the time of the 1881 Census for the Parish of Saint Werburgh's, Derby, William and his wife Caroline, who had also been born in Broseley, and was aged 56, were living at 86 Normanton Road, Derby, where his occupation was described as "Modeller in China Works". With them at the same address was their neice, Emma Carfield, who was a general servant aged 14, who had been born in Broseley in 1867.

Although it is not known exactly when William Stephan ceased working at King Street, there is a William Stephan recorded as being employed by the Osmaston Road factory in the 1880s (3).

GEORGE STEVENSON
Proprietor and former draper

Details of George Stevenson can be found in Chapter One.

ANNIE SWAINSON
China patter

The daughter of Samuel and Sarah Swainson, of 38 Franchise Street, Derby, Annie Swainson was born in Derby in 1862. The elder sister of the King Street modeller Edward Swainson, Annie is believed to have worked at the King Street factory. In the 1881 Census for Saint Werburgh's Parish, Derby, her occupation is shown to be a "china patter".

EDWARD SWAINSON
Modeller

Whilst Samuel Brassington was employed as a modeller at King Street, he produced a bust of the modeller Edward Swainson. The bust from which the photograph on p.187 was taken was produced from the orginal mould but at a later date, being commissioned by Maurice Brassington, the son of Samuel Brassington. Maurice Brassington discovered the original mould at his parents' home.

The son of Samuel and Sarah Swainson, and younger brother to Annie Swainson, a china patter, Edward was born in 1866 in Derby.

In the 1881 Census for Derby he is shown to be an apprentice brush maker, living with his parents and their family at 38 Franchise Street, Derby, in the parish of Saint Werburgh's.

*Left: Edward Swainson, modeller.
Private Collection.*

*Below: Edward Swainson, modeller.
Twitchett & Bailey, "Royal Crown Derby."*

Samuel, his father, is shown to be a brushmaker.

Edward is believed to have acquired his skills from the survivors of the group of craftsmen from the former factory on Nottingham Road (1). He commenced his career at King Street in the early 1880s, following a visit by his brother Thomas, who worked on the Midland Railway, to see Sampson Hancock. Thomas knew of Edward's secret desire to become a potter and following his meeting with Sampson Hancock, Edward was invited to work at the china manufactory, and began his career as a potter.

In his early days at the china works Edward remained behind after work to practise his art, working by candlelight until the introduction of oil lamps. He is known to have modelled flowers which were given to a daughter of Samuel Brassington. She in turn recalled to her brother Maurice several years later that she wished they were still in her possession (2).

An unassuming and quiet gentleman, he was believed to be the oldest employee at King Street in 1930. He remained with the company until its takeover in 1935 when he retired. Although working for the firm for more than 50 years he did not receive a pension, instead he was given a porcelain group of the "Virgins awakening Cupid", made at King Street, as well as a Tythe Pig Group which were still in the possession of his daughter several years ago.

Known as Teddy, he died in 1937.

A photograph of the bust of Edward Swainson, modelled by Samuel Brassington.
Private Collection.

187

JOSEPH TAYLOR
Modeller

Joseph Taylor, modeller, seen here with John Marshall, potter.
Twitchett & Bailey, "Royal Crown Derby."

Born in Derby, Joseph Taylor is said to have been apprenticed at King Street on leaving school. He was employed as a potter and remained at King Street throughout his life (1).

He may have been a descendant of the Taylor mentioned by Haslem (2) who was recorded as one of the first boys employed at the Nottingham Road works.

He married Edith Le Lacheur on 20 June 1908 in Derby.

He died in 1916 (3).

There were two members of the Taylor family who were mentioned on the 1832 list, Benjamin Taylor a potter, and Hannah Taylor a burnisher. A William Taylor, who was a china painter, married Elizabeth Wright at Saint Werburgh's Church, Derby on 2 February 1769, and a George Taylor was listed as a china painter living in Siddals Lane in the 1843 Glover's *Directory for Derby.*

It is most probable that Joseph Taylor may have been a relative of those mentioned above.

Figure group of Three Lambs

Description:	Three lambs, (one recumbent, and two standing), inside a fenced enclosure,attached to a tree. All on an oval grassy mound base, and decorated in enamel colours. All three lambs wear gilt collars.
Modeller:	Probably Joseph Taylor.
Marks:	Red crown over crossed swords and D, two sets of three dots and initials S and H. Also the mark of two parallel lines in red.
Measurements:	Height 11cm. Length 11cm. Width 7cm.
Date:	Early twentieth century.
Location:	In a private collection.
Literature:	A similar group illustrated in Twitchett and Bailey, *Royal Crown Derby*, Antique Collectors' Club, p.14.

THOMAS WATERHOUSE
Possible Potter

On 11 July 1864, Thomas Waterhouse, "Potter" of Goodwin Street, married Ann Brundall at Saint Alkmund's Parish Church, Derby.

There is the possibility he was employed at King Street.

MINNIE WELLS
Gold burnisher

Living with her stepfather and her mother at 8 Darley Lane, in the 1881 Census for Saint Alkmund's Parish, Minnie Wells was aged 14. The daughter of Walter and Myra Wells, her mother's second marriage to Robert Musson, a Midland Railway labourer, took place on 31 March 1877 at Saint Alkmund's, Derby.

Minnie was born in Derby in 1867, and her occupation in the 1881 Census was shown as a "Gold Burnisher China Factory".

J. WENCKER
China painter

Wencker was of German origin and worked at King Street in the 1930s prior to the takeover in 1935 (1).

Saucer

Description:	A saucer decorated with five full blown roses and gilt line around the rim.
Painter:	J. Wencker.
Marks:	Signed "J. Wencker" alongside the stem of a rose. Red crown over crossed swords and D, with two sets of three dots and initials S and H. Also in red the crossed Ps mark of proprietor Paget and his wife.
Measurements:	Diameter 14cm.
Date:	Circa 1933-1935.
Location:	In the collection of Dr. J. R. Freeman.

Cup and Saucer

Description:	A tea cup and saucer, both decorated in enamel colours with alpine scenes depicting snow capped mountains and a log cabin.
Painter:	J. Wencker.
Marks:	Signed " J. Wencker" near the cup handle. Puce crown over crossed swords and D, two sets of three dots and initials S and H. Also on both, in puce, the crossed Pˢ mark of proprietor Paget and his wife.
Measurements:	*Cup*: Height 5.5cm. *Saucer*: Diameter 14cm.
Date:	1933-1935.
Location:	On loan to Royal Crown Derby Museum.

Teapot

Description:	A globular shaped teapot with cover, decorated in enamel colours with anemones on a mottled yellow ground.
Painter:	J. Wencker.
Marks:	Signed "J. Wencker" in the painting. Red crown over crossed swords and D, with two sets of three dots and initials S and H.
Measurements:	Height 11cm.
Date:	1930-1935.
Location:	Royal Crown Derby Museum.

Box and Cover

Description:	A circular box, with straight sides and separate domed cover. Decorated in enamel colours with clematis flowers and green foliage on a mottled yellow ground. The rims and footrim are gilded.
Painter:	J. Wencker.
Marks:	Signed "Wencker" on cover. Red crown over crossed swords and D, with two sets of three dots and initials S and H, on both box and cover.
Measurements:	*Box, including cover*: Height 4.5cm. *Cover*: Diameter 9cm.
Date:	Circa 1930-1935.
Location:	Private collection.
Literature:	Illustrated in the booklet "The Factory at King Street 1849-1935", by A. Bambery and R. Blackwood, Derby Museums and Art Gallery, October 1993, plate IV.
Exhibition:	On display in "The Factory at King Street, 1849-1935" Exhibition held in 1993 at The Museum and Art Gallery, Derby. Catalogue number 59.

F. WERNER
Factory manager

A few years prior to the takeover in 1935, Werner was appointed manager of the factory by F. Howard Paget to take care of the business during his absence.

T. WILKINSON
Modeller

There is the possibility that someone by the name of T. Wilkinson was employed at the factory, however, it has not been possible to establish his whereabouts.

MARY ANN WILLAT
China burnisher

At the time of the 1851 Census for the Parish of Saint Alkmund's, Derby, Mary Ann Willat was recorded as a "China Burnisher" living at 16 William Street, with her husband Charles and four children. Born in Gloucestershire, she was aged 47.

Hilda Moore also records her as a "china burnisher" (1).

JOHN WINFIELD
Gilder

Baptised on 30 December 1812, at St. Werburgh's Church, Derby, John was the son of John Winfield and his wife Mary Moore. The baptism entry records that John's father was employed as a labourer. The marriages of John's siblings which appear in the Parish Registers of St. Alkmund's, and St. Werburgh's, Derby, record John's father had become a "potter" by 1840.

Hilda Moore records that by the time of the 1851 Census, John Winfield (1812), was living in William Street, Derby.

It has not been possible to locate John Winfield in the town for the years 1861 and 1871, however he and his family were residing at 42 Hope Street, Stoke upon Trent, at the time of the 1881 Census for Staffordshire. Aged 68, born in Derby, he is recorded as a "Potters Gilder". At the same address are his wife, family and two boarders, the latter two being Charles Judd, also a gilder, and George Graham, a pottery painter.

The initials JW are often found on King Street china and occasionally appear alongside artists' signatures or initials, in particular those of Edwin Prince, which leads the authors to believe the initials JW were attributable to a gilder.

In view of the fact that Edwin Prince was employed by the factory as an outside decorator, it is possible that John Winfield carried out gilding on behalf of the King Street factory whilst living in Staffordshire.

His death on 12 October 1899 when aged 87, at 146 Gerrard Street, Derby, is recorded in the Red Book located at Derby Local Studies Library, which suggests that he may have returned to the town some time after the 1881 Census.

There are several members of the Winfield family who were connected with the china industry at the earlier Nottingham Road factory. John Winfield, a glaze dipper, and Mary Winfield, a burnisher, appear on the 1832 Nottingham Road List. A further John Winfield also appears on the 1832 Nottingham Road List. The registers of All Saints Church, Derby record a William Winfield, "china man", had married Sarah Jones, on 14 August 1815.

His signature has been recorded on a plate produced at the King Street factory.

Jug

Description:	A squat jug with loop handle. The neck is decorated in patterned gilding and the body in leaf design gilding on a blue ground.
Painter/Gilder:	Probably J.Winfield.
Marks:	Red crown over crossed swords and D, with two sets of three dots and initials S and H. Also inscription "JW12" in red.
Measurements:	Height 5.5cm.
Date:	Later nineteenth century.
Location:	Private collection.
Notes:	This is the first recording by the authors of the inscription "JW12" on its own and not accompanying the work of another artist. This jug points once again to "JW" being a gilder and probably J. Winfield.

EDWARD YATES
Retired china painter

Born in 1788 in Derby, Edward Yates was recorded as a retired china painter living in Henry Street, in the 1871 Census for Derby (1).

An Edward Yates appears as a gilder on the 1832 Nottingham Road List, and it is thought this may well be the same person. There is a person of this name who was recorded in the 1851 Census for the Parish of Saint Alkmund's, Derby, whose occupation is shown to be a "Proprietor of houses", and who was aged 62.

It is not known whether Edward Yates worked at King Street since he does not appear in the 1852 Freebody's *Directory for Derby*, which leads the authors to think he may have moved away from the area in order to find work following the closure of the Nottingham Road factory, returning to Derby at a later date.

However his name has been recorded in case any new information comes to light in the future.

LIST OF PRICES FOR PAINTING AND GILDING

A very small pocket book with clasp, bearing the date 1867, records some of the prices believed to have been paid to artists for decorating King Street productions. A small proportion of the entries are illegible, however the majority have been transcribed and are as follows and are presented in the order in which they appear in the book, followed by some notes.

Set of Seasons B & NP & Gilt	11/-	
Set " " No B & N " "	9/-	
Swiss Peasant	3/6	each
Greyhound Group	1/6	each
Christ	3/6	each
Theatrical Figures Painted & Gilt & chased	9/8	pr.
French Grape Gatherers	1/4	pr.
Match Bases	2/-	Dozen
Rustic Flower Holder	1/4	pr.
Fruit and Flower Figures	1/8	pr.
French Throwers	2/-	ea
No. 8 FiguresB & N	2/8	pr.
No. 8 " No B & N	1/4	pr.
Welsh (sic) Tailors P & Gilt	2/6	pr.
Large Samuel & Mary	1/-	pr.
Small " "	8d.	pr.
French Shepherd	2/6	pr.
Tinker & Gipsey (sic)	4/-	pr.
French Shepherd B & N	3/6	pr.
Parian Figures	3/-	each
Reclining Figures	11/-	pr.

1 Choclate (sic) Cup Complete Painted		
& Gilt to sevres pattern Yellow Ground	10/ 2^1/$_2$	
Small Ewers Raised Flowers	3d.	each
Water Bottle Raised Flower, embossed Sprig		
Painted & Gilt	3/6	each
Lily and Convolules (sic) Tapers Painted	3d.	each
Large Incencers (sic) Raised Flowers Painted		
Gilt and Grounded	5/-	each
Small W.W. Baskets	18d.	each
Paul & Virginia	5/-	pr.
Large Goldfinches	4/-	Dozen
Large Canarys	2/6	"
Small Canarys	1/3	"
Small Goldfinches	2/6	"
Small Tomtits	2/6	"
Parrotts (sic)	5d.	each
Butterflies	3/6	Dozen
Cats Col^d	1/3	"
Cats White and Gold	6d.	each
Stags Col^d	6d	each
Stags White and Gold	2d.	each
Cows Col^d	1/9	Dozen
Small Standing pugs Dresden	5d.	ea
Small " " " Col^d.	2d.	ea
Small " " " White and Gold	1d.	ea
Sitting Pugs on Stands Col$^{d.}$	2/3	Dozen
H. Sitting Pugs Dresden	6d.	each
Mid Size pugs White and Gold	1/6	Dozen
H Pugs " "	2/6	Dozen

No.				s. d.
No.	301	Teas	Dozen	1/6
No.	304	Teas	"	3/6
	269	Teas	"	2/6
	366	Teas	"	2/-
	287	Teas	"	2/9
	319	Teas	"	2/6
	201	Teas	"	2/-
		Teas	"	1/6

No.				s. d.
	312	Teas	Dozen	1/9
	320	Teas	"	2/-
	220	Teas	"	2/6
	279	Teas	"	2/3
	308	Teas	"	2/6

| 289 | Teas | " | 2/- |

1 Dessert Plate Col^d. & Gilt.		2/-
1 " " " & Chased		2/6
1 " " " & Fruit		2/3
1 " " " & Birds		2/-
Large Size Dogs without tracing		1/9
1 " " " with "		2/3
Small Size Frames		1/3
No. 2 " "		2/-

No. 2 New Shape Frame   3/-
Mrs. Gamps (crossed out) Small
Set of New Season Figures
Pig Group   2/6
Mrs. Grants Large   2¹/2d.
Hands   6d.
Shakespeare & Milton   6/-
" " with (illegible)

Elephants   1d   each
Small Sized Vases Blueing Witches
Japan, Painting & Gilding   1/1   each
? Groups of Kettles, Doeing same   1/1
Painting & Gilding   5d.
Egg cups same price

Small size 6in Pugs on Vase.
Painting and Gilding Witches   1/-   each

Small Kettles Painting Gilding & Blueing
Partridge Japan   1/1 per 8" plates.

Syntax Painted & ? .   6d. ea
Queens   5d. ea
Volenteer (sic)   6d.
Paul Pry & Madam Vestris   2/6
Syntax Sketching   1/3
Topers   1/3

Notes: 1. Despite many enquiries being made, no explanation has been found for "B & N" and "No B & N", a smaller remuneration being paid for the latter.
2. "Painted" is sometimes abbreviated and shown as "P".
3. Many of the prices shown are for the decorating of figures, the names of which are self-explanatory. The "Volenteer" (sic) is possibly the small figure of a soldier with rifle illustrated on p.302. The "Pig Group" is probably the Tythe Pig Group, consisting of Parson, Farmer and Farmer's Wife.

4. The two sizes of "Frames" will be mirror frames and the price against "Match Bases" being for the single gilt band encircling the match holders, over which fit candle extinguishers.

Following the lists of prices paid to artists is a single entry dated May 16/81, referring to the year 1881, which is as follows:

Adrefs (address) for Man,
Painter and Gilder Cheap
C Norris
8 Conningsby Place
Blakefield
St. John's
Worcester.
C. Norris appears to be an outside decorator used by the King Street factory at this time. Some ten years later items signed by him were still for sale at the King Street factory.
Amongst the items listed for sale at an auction held on 23
December 1895, following the death of Sampson Hancock,were the following:
From King Street*
Item 129 One ditto blue and gild cup and saucer, painted panels by *Norris.*
Item 140 Pair of green bottles, painted with views by *Norris.*
Item 142 Pair of small pink and gold ewers, painted flowers by *Norris.*

.* Refers to items which were for sale at the factory rather than from the personal collection of Sampson Hancock which was located at Bridge Gate, Derby.
Note: A person by the name Conningsby Norris, who was a china painter, was living at the address 8 Conningsby Place, Blakefield, St. John's. Worcester in the 1881 Census, and is most probably the C. Norris referred to in the pocket book.

2. REFERENCES

(1)   1881 Census Returns for the town of Derby.St. Alkmund's Parish, Public Record
       Office Ref. No. HO2736 Folio 136-136d, 137-145
(2)   Gilhespy, F. Brayshaw, & Budd, D., *Royal Crown Derby China*. C. Skilton Ltd.,
       1964, p.55

Richard Ablott
(1)   Haslem, J., *The Old Crown Derby China Factory*. G. Bell & Sons, 1876,
       p. 123
(2)   Haslem, Op. Cit., p. 124
(3)   Gilhespy & Budd, Op. Cit., p.45

Baddeley
(1)   Williamson, Fred, Typed and handwritten notes. Derby Local Studies Library, Ref.
       BA738.2 (46159)

Annie Bailey
(1)   Moore, Hilda, "Workers at King Street." *DPIS Newsletter*, No. 8. April 1987, p.17
(2)   Gilhespy & Budd. Op. Cit. p.55

James Barnett
(1)   Haslem, Op. Cit., p.238

Ann Beeson
(1)   Bradley, H. G., "The King Street Factory." *DPIS Newsletter*, No. 18, May 1990,
       p.43

Robert Booth
(1)   Bradley, H. G., Op. Cit., May, 1990, p.43

Lewis Bradley
(1)   Haslem, Op. Cit., p.162

Samuel Brassington
(1)   Brassington, Maurice, "Samuel Brassington 1883 –1951," *DPIS Newsletter*, No.
       10, September, 1987, p.27

Joseph Broughton
(1)   Haslem, Op. Cit., p.137
(2)   Haslem, Op. Cit., p.137
(3)   Williamson, F., Notes. Derby Local Studies Library.
(4)   Williamson, F., Handwritten notes.

Frank Bucknall
(1)   Gilhespy & Budd., Op. Cit., p.47
(2)   Moore, Hilda, "Porcelain Manufacture At King Street." *Antique Collecting
       Magazine*, Antique Collectors' Club, September 1983, p.43

Ethel Burns
(1)   Moore, Hilda, Op. Cit September 1983, p.43

Hilda Castledine
(1)   Bambery, A., & Blackwood, R., *The Factory at King Street, 1849-1935.*
        Derby Museums and Art Gallery, p11
(2)   Moore, Hilda, Op. Cit., September 1983, p.43

Frederick Chivers
(1)   Twitchett, J., & . Bailey, B., *Royal Crown Derby.* Barrie & Jenkins, Antique
        Collectors' Club, 1988, p.231

Joseph Cope
(1)   Moore, Hilda, Op. Cit., September 1983, p.43

Mary Dawes
(1)   Moore, Hilda, Op. Cit., September 1983, p.43

Edwin Fearn
(1)   Bambery, A., Handwritten notes.
(2)   1851 Census for the town of Derby, PRO Ref. No. HO2142 p.306

Thomas Gadsby
(1)   Major Tapp's Notebook, Derby Local Studies Library, Ref. DL350
        Microfilm Manuscript. p.133

Gwen Goodwin
(1)   Moore, Hilda, *DPIS Newsletter,* April, 1987, p.19

Albert Gregory
(1)   Gilhespy & Budd, Op. Cit., p.55
(2)   Gilhespy & Budd, Op. Cit., p.50
(3)   Twitchett & Bailey, Op Cit., p.224

Albert Haddock
(1)   Twitchett & Bailey, Op. Cit., p.225
(2)   Information provided by Mr. Mike Morris.

Harry Sampson Hancock
(1)   An extract from ten pages of handwritten notes, dated May 1964, and now in a
        private collection. The source of these notes is not known, but both the owner and
        the authors consider that they were written by someone closely connected with the
        King Street factory – possibly a worker who had been employed there, and as
        such, should be recorded.

Henshall
(1)   Hilda Moore, Op. Cit., April 1987 p. 19

Hopkinson
(1)   Haslem, Op. Cit., p.136
(2)   Williamson, F., Notes.

George Jessop
(1)   Twitchett & Bailey, Op. Cit., p.230
(2)   Brock's MSS Notebook, Royal Crown Derby Museum Archives.

Herbert Jewitt
(1)   William Henry Goss, *The Life and Death of Llewellyn Jewitt FSA., with fragmentary memoirs, William Henry Goss.* Henry Gray, London, 1889. p.205

Iris Johnson
(1)   Bradley, G., Op. Cit., May 1990, p. 45

W. Jones
(1)   Twitchett & .Bailey, Op. Cit., p.230

Elsie Larcombe
(1)   Moore, Hilda, Op. Cit., April, 1987, p.18

Leonard Lead
(1)   Haslem, Op. Cit., p.107
(2)   Haslem, Op. Cit., p.107
(3, 4 & 5)   Tapp Notebook p. 81
(6)   Haslem, Op. Cit., p.107
(7)   Tapp Notebook, p. 81

William Lovegrove
(1)   Haslem, Op. Cit., p.136

Arnold Machin
(1)   Gilhespy & Budd., Op. Cit., p.55

John Marshall
(1)   Moore, Hilda, Op. Cit., April 1987, p.19

Olive Meakin
(1)   Moore, Hilda, "Porcelain Manufacture at King Street." *Antique Collecting Magazine*, Antique Collectors' Club, September, 1983, p.44

Mrs. Minor
(1)   Moore, Hilda, *DPIS Newsletter,* April 1987, p.18

Miss E. H. Mosley
(1)   Williamson, F., Notes.

William Edwin Mosley
(1)   Bambery, & Blackwood, Op. Cit., p.13
(2)   As reference 1 for Harry Sampson Hancock.
(3)   Gilhespy & Budd, Op. Cit., pp.57-9

John Mountford
(1)   Williamson, F., Notes.
(2)   Head, C. D., "I was born in China so to Speak, (the life story of Sampson Hancock.)" *Derby Porcelain International Society Journal 4*. 2000, p.100

Isaac Newton
(1)   Tapp Notebook, p.176

Doris Louise Pacey
(1)   Moore, H., Op. Cit., April 1985, p.18
(2)   Bambery, A., Handwritten notes.

Alice Pates
(1)   Moore, H., Op Cit., April 1985, p.19

Edwin Prince
(1)   Twitchett & Bailey, Op. Cit., p.235
(2)   Murdoch. J., &. Twitchett, J., *Painters & The Derby China Works*. Trefoil, 1987, p.58. Fineran, J., MA., *The Index of Derbyshire China Painters, Modellers and Gilders, connected by Birth, Education, Employment or Domicile.* Private Publication. 2000.
(3)   Haslem, J., Op. Cit., p.123-5
(4)   Murdoch, & Twitchett, Op. Cit., p.58

Jack Ratcliffe
(1)   Twitchett & Bailey, Op. Cit., p.236
(2)   Twitchett & Bailey, Op. Cit., p.296

Mr. Redfern
(1)   Moore, Hilda, Op Cit., April 1985, p.19

James Rouse
(1)   Messenger, Michael, *Coalport 1795-1906*. Antique Collectors' Club, 1988, p.155
(2)   Haslem, J., Op. Cit., p.121
(3)   Godden, Geoffrey, *Victorian Porcelain*. Herbert & Jenkins Ltd., 1961, p.40

Thomas Rouse
(1)   Bradley, H. G., Op Cit., May 1990. p.47

Amy & Eva Sadler
(1)   Moore, Hilda, Op Cit., April 1987, p.18
(2)   As reference 1 for Harry Sampson Hancock.

F. Schofield
(1)   Bradley, H. G., Op. Cit., May 1990, p.47

Shardlow
(1)   Moore, Hilda, Op. Cit., April, 1987, p.17

Shaw Jnr
(1)   Moore, Hilda, Op Cit., April 1987, p.18
(2)   An extract from ten pages of handwritten notes, dated May 1964 and now in a private collection. The source of these notes is not known, but both the owner and the authors consider that they were written by someone closely connected with the King Street factory – possibly a worker who had been employed there, and as such, should be recorded.

Shufflebottom
(1)   Haslem. J., Op. Cit., p.238.

William Slater
(1)   Bradley, H. G., "King Street Factory", *DPIS Newsletter*, No.18 p.47

Ann Stanley
(1)   Bradley, H. G., "King Street Factory", *DPIS Newsletter*, No.18 p.47

Horatio Steele
(1)   J. Haslem, Op. Cit., p.120
(2)   Bradley, H. G., "King Street Factory", *D.P.I.S. Newsletter*, No.18, p.47
(3)   Haslem, J. Op Cit., p.205
(4)   Haslem, J., *A Catalogue of China (Chiefly Derby) 1879. The property of J. Haslem.* Reprinted facsimile limited edition, Reference Works, Dorset, 1988.

William Stephan
(1)   Messenger, Op. Cit., p.215
(2)   Messenger, Op. Cit., p.238, ref. 58
(3)   Twitchett, & Bailey, Op. Cit., p.239

Edward Swainson
(1)   Moore, H., *Porcelain Manufacture in King Street.* Derby, Information Sheet, City of Derby Museum and Art Gallery. nd.

Joseph Taylor
(1)   Twitchett & Bailey, Op. Cit., p.240
(2)   Haslem, J., Op. Cit., p.163
(3)   Bambery, A., and Blackwood R., *The Factory at King Street, 1849-1935.* Derby Museums and Art Gallery, p.11

Wencker
(1)   Twitchett & Bailey, Op. Cit., p.242

Mary Ann Willat
(1)   Bradley, H. G., Op. Cit., Newsletter No. 18, p.48

Edward Yates
(1)   Bradley, H. G., Op. Cit., Newsletter No. 18, p. 48

Note: Concerning the above references, the authors have tried, without success, to contact the copyright owners C. Skilton Ltd.

For quick reference, the following table of the main factory marks is provided. This is followed by a more detailed account of each one and notes on other marks.

MARK		COLOUR	IN USE
1		red or blue	1849-c.1861
2		puce	c.1849-c.1859
3		puce	c.1859-c.1861
		blue	Later nineteenth century
or			
4		red	c.1861-1935
or		puce	c.1915-1935
5		red or puce	c.1915-1917
6		red or puce	c.1917-1933
7		red or puce	c.1933-1935

| 8 | | gilt moon and black zeppelin | 1916 |

| 9 | **BCM/PUG** | red or puce | 1930s |

Mark 1   1849-c.1861

This hand-painted mark of crown, crossed batons (not swords), with two sets of three dots over a script D, is the same as that used at the earlier factory on Nottingham Road. It is likely that this mark was used on ornamental wares originating from the King Street factory for the twelve years prior to 1861.

In the last few years six such pieces bearing this mark – four in red and two in underglaze blue – have been identified. They clearly were produced at King Street and not Nottingham Road. They are all ornamental objects and this mark has not been found on any King Street tablewares.

The introduction to the King Street factory Sales Catalogue of 1934-35, when referring to this mark, includes the following statement: "In most cases it is impossible to tell which ware was late Bloor and which was King Street before the "S.H." was added at that date" (c.1861). It is therefore understandable that more examples of King Street wares bearing this mark have not come to light. Collectors are under the impression that if something bears a mark of the Bloor period at Nottingham Road, then it was produced in that factory. Why should they think otherwise?

In 1861 Llewellynn Jewitt, the ceramic historian, persuaded King Street to cease using this mark, claiming that it was "bad policy and may lead to confusion" (1). Let it be stressed that it has misled in the past and continues to at the present time.

Mark 2   c.1849 – c.1859

This mark embodies the words "Locker and Co. Late Bloor, Derby". It is likely that it was superseded by Mark 3, following the death of the proprietor William Locker in 1859. Found in puce.

Mark 3   c.1859-c.1861

This short-lived mark reads "Stevenson Sharp & Co." around "King St. Derby" which is placed in the centre. George Stevenson joined the partnership on Locker's death and Samuel Sharp was one of the three potters who were amongst the original six workmen who had founded the business. Found in puce.

Note: Marks 2 and 3 are seen infrequently and were in use on tablewares during the twelve years 1849 – 1861 whilst mark 1 was being applied to decorative wares.

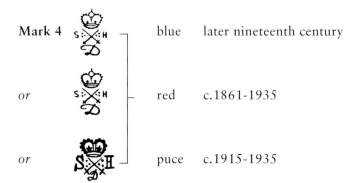

Mark 4   blue   later nineteenth century

or   red   c.1861-1935

or   puce   c.1915-1935

Mark 4, in its slightly varied form, has become well known, having been in constant use for around seventy-four years. It met Jewitt's requirement of not being confused with the Nottingham Road mark, and he said of this new mark:

"While it is sufficiently identical with the old Derby mark, is yet distinct enough for it to be recognised as the work of a different period from that in which the old one was in use" (1).

The differences are the addition of hilts to the crossed batons of the earlier mark, turning them into swords and adding the initials S and H. These initials originally stood for the proprietors George Stevenson and Sampson Hancock. After Stevenson's death in 1866, the mark continued unchanged, the same initials standing for Sampson Hancock, who became the sole proprietor.

As shown below, this S and H mark was registered with the Trade Marks Registry in 1877, just two years after the passing of the Trade Marks Registration Act (2). This was done during the complicated negotiations that took place between the partners of the new factory in Osmaston Road and Sampson Hancock, regarding the use of all, or part of the King Street mark. Hugh Gibson has recorded the details of these dealings in his book *"A Case of Fine China"* (3).

No doubt, under the heading "Description of Goods", Sampson Hancock would have covered all possible eventualities. So far there is no evidence to suggest that the factory turned out wares in terra-cotta.

The final column of the entry in the Trade Marks Journal shows Sampson Hancock recording that the factory commenced using the S and H mark in 1848 (1875 – 27 years = 1848). It was not until the early 1860s that they were persuaded to adopt this mark, making this an inaccurate declaration.

No. 11,493.

Trade Mark.	Name, Address, and Calling of Applicant.	Class of Goods.	Description of Goods.	Number given by Registrar.	Date of Application received.	If Mark used prior to 13th August 1875, how long used.
	SAMPSON HANCOCK, Derby; China Manufacturer.	16	Porcelain, Earthenware, Stoneware, and Terra-cotta.	11,435	28th Mar. 1877.	Twenty-seven years before 13th Aug. 1875.
No. 11,493 (see above).	ELIJAH ROBINSON, of and on behalf of the Firm of ROBINSON AND SONS, Stockport; Tobacco Manufacturers.	45	Tobacco, Manufactured or Unmanufactured.	11,493	31st Mar. 1877.	Not so used.
	THOMAS GUEST, trading as THOMAS GUEST AND COMPANY, 45, Carnarvon Street, Cheetham, Manchester; Manufacturing and Wholesale Confectioners.	42	Confectionery of all kinds.	11,502	3rd Apr. 1877.	Two years and a half before 23rd Mar. 1877.
	THEODORE TURLEY, of Shenstone, Hagley Road, Edgbaston, Warwickshire, on behalf of Self and Partners, SAMTSON HANBURY, of Bishopstowe, Torquay, Devonshire, and HANBURY BARCLAY, of Middleton Hall, Tamworth, Warwickshire, trading as THE ANCHOR TUBE COMPANY; Tube Manufacturers.	5	Unwrought and partly Wrought Metals used in Manufacture, such as Iron and Steel, Pig or Cast; Iron, Rough; Iron, Bar and Rail (including Rails for Railways); Iron, Bolt and Rod; Iron Sheets and Boiler and Armour Plates; Iron Hoops; Iron Wire; Lead, Pig; Lead, Rolled; Lead, Sheet; Copper; Zinc.	11,563	6th Apr. 1877.	Not so used.

Entry in Trade Marks Journal, 1877.

Single examples of mark 4 have been recorded in black and green, but the main colours used were blue, red and puce and each of these is dealt with below in more detail. This mark is also seen incised.

a) Blue

The S and H, mark 4, in blue, was mainly used on biscuit and glazed white wares. Research continues, but it is so far not possible to accurately state the period over which this colour was used. An assumption is that it was in use from around 1861 until the end of the nineteenth century. The factory showed a tendency to alter marks when proprietors changed, so perhaps the blue mark ceased to be used around the time of Sampson Hancock's death in 1895.

The blue mark is usually applied under the glaze, but if no glaze is present where the mark appears, it is often, but not always, covered with a small dab of glaze specially applied.

It is sometimes found in this colour on decorated wares. It is suggested that these wares were surplus to requirements in the white, or were decorated to meet special orders placed by customers. On rare occasions a red mark is found as well as one in blue, both on the same specimen.

b) Red

Of all the marks used at King Street the S and H mark in red is the most difficult to date. By observing over the years the colour of the marks used, and assisted by artist signed and commemorative wares, which can be dated, it is clear that mark 4, painted in red, was used continuously from 1861 until the factory closure in 1935. When there is nothing else to help, sometimes the style of decoration can be of assistance in arriving at an approximate date of manufacture. Also, in the twentieth century, the proprietors and other marks 5–9, covered later, can act as a useful guide.

Wares decorated in Imari patterns almost always bear mark 4 in red and not blue or puce.

c) Puce

It is suggested that the puce coloured version of the S and H mark was introduced in 1915 or 1916. Mrs. Willoughby Hodgson in *Old English China* (4) published in 1913 states that: "The mark now employed is a red crown with crossed swords and dots surmounting a script D and on either side the letters S and H". This implies that the puce mark had not yet been introduced. Several pieces that can be accurately dated to January 1916 do bear puce marks. It is possible that the introduction of the mark in puce marked the arrival of William Larcombe, who took over the lease of the factory in 1915.

From around 1915 to 1935 we have both red and puce coloured S and H marks being used simultaneously. Regrettably, so far no reason has been established which shows what led the factory to use one or other of these colours on a particular piece. It is likely that there is an explanation, as apart from the occasional signs of marks being carelessly applied, the factory appears to have taken the marking of its products quite seriously.

Notes on Marks 4a, b, & c

(i) These marks were painted with and without jewels (small dots encircling the crown). There is no explanation for these minor variations, but maybe some decorators paid more attention to detail than others.

(ii)   In the main these marks are painted by hand, but infrequently printed marks are seen, these mainly being on nineteenth century pieces.

(iii)   Very occasionally one or both of the initials S and H which flank the crossed swords, are omitted. This also applies to the two sets of three dots.

d) Incised

The S and H mark 4 is occasionally seen incised rather than painted or printed. This is mainly on undecorated biscuit or glazed white wares.

Certain other main factory marks, as opposed to workers' marks, were applied in addition to the S and H mark and are usually in the same colour, red or puce and are as follows:

Mark 5   c.1915-1917

Applied in red or puce, this is the monogram of proprietor William Larcombe and was in use in 1916.

Mark 6   c.1917-1933

When Captain Paget joined Larcombe as a proprietor in 1917, their joint monogram came into being. Again, seen either in red or puce.

Mark 7   c.1933-1935

After January 1933 Larcombe was no longer a proprietor, leaving Paget on his own in control of the works. He adopted the symbol of crossed Ps seen above. These stood for the nicknames of Pug and Peg, given to Paget and his wife (5). Found in red or puce.

Mark 8   1916

On 31 January 1916 there was a German air-raid on Derby, by a zeppelin. To commemorate this event the contents of one kiln had the above mark added in addition to the usual S and H mark. The moon was painted in gilt and the zeppelin in black.

An unknown person who it is considered had close connections with King Street wrote in more detail about this episode, as part of notes created in 1964.

"The story of the airship mark on certain of the King Street porcelain, happened as follows. It appears that during the first world war the factory had a kiln full of china which had reached a crucial stage in its firing when the air-raid warning was sounded which meant the necessity of drawing and dowsing the kiln fires. Thus it was left until the last moment and when it was ultimately done it was not known whether the contents of the kiln would be spoiled or not. However when the kiln was emptied it was found to be the contents were well fired, and in memory of the event the kiln contents were marked with the "airship" mark" (6).

Mark 9 **BCM/PUG** 1930s

This mark is the telegraphic address adopted by the firm and is seen in red or puce.

MARKS POSSIBLY IN USE

These three marks used at Nottingham Road. at various times between c.1825 and 1848.

It was recorded in 1925, that King Street still had in its possession three copper plates for the Bloor transfer marks, based on the Gothic crown, which are shown above. These, it is stated, were amongst the equipment that the founding partners were able to take with them from Nottingham Road (7).

Having these plates in their possession, the question has to be asked, did they use them? As already shown under the heading mark 1, the factory used the Nottingham Road painted crown and crossed batons mark for twelve years. It is going to be difficult to prove, but a possible explanation is that these marks based on the Gothic crown were applied to the Bloor replacement wares that were turned out at King Street.

MARKS OF FACTORIES OTHER THAN DERBY

When it was learned that amongst the items that Howard Paget presented to the British Museum there was a copper plate, it was expected to be engraved with one or more of the Bloor Gothic crown marks.

As can be seen from the following illustration, the British Museum plate is something entirely different, being engraved with two Rockingham marks and one for the Worcester factory. Reproduced below, in full, is a letter from Howard Paget which makes mention of this plate. This letter to King, who was Deputy Keeper at the British Museum at that time, suggests to the authors that like the Gothic crown copper plates, this one also came from Nottingham Road. There is no hint from Paget that this plate may have been used at King Street. This letter is attached to Derby Pattern Book Number Two, British Museum Registration Number 1936 7-15 141.

Rockingham and Worcester marks,
engraved on copper plate.
British Museum

June 28. 1936

Dear King

Seven Stones
South Cliff
Broadstairs.

Many thanks for your
letter. There has always
been a tradition among the
old hands at Derby, that
the O.C.D.C.* works used to
make goods for Rockingham,
when the latter were coming
to an end. The 2nd Book of
patterns, or any how the
early ones, for many have
been added later at King Street
suggest Rockingham more
than Derby & taken in
conjunction with the Rockingham
mark on the copper plate,
we always suppose they sent
this book for Derby to copy
from. Purely a guess and no
foundation of fact.

You notice the ribbon
underneath the crest, & holding
motto is not as usually found.
One is straight, the other curly.
I forget which is which.

Yours Sincerely
            F. Howard Paget.
* Old Crown Derby China.

215

Although it may not have been put into use at King Street, this plate has a rightful place in this chapter, as it came to the British Museum from the last proprietor of the factory and was probably at King Street for the entire life of the factory. It may well turn out to be of more significance to researchers of early Derby, Rockingham and Worcester, than to those of King Street.

INCORPORATING THE CROWN INTO
THE MARK OF THE DERBY CROWN PORCELAIN COMPANY

Prior to the start of production in 1877 in Osmaston Road, Derby, the new firm approached Sampson Hancock seeking permission to incorporate the crown used in the S and H mark into their new factory mark. After lengthy discussion involving the Trades Marks Registry and solicitors, Hancock agreed that the crown could be used and for granting this permission he was paid the sum of £10 (8).

USE OF THE S AND H MARK AT THE
ROYAL CROWN DERBY FACTORY

Having purchased the King Street concern in 1935 and closed it down, the Royal Crown Derby Porcelain Company as it was by then known, was fully entitled to use the S and H mark and there is a known period when they did this.

1960s

In the early 1960s the factory agreed to make good customers depleted sets of figures of Seasons and Elements which had originally been turned out by the King Street factory and for these to bear the original S and H mark.

Owing to a misunderstanding, more of these replacement figures were produced than were required to meet customers' needs. These R.C.D. figures appear in the market place from time to time. They differ from the original figures and to avoid confusion in collector's minds, these variations are listed below.

a) The weight of the replacement R.C.D. figures is noticeably less than that of the original ones.

b) The S and H mark in red on the base of the R.C.D. figures is larger and more spread out than is ever seen on King Street wares.

c) The R.C.D. replacements often bear the name of the artist on the base, which is helpful in identifying them as originating from Osmaston Road.

d) The subject name is also found on the substitute figures and this is not found on the original King Street versions of The Seasons or The Elements.

In addition to figures of Seasons and Elements, a pair of Mansion House Dwarfs, produced at Royal Crown Derby, but bearing the S and H mark in red is known, in a private collection. Both figures are signed J. Gould and were probably produced in the 1960s. Because these figures have not been handled by the authors, no other information can currently be provided.

Less easy to explain is the marking of a coffee can and saucer signed in the painting by W. E. J. Dean, which are known in a private collection. Both are decorated with landscapes depicting Derbyshire scenes and have gilt rims.

Cup and saucer are inscribed on the base "ILAM ROCK, DOVEDALE" in black and carry a very normal looking S and H mark in red. Also, close to each footrim is a small untidily painted "R" in red.

There is no indication that "Billy" Dean, who worked at Osmaston Road from c. 1890 until the 1940s, ever worked at King Street and the use of a small script "R" has not been previously recorded on King Street pieces. This therefore looks like another set of circumstances in which Royal Crown Derby used the S and H mark, but in this case the authors have not established a reason.

ENGLAND AND MADE IN ENGLAND

Only two examples marked "ENGLAND" are known to the authors and none bearing "MADE IN ENGLAND." This implies that the factory did not, like many others, comply seriously with the American McKinley Tariff and Trades Act, calling for one of those marks to be applied: "ENGLAND" from 1891 and "MADE IN ENGLAND" from c.1920.

Had the business continued and not closed in 1935 things regarding these marks would have changed. A note from an unknown source stated in 1964:

"The King Street factory seems to have suffered badly during the great coal strike. They had a large American order in hand, but owing to the failure of coal supplies they fell behind in delivery and the order was cancelled, and this seems to have been the beginning of the end." (6)

It is also likely that sales were made to American visitors who went to the London shop in Brook Street.

REGISTRATION MARKS AND NUMBERS

The diamond-shaped device, which shows that a pattern or shape has been registered with the Patent Office to prevent its use by other manufacturers, has not been found on any King Street wares.

RETAILERS' NAMES

The rarely seen printed mark, shown on the left, was used in puce. It has been recorded in some earlier publications that this mark was oval rather than round, but four known marks, two on cups and one on a separate saucer, and one on a plate, are round. It cannot be dated accurately, but was most likely in use from c.1849 –c.1862.

Thomas Courtney had been the London agent for the Nottingham Road factory and after Robert Bloor's death traded with King Street.

One example has been recorded of "T. Goode & Co." appearing with an S and H mark, both being in red, on a coffee cup and its saucer.

OVER-PAINTED MARKS

Four decorated pieces have been recorded which bear an original S and H mark in blue, which has been carefully over-painted in puce, the colour that made its appearance with this mark around 1915. On one of these, a pot-pourri and cover, the latter looks like a twentieth century replacement for an original broken pierced lid.

The remaining wares with over-painted marks more likely started life in the white, with their correct blue mark for the later nineteenth century and, when decorated at a later date, had the colour of the mark updated at the same time.

It is not clear why this was done, but there does not appear to be any deception involved, as an earlier mark is replaced by a later one.

FAKE MARKS

Just occasionally faked marks are encountered. The reason is usually to "age" the piece concerned. With the similarity of the Nottingham Road mark and King Street mark, this is not too difficult. Erasing the initials S and H is carried out, but sometimes it is forgotten that also the hilts should be removed from the swords, turning them into the batons contained in the Nottingham Road mark.

WORKERS' AND OTHER MARKS

The authors are conscious that more research is required in this area. However with the scarcity of records and the passage of time, it is probably realistic not to expect that a great deal of progress will be made. There follows a list of these marks that have been recorded and on the few occasions that there is any useful information to accompany these workers' marks, this is also given.

Painted Workers' Symbols

// Red and Puce

This mark, positioned not as an eleven would be, but as two parallel lines, is the most frequently seen workers' mark. It is found on numerous twentieth century puce marked pieces (c.1915-1934) and on many red marked items apparently dating from the twentieth century.

For the last ten years or more it has been suggested that this mark of two parallel lines was used by Harry Sampson Hancock.

Two recently discovered pieces of information support this view:

a)   The first provides strong, factory based evidence. In a letter, transcribed on p.417 proprietor Paget, when writing to a customer in May 1918 regarding a special commission, states that the plate concerned was painted by "Harry Hancock". Painted on the reverse are two parallel lines.

b)   The second is a statement from an unknown source, that reads as follows:

"Harry Hancock was the last at Derby of a long line of ceramic artists of this town. His mark on china was two parallel marks on the back of the piece, thus "//" ."(6)

In the light of the above, especially that set out in a), it would now seem in order to state with some confidence that Harry S. Hancock was the decorator who so frequently used this mark, when not signing his name in full.

H. S. Hancock was employed at King Street, without a break, for more than forty years. As the amount of work signed with his name is quite limited, one has to ask, what was he doing for the rest of his time? We now have the answer; he was painting or gilding, and marking his work thus "//."

※	Red
X	Red and underglaze blue
Δ	Red and underglaze blue
▪ ▪	Blue, on footrim of dish – twentieth century style decoration
(	Underglaze blue
✓	A tick or v in underglaze blue
1	Puce, on the inside of a thimble
αⱼ	Red, inside footrim of a cup
Ǝ	Blue, on the base of a vase
U̇	Red, on a dessert plate
Ŧ	Puce, on a pastille burner signed by W. E. Mosley. Probably a gilder.

Names and Initials, other than those of known artists

a). Painted

B.B.	Red
HW	Puce, on a figure dated c.1915-1935
WR	Red
VS	Stamped letters on a pin tray

P   Puce

b) Incised or Impressed: Initials and words.

Hilda Moore, in an article,
suggests some of these
initials marked in the body
could be those of the modeller
Edward Swainson (9).

Derby   Seen, incised or impressed, on four dessert plates, both nineteenth
and twentieth century, and on two saucers. These may have been
bought in as blanks from Royal Crown Derby, where this mark was
used.

Gamp   Incised into the base of the match holder that goes with the candle
extinguisher based on the figure of Mother Gamp.

NUMERALS

The 1934-35 factory sales catalogue and separate price list show a number against each
entry. These were probably sales reference numbers. Relatively few actual pieces bear painted,
impressed or incised numerals and, where these were used, they bear no relation at all to the
numbers in the catalogue. The following numbers have been recorded but their significance
is not known:

3   Incised, on a figure and painted in underglaze blue on a cup.

12   Painted in red. This number has been found on several pieces signed by E. Prince, preceded by the initials JW, possibly those of the Gilder John Winfield.

14   Painted in red on a small toilet pot – Imari pattern.

16   Incised, on an enamelled figure of a greyhound.

19   Incised, on a dish.

25   Impressed, on the figure of Air from the Four Elements.

N 58   Incised, on the female figure of a glazed white pair, comprising a boy and girl, each holding a small basket.

N 60   Incised, on both figures making up a pair of spill vases in the white.

N 129 Incised, on the biscuit group, Cupid awakening the two Virgins.

Note.

The script *N* that precedes the 58, 60 and 129 is very similar to those used on the base of Nottingham Road produced figures. None of these King Street numerals bears any relation to the earlier figures listed under these numbers in either the Haslem or Bemrose lists, so their significance is unknown.

3. REFERENCES

(1)   Jewitt, L., "Old Derby China Works, a history of the Derby Porcelain Works", *The Art Journal, London,* 1 January 1862, p.4

(2)   *Trade Marks Journal,* 23 May 1877

(3)   Gibson, H., *A Case of Fine China.* The Royal Crown Derby Porcelain Company Limited, 1993, pp. 34-37

(4)   Mrs. Willoughby Hodgson, *Old English China.* G. Bell, 1913 p.62.

(5)   Twitchett J., & Bailey, B., *Royal Crown Derby.* Antique Collectors' Club, 1988, p. 254

(6)   An extract from ten pages of handwritten notes, dated May 1964, and now in a private collection. The source of these notes is not known, but both the owner and the authors consider that they were written by someone closely connected with the King Street factory - possibly a worker who had been employed there, and as such, should be recorded.

(7)   Gibson, Op. Cit., p.33

(8)   Williamson, F., An Article in the *Derbyshire Advertiser,* 13 February 1925. Ref. BA 738.2 (46159), Derby Local Studies Library.

(9)   Moore, H., "Porcelain Manufacture in King Street, Derby," an article in *Antique Collecting Magazine,* The Antique Collectors' Club, September 1983, p.44

4. NINETEENTH CENTURY INVOICES

A large part of the King Street records relate to invoices retained for the period of the 1860s to 1880s. There are about 350 of these and they are pasted into a book 28cm.x 21.5cm., several to a page and often folded over.

No documents have come to light which show if this careful preservation of invoices was also carried out before or after the period that these particular ones cover. Could this have been the work of just one very enthusiastic clerk?

Those to be considered in this chapter relate to china bought in from other manufacturers and suppliers and cover the purchase of raw materials. Others, associated with maintenance of factory buildings, plant and equipment, help to build up a picture of daily life at this small concern during a short period in the nineteenth century.

BOUGHT IN WARES

Like other manufacturers, King Street bought in china in order to supplement their own output, which in turn would have allowed a wider range of wares to be offered for sale. It would have been useful to have provided readers with an estimate of the proportion of the total factory sales that were sourced from outside suppliers. Hampered by the lack of sales records for the period being considered, or for any other time during the life of the factory, it is felt that this could not be produced with any degree of accuracy.

No documentation has been discovered which shows if this practice of buying in china continued into the twentieth century. It is the authors' opinion that it did and this is based on the sometimes wide variations that are found in the components of services which can be dated to the twentieth century, indicating different suppliers being used.

THREE MAIN SUPPLIERS

James Beech
China manufacturers

James Beech and Son of Albert and Sutherland Works, Longton, Staffs., in business from around 1850 to 1890 was the main supplier of tableware to King Street. Some was in the white (glazed, but undecorated), some part decorated and others fully decorated.

During the period covered by the available invoices, these facts emerge:

> Period covered 1870-1881
> Total invoices 58
> Total spend around £330.

It is interesting to note an invoice dated 31 August 1871 which reads, "1 Teapot 1/5d. Taken by Mr. H.", showing that Sampson Hancock was visiting his main supplier of china. Included in these invoices are some single items, but many were bought by the dozen and almost entirely tablewares. Mugs, Muffin dishes and Toy Teas feature in several of these invoices. There is one record of King Street purchasing seconds, "6 doz. Teas 2^{nds} white, 18/-". The same quantity of "Best White" teas cost £1-4-0.

An indication of how interwoven the world of china manufacturers was, is illustrated by one entry in an invoice dated 2 September 1871 which lists "12 Teas Wor. Broseley, 2/4^{d}". Broseley was a pattern produced for teawares by Grainger, Worcester, used here by Beech, then bought by King Street, for sale to the public.

Despatch to Derby was in baskets or hampers by rail, sometimes listed as "passenger", this probably for the most urgent orders. Receipts show that accounts were settled in a mixture of cash and postal orders. One dated 6 April 1872 thanks Mr. S. Hancock for "Two five pound notes and Postal Orders for three pounds seven shillings and sixpence".

John Aynsley
China manufacturer

John Aynsley of Portland Works, Longton, Staffs. is still in production at the present time. During the period of six years being considered here, King Street spent less per annum with John Aynsley than with James Beech.

Period covered 1869-1875
Total invoices 30
Total spend around £132.

Again it is tablewares that are being purchased, many of them in Aynsley's "Newcastle best white". Tall and low comports feature regularly and this supplier also provided Muffins and Mugs in the white.

Nestle and Huntsman
Wholesalers and Exporters

Nestle and Huntsman, of Bohemia House, Bishopsgate, London, although not a manufacturer, is the third largest supplier of wares:

Period covered 1870 – 1872
Total invoices 11
Total spend around £46.

Nestle and Huntsman's letterheads show that they dealt in a number of specialist areas and King Street availed itself of a number of these.

There are several orders for shades at specific sizes, often with the material "chenille for shades" and sometimes black stands were asked for. Perhaps this tells us that these shades, which were probably of glass, and the other materials were for use with lamps that King Street produced, but none of these has so far been recorded.

Painted china paperweights along with painted and gilt card trays were purchased. Small quantities of bronzed lava oval dishes and lava flower pots were ordered. Lava wares were made of coarse stoneware clay and slag from iron smelting, with a hard glaze fired at great heat. It could be that these lava wares were for sale in the factory shop and nothing to do with production.

"Ruby plain linings" were supplied by Nestle and Huntsman and also obtained in 1870 from Boyle and Co. of Birmingham. Towards the end of the nineteenth century the Derby Crown Porcelain Company was turning out pierced vases with coloured glass linings. This is put forward as a possible use for these at King Street, but on the other hand as pierced wares were being bought in from John Aynsley maybe the factory did not undertake this very skilled work.

Other Suppliers in this group

Of the remaining eleven suppliers, the following are worthy of mention:

Nevitt Oswell

Nevitt Oswell of 30 Wharf Street, Longton, Staffs. is not recorded as being a china manufacturer, but his correspondence with Sampson Hancock suggests that he was both experimenting with and making ornamental china baskets for King Street. During the years 1872 to 1874 he supplied a total of forty-six baskets, both round and oval in shape.

Oswell also supplied brooches to King Street, priced at 4d, 6d. and 7d. each. He charged 9/- for a large china basket.

Robin Blackwood is continuing research, with a view to identifying these bought in baskets, compared with those that originated at King Street.

James Hancock
Dealer in china

Sampson Hancock's relationship with his cousin James of High Street, Longton, Staffs. was a short one. Just three transactions are recorded for the years 1869-1870, when James supplied King Street with vases at 1/- each and some tablewares.

Minton & Co., later Mintons
China manufacturers

Five small orders are recorded between 1869 and 1874, mostly for tablewares, the total spend was £7.

James Barlow

James Barlow gives his address as 55 Carlisle Street, Dresden, Staffs. There are only two small orders recorded. A letter sent by Barlow to Sampson Hancock in 1878, which is transcribed below, requests secrecy regarding their transactions.

55 Carlisle St. Dresden
March 5 1878
Sir,
I shall forward your ware tomorrow – Monday. I have sent you 2 comb trays , 1 taper 1 Ring Stand. I had to make 2 packages. I think with the additions and Box and hamper you must send me £2-0-0 make it payable at Dresden post office. To Catherine Barlow as I am not at home in post hours. Let this little transaction be strictly private as I am not in

business now and I hold a good situation.
Hoping you and your family are well,
I remain
Yours respectfully
James Barlow.

Joseph L. Carter
Glass and china showrooms

Carter, of 8 Market Head, Derby, was sole agent for Royal Worcester and Coalport China. The five invoices dated between 1871 and 1875, which are all for small amounts, suggest that Sampson Hancock was using this retailer for his purchases of other manufacturers' finished goods, perhaps with a view to copying them.

One Worcester "Group of Pugs" purchased for £1-2-0 in 1872, is an example of this, as the King Street group of three pugs in the white, on an oval mound base, is very similar to that produced at Worcester.

There is also one invoice from Worcester Royal Porcelain dated 4 February 1874, but this just reads "to goods supplied 13/-," which was paid by postal order.

MATERIALS FOR MIRROR PRODUCTION

The Patent Silvering Co. Ltd.

This company, of Lower Kennington Lane, London, S.E., supplied glass cut to size, for use in the elaborate china frames produced at King Street:

> Period covered 1870-1873
> Total orders 14
> Total spend around £31.

J. & O, C. Hawkes

Hawkes of Bromsgrove Street, Birmingham, appear to have taken over as looking glass supplier when The Patent Silvering Company ceased in 1873:

> Period covered 1873- 1875
> Total orders 11
> Total spend around £36.

E. H. Heapy

Heapy, of 37 King Street, a near neighbour to the factory, was an upholsterer, paperhanger and decorator and made mahogany and velvet covered backs for the factory's mirrors.

> Period covered 1872 – 1875
> Total orders 21
> Total spend around £50.

The invoices from these three concerns indicate the importance of mirror frame manufacture. The first supplier of glass for the mirrors, The Patent Silvering Co. Ltd. provided no less than 594 pieces of glass in several different sizes in the years 1870-1873. Glass in twelve different sizes was ordered, some only as single pieces, but three sizes were ordered in much larger quantities, these being:

$6^{1}/_{2}$" x 5"   169 pieces
$10^{1}/_{4}$" x $7^{3}/_{4}$"   283 "
15" x $11^{3}/_{4}$"   110 ".

As the glass was thick, it is unlikely that many breakages occurred. King Street would therefore have been making on average about three mirrors a week, a great deal of work going into the production of each one, as can be seen from the illustration below. This mirror uses the glass size $6^{1}/_{2}$" x 5".

Oval mirror, glass size $6^{1/2}$" x 5". Private collection.

RAW MATERIALS

Jesse Shirley, later Shirley Brothers

Shirley's of Etruria Bone Works, Staffordshire Potteries, and agent for E. Luke and Sons, china clay and stone merchants, Cornwall, was the main supplier of raw materials for china manufacture.

> Period covered 1869-1876 and 1882
> Total orders 35
> Total spend. around £306.

The invoice shown below covers the three ingredients supplied by Shirley's, namely china clay, ground bone and ground stone with the prices paid for these materials in 1871 and includes £5-9-3d. owing from an earlier account. It is thought that the numbers against the ground bone and stone are sieve mesh sizes. The extra cost of carriage from Liverpool to the Potteries is interesting. In certain body recipes which are considered in Chapter Five "Cornish or Cornale" clay is specified. Does this extra carriage cost indicate that this was Cornish Clay transported by sea from Cornwall to Liverpool and then this was sent on to the Potteries?

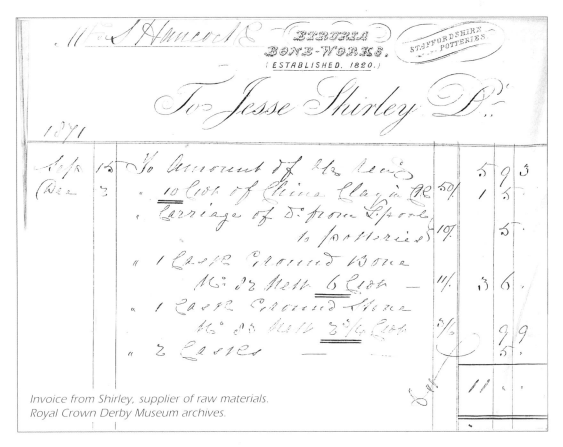

Invoice from Shirley, supplier of raw materials.
Royal Crown Derby Museum archives.

James Woodward (successor to John Hunt), Swadlincote Fire Brick Works, Burton-on-Trent

> Period covered 1867-1877
> Total orders   14
> Total spend   around £65.

Woodward provided fire clay (as opposed to china clay) and ground brick, for use in the kilns.

Robert Jones, of Hanley, Staffs, and **Ian Cartwright**, of Swadlincote, received four orders between them for raw materials during the years 1863 to 1882.

COLOUR SUPPLIERS

James Hancock, of Diglis Color (sic) Works, Worcester

> Period covered 1870-1873
> Total invoices   10
> Total spend   around £22.

His cousin, James Hancock at Worcester, met all of Sampson's requirements for colours for decorating, with the exception of a single small order placed with F. Emery, of Cobridge, Staffs.

TIMBER SUPPLIERS

Pipes and Yates
   Timber and slate merchants, City Road and Mansfield Road, Derby

In 1870 and again in 1873 orders were placed with this firm for a total of over one thousand pieces of wood, cut to various sizes. This could have been used for making packing cases in addition to the baskets used. The factory purchased ten packing cases from Thomas Mosedale of Derby in 1872, but as only one order is recorded, perhaps they were happier producing their own?

COACH BUILDERS

Wells and Pool, King Street, Derby

In 1872 and 1874 this firm carried out repairs to a "basket gig" and a pony trap. Cart, gig and trap were sometimes used in different parts of the country to describe the same thing. The one illustrated below, showing it in the factory yard, is taken from a photograph dated early twentieth century and could be the same one mentioned in the invoices. This heavy duty general purpose delivery vehicle was described to the authors by an expert, as the "white van" of its day and may well have been used to transport the baskets of finished china to Derby station or local customers.

Cart, in factory yard.
Alice Robinson's scrapbook, in a private collection.

There is no record of fodder having been purchased for the horse, but one could have been shared with another local supplier who stabled it, or one hired from one of the Job Masters Yards that existed for this purpose.

INSURANCE

Receipts show that for a year's insurance of the works for £700, the premium was £1-14-4d., this being with the Sun Fire Office, for the year ending Christmas Day 1875.

Sampson Hancock had a life assurance policy for £200 with Sun Life Assurance Society, for which he paid an annual premium of £10-17-2d. in 1874.

MAINTENANCE

During the period 1867-1875 the factory employed nine local firms to carry out their maintenance, including two Haslams (not Haslem), Edwin and William, and two Haywoods, Edward and James.

Edward Haywood, 22 King Street, Derby

On 30 September 1869, Edward Haywood presented a bill of £1-5-0 for "Painting walls and writing name on 2 sides". These "names" were probably those that can be seen from the road and are shown in the photograph on the half title page at the front of the book.

William Haslam, Brass and Iron Works, Derby

In 1867 and 1868 William Haslam carried out seventeen jobs for a total cost of only £1-18-5d. This illustrates the large number of small repairs that were carried out to tools, rather than purchasing new ones, e.g. "Repairing large poker, 4ᵈ.".

T. Stanesby, Queen Street, Derby

Stanesby supplied and repaired the sieves used in the factory. The paid invoice shown below is typical of those submitted by this firm and it must have been nice for his customers to know that they could also get their bacon smoked, as shown in Stanesby's letterhead.

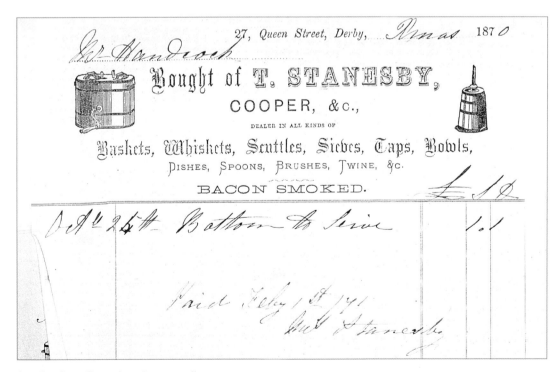

Invoice from Stanesby, sieve supplier.
Royal Crown Derby Museum archives.

4. REFERENCES

The invoices considered in this chapter are held in the Museum at the Royal Crown Derby Porcelain Company Ltd.

5. Recipes

Several hundred recipes for producing the body, glaze, colour and flux, gold and a few unrelated to porcelain, exist in the King Street archives held in the museum at the Royal Crown Derby factory. These are in five separate small books, some only partially filled with entries, and a small number of recipes are on loose sheets of paper, which John Twitchett has placed safely in envelopes. Many of these recipes were not originated at King Street as they bear dates long before the factory came into being. As it is thought they were all saved with other papers, when King Street closed, it is possible that any of them could have been put into use there and hence should be briefly considered in this chapter.

Sadly, a considerable number of these recipes are extremely hard to understand due to fading, poor handwriting and the copious use of abbreviations. The number of recipes headed "Trial" is considerable and in many instances variations on one particular recipe are listed, with an occasional comment added regarding their performance when put into use.

An attempt has been made to identify the source of these recipes, using the occasional dates that appear, the spelling and handwriting used and mention will be made of a selected few, placing them into two main groups; firstly pre-King Street, followed by those thought to have originated there.

RECIPES PRE-KING STREET (1849)

BOOK ONE

15.5cm. x 10.5 cm. with a faded yellow parchment cover. Based on the few dates that accompany the recipes this is the oldest group, the earliest date being 1805, with several in the 1820s and 1830s.

There are certain entries in this book which are strong pointers to it having been handed down to Sampson Hancock by his father James (1785 -1865), who was in the Worcester area at the time of his marriage in 1814, and who later joined the Chamberlain's porcelain works where he was employed as a colour maker, having responsibility for bodies and glazes(1).

It is believed that James may later have been employed by Messrs. Richardson of Wordsley, near Stourbridge, which was not too far away from Worcester, where his elder brother George had been engaged to decorate glass ornaments(2).

The notes that follow are taken from Book One, being found amongst the recipes and they support the link between this book and the earlier members of Sampson's family that are mentioned above.

"Entered Mr. Chamberlain hous (sic) december 14, 1825.
Paid the first Weeks Rent December the 18, 1825."

In same hand as above,

"James Hancock Born November 27. 1825."

This is the son of James mentioned previously, who was younger brother to Sampson.

There are two references to Shelton, near Shrewsbury, and one of these reads:

"March the first heeteen (sic.) hundred and twenty five
James Hancock
Shelton."

Amongst the recipes was the following entry, the significance of which has not yet been established:

"4th February 1830 O' Conol took is (sic.) seat as Member of Parliment (sic.)."

This could refer to Daniel O'Connell (1775-1847), an Irish political leader. He was elected M.P. for Clare in 1828, but being a Catholic was prevented from taking his seat. The Catholic Emancipation Bill having been passed, he was then able to take his seat, when re-elected in 1830.

Colour

The formulations in this book are mainly for colours and fluxes, the latter being substances added to colours to assist in their fusion during firing.

The following recipes show how modifications to one basic recipe produce three different colours and are typical of the way in which many of the formulations in these books are set out.

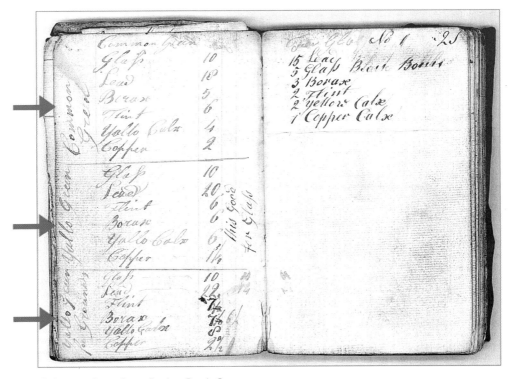

Colour recipes, from Recipe Book One.
Royal Crown Derby Museum archives.

Notes:

    a)   For glafs read glass.

    b)   Calx is Calcium Oxide.

Flux

The same remarks apply to flux recipes as for colours, there being as many as four formulations on one small page, with only minor variations in each.

Body

Only three recipes for bodies are given in this book and two are recorded here from a page containing the dates 1830s and 1850. They are quoted here as they may be of interest to anyone wishing to compare them with recipes of a later date. It is suggested that the wide gap in dates appearing on the same page is due to space in the book being filled in later rather than wasting it. The date of these recipes is circa1830.

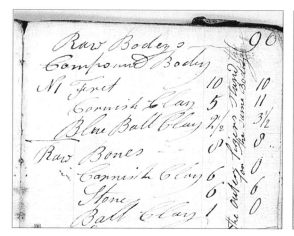 

Two body recipes, from Recipe Book One.
Royal Crown Derby Museum archives.

Notes:

The top left hand recipe, containing N 1 Frit, is the compound body, being a two-stage process with the separate recipe for the frit being given on the right.

    Frit is the name given to substances mixed together, fired and ground to a powder for inclusion in formulations as required.

Factory or Home Brew

Although unconnected with china, someone considered it of sufficient importance to include in this book the following nineteenth century recipe, which readers may be tempted to try.

Factory or Home Brew recipe, from Recipe Book One.
Royal Crown Derby Museum archives.

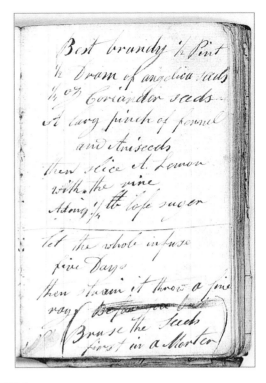

BOOK TWO
18cm. x 11cm. with a brown leather cover. A label on the front cover reads:

"Old Recipes for Bodies, Colours, etc."

There are only two dated recipes and these are for 1820 and 1840. There are references in this book to Hancock's Fluxes and Hancock's Gold, but this is to be expected with the prominence of the family in the field of ceramics, but unlike Book One there is no indication that a member of the family was directly involved in compiling it. In addition to the Bodies and Colours mentioned on the cover of the book, there are also recipes for glaze, flux and gold. It seems likely that this book was brought with other items from Nottingham Road to King Street. It perhaps should be borne in mind that Sampson's uncle, John Hancock (1777 –1840), was colour maker at the Nottingham Road factory from 1819 until his death in 1840, which may help to establish from where this book originated.

Body
A wide variety of different bodies are dealt with including the following:

Green	Peeover's
Flesh coloured	Wedgwood's Jasper
Chalk	Parian
Green drab stone	E. Ps. Brooch

It is interesting to note that the modern day colouring agent turmeric was included in the recipe for flesh coloured body.

Flux

As in Book One the number of flux recipes is considerable, often being for a particular purpose. Under the heading of Hancock's fluxes the number allocated to the final recipe on the page is sixteen, providing a wide choice from which to choose when selecting one for use with a particular colour.

Glaze

Amongst the glaze formulations the following names are given to them:

Bailey's.	Green.
Wilson's.	Chalky.
Rockingham.	Black.
	Drab.

One recipe for glaze is given below, showing that it is a two-stage process. There is a date of 1842 on the previous page.

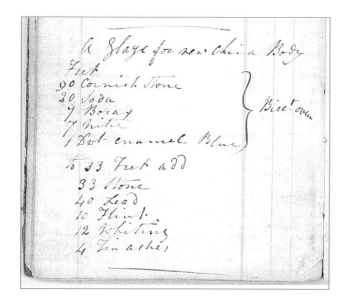

Glaze recipe, from Recipe Book Two.
Royal Crown Derby Museum archives.

Notes:
a) A Dwt. is an abbreviation for pennyweight in the Troy weights system. 1 Dwt. = .050 of a troy ounce, the Troy system being used for precious metals and gemstones.
b) The frit would have been fired in the biscuit oven as instructed before being ground and then added to the rest of the ingredients.
c) Niter is sodium nitrate.

Colour

Amongst the colour formulations familiar names appear including:

Worcester Brown.
Coalport 2.
Caughley green.

Other titles given are:

R. Wynn's.
Garrard.

A heading "Pale Brosely Blue" is interesting, Brosely being the name given to a pattern at Chamberlain's, Worcester.

Gold
There are several recipes for the preparation of gold. Again the name Hancock appears and the formulation headed "Hancock's Gold" is as follows:

Recipe for Hancock's Gold, from Recipe Book Two.
Royal Crown Derby Museum archives.

Note: Quicksilver is another name for mercury.

BOOK THREE

18cm. x 11.5cm. with a green leather cover. Only eleven pages of this book have been used. John Twitchett states that the paper used is watermarked 1824 (3), but it is most likely that the recipes contained in it were entered much later. The one titled "China Body to be made at the New Works, King Street, Derby," indicates that these few recipes, all written in the same hand were recorded not long before 1849, when production started at King Street.

Body
The important recipe mentioned above is as follows:

*Body recipe, from Recipe Book Three.
Royal Crown Derby Museum archives.*

Note: It is likely that Bale clay is Ball clay, used to increase the plasticity of the body.
In addition to the above, there are others headed:

Mountford's.
Close China.
John Hancock's.

There is no documentary evidence to support it, but a suggestion is put forward that John Mountford, who was at Nottingham Road right up to its closure in 1848, may have had a hand in writing the recipes in this Book Three. He was an expert on the formulation of porcelain bodies and a friend of Sampson Hancock, for whom he later worked at King Street.

RECIPES PROBABLY WRITTEN UP AT KING STREET

BOOK FOUR
16cm x 9.5cm. cover lacking. Only four pages are dated and these are all in the 1860s. Body, flux, glaze and colour recipes are included, but none for gold. Of all the books studied this is by far the most difficult to read, the handwriting is poor and many recipes do not indicate what the end product is intended to be. Two trials are of interest, the first being for "Insulator body", suggesting an interest in supplying the electrical industry with wares. Another shows "Pitcher" trials, pitchers being broken, or scrap china, indicating a cost conscious management. In Book Five a body recipe is given for using these pitchers.

BOOK FIVE
14cm. x 8.5cm., with green cover. This book is written by the same hand as the previous book, but fortunately a different pen would appear to have been used and many of the recipes contained within it can be read. The four dates that are recorded follow on from those in the previous book and range from 1869 to 1878. The recipes cover body, flux and glaze only.

Body
A single process body recipe for 1878 is given as follows:

Body recipe, from Recipe Book Five.
Royal Crown Derby Museum archives.

   As in Book Four there are recipes for "Insulator Body" and "New Insulator body" but here no mention of trials, so perhaps production was contemplated.

Glaze
A considerable variety of glaze recipes are given, some of the titles being:

Earthenware.	Hard.
Crown.	Soft.
Rose's Biscuit Blue.	Parian.
For Hollow Wares.	New China.
New Vitreous.	White Enamel.

Insulator.

MISCELLANEOUS RECIPES

A few recipes are found in books that contain information other than recipes and, as mentioned earlier, some are on loose sheets of paper. The dates of these, classed here as miscellaneous recipes, range from 1869 to 1915 and mention is now made of those felt to be of significance:

Body
For the first time a special body for teapots is mentioned, with a comment against it reading:

   "This clay seldom cracks in firing."

   There are also recipes for the following:

   Converting useful clay to make it suitable for casting china figures and other ornaments.
   Spode's body.
   Mason's china.
   Mauve ground.
   China body for using up biscuit Pitchers (dated 1873).

   There are also lengthy instructions of how
   "To make china body as it was made at Derby for 36 years by T. Wardle",
   but these are undated.

239

Glaze
The headings for glaze include the following:

> To make glaze soft.
> To make Hard Glaze for Portickeler (sic.) use.
> Ridgways glaze for china.

Gold
There are several sets of instructions for gold preparation including the following:

> Hard Gold for regular grounds.
> Unfluxed Gold.
> Mr. R.ˢ· Specimen grinding.
> Printing Gold.
> Regular Gold.

Colour Pots
In the Reserve Collection in the British Museum are six small pots with covers which contain colours in powder form. Four of these also contain small "puffs" made up of folded material. There is also a pestle, but no mortar to go with it.

These pots of colour and the pestle (B.M. Accession Numbers, 1936. 10-15, 1 to 7) were presented to the Museum in 1936 by Howard Paget, the final proprietor at King Street. These have been well-used and the bodies of the pots are covered in a thick grime, where they have constantly been handled. All are round, except for one which is oval, and all are about 14cm. high and may well have previously been discarded sucriers from the Nottingham Road factory.

The only names that can be read on the pots, some in script on labels and others painted on the pots, are as follows:

> Exeter Blue.
> H. K. Green N.10
> Torquorse (sic) to gold on
> Glaze Kiln Drab.

In addition to these pots and the pestle, Paget presented 142 items of fine porcelain from his own collection and from the factory, two pattern books and a copper plate engraved with factory marks. As the paperwork connected with his presentations throws no light on the strange gift of the pots and pestle, assumptions seem in order.

Would Paget have considered that of his total presentation to the museum, those items coming from the factory were under represented, when compared with his large personal gift of porcelain? These pots, which may have come from Nottingham Road to King Street and could have been used at both factories, are excellent examples of everyday working equipment and materials, which Paget perhaps felt were worth preserving. It is difficult to put forward alternative reasons for this unusual gift.

Milton and Shakespeare
This unexpected heading, in a chapter dealing with recipes, is placed here because sandwiched between recipes in the King Street Archives is a sheet headed, "Inscription in Ger-

man for Milton and Shakespeare", which probably dates from the early nineteenth century.

The later figures of Milton and Shakespeare from Nottingham Road both had inscriptions on the scroll that each figure held. Shakespeare's came from his work The Tempest and Milton's from Book VII of Paradise Lost, written by him in the later seventeenth century.

It is suggested that the reason for these two inscriptions being translated into German was perhaps to assist a customer from Germany, who had purchased a pair of these figures and was interested in the inscriptions.

To close this chapter, a mixture of recipes, believed by his descendants to have been written by Sampson Hancock, are illustrated here in their original form. It gives an idea of the rather complicated manner in which many of the more legible recipes are set out, but no doubt they were straightforward to those who wrote and used them, over a hundred years ago.

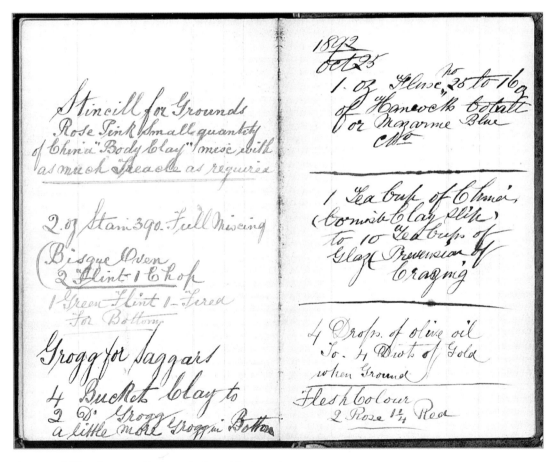

A page of Miscellaneous Recipes, believed to have been
written by Sampson Hancock.
Royal Crown Derby Museum archives.

Notes:
a) Grogg is pulverised damaged pottery, which when used can reduce shrinkage.
b) Saggers are used to protect wares during firing as shown in the illustration on p.242.

c) The recipe for prevention of crazing is not unexpected. A glaze formulation on another page has the following comment against it:

"To Be dipt (sic.) thin, shows
the pattern through, it improved
the colour, and does not craze".

Kiln, partly filled with saggers, c.1900.
Alice Robinson's scrapbook in a private collection.

This brief study of the many specialist recipes, some with several variations, and the wide range of ingredients used, has been most enlightening for the authors. It has given them a further insight into the complexities of china manufacture.

5. REFERENCES

(1)   Haslem, J., *The Old Derby China Factory*. G. Bell and Son, 1876, p.133
(2)   Haslem, Op. Cit., p.130
(3)   Twitchett, J., *In Account with Sampson Hancock 1860s-1880s*. D.J.C. Books, 1996, p.79

The recipes considered in this chapter are held in the Museum at the Royal Crown Derby Porcelain Company Ltd.

6. THE PRODUCTS, THEIR SHAPES AND PATTERNS

King Street continued to produce shapes and patterns, in both ornamental and useful wares, that had been in use at the Nottingham Road factory, but also turned out different models and introduced fresh patterns.

With virtually no sales records it is also difficult to estimate what the balance of output was between the two. Haslem gives us a clue, when he wrote in 1876, "of late years attention has been specially directed to the making of a larger class of figures, and more particularly of ornamental ware, in which modelled flowers have been a chief feature." (1)

At the close of this chapter details and illustrations of a wide range of King Street products are given. These are in addition to those recorded in Chapter Two, which could be attributed to a specific artist.

Firstly, some general notes which cover the various types of wares produced and provide some comments on shapes and patterns.

TYPES OF PRODUCT

These fall into the seven categories listed below:

> Unglazed biscuit
> Glazed white
> Enamelled, often with gilding
> Underglaze blue decoration
> Coloured bodies, usually with applied white flowers
> Earthenware
> Possibly Parian

Unglazed biscuit
About twenty models turned out in this manner have been recorded, these being mainly figures. A fine example of the group, Two Virgins awakening Cupid, is illustrated in this chapter. These biscuit figures were probably all produced in the later nineteenth century. The finish on the biscuit wares turned out at Nottingham Road shows some variation between appearing almost slightly glazed, or being a little dry and chalky. The known King Street figures are reasonably consistent in this respect and fall between the two extremes of the earlier factory's models.

Glazed white
A large range of glazed white wares was produced in the later nineteenth century, being mainly decorative and some are illustrated in this chapter. The use of modelled flowers and fruit applied to the wares in this group was extensive. Several different mirror frames and ornamental baskets were made, as well as bowls, vases and many figures, human and animal, and a range of miniatures.

Robin Blackwood has made a separate study of these wares in the white and has produced a private edition catalogue illustrating and giving details of some two hundred different items. Should readers wish to refer to this catalogue, copies are available at the Museum and Art Gallery, The Local Studies Library, and the Royal Crown Derby Museum, all of which are located in Derby. Alternatively it can be viewed via the Web at the following address: www.jupiterantiques.co.uk where it is located under the educational section.

The Glaze
Usually the application of glaze is thick but occasionally on the heads of figures it is sparse, where it has run off. At one time it was thought that the lack of definition on the faces of some figures was due to the use of worn moulds, but several recent comparisons of biscuit figures with like glazed figures, highlight the thick covering of glaze. This is illustrated by the heads of the figures that King Street called the French Shepherdess, which are shown below.

Unglazed biscuit.
Private Collection.

Glazed.
Private Collection.

In many cases the glaze is crazed, although perhaps to a slightly lesser extent in the twentieth century. Usually this is pronounced enough to be seen by the naked eye, but if not, clearly when magnified. On figures, especially those with crevices, the glaze settles thickly in these and here bad crazing is often found. The glaze in these areas takes on a greenish tint. Minute pinholes can often be detected where the glaze has not provided a total cover.

Enamelled
As shown in Chapter Four, a wide range of wares was bought in from other manufacturers, mainly, but not wholly, in the white. This led the authors to the conclusion that any compo-

sitional analyses, carried out by an expert in this field, might be of limited value. This view was supported by the fact that as the basic body is bone china, there would be less variation to be found than in the earlier porcelains.

In general the factory potting is a little thick and heavy, but on the occasional piece that is eggshell thin, the translucency is good. These comments are made based on a study of the large range of wares turned out in the white, as it is almost certain, based on details contained in the invoices covering bought in wares, that the majority, but not all of these, were King Street produced.

Variation is a most noticeable feature of the finished wares. In the case of tablewares this is understandable as the factory obtained supplies from a variety of sources in the white, for decoration at King Street. The difference in thickness, and hence the weight of cups or saucers, within the same tea service is sometimes most obvious. These fluctuations are found in addition to those due to any changes in recipe, or experimentation that would have taken place on wares potted within the King Street factory.

Underglaze blue decoration
Only one example of blue decoration painted beneath the glaze is known and it is on a wall vase that is in the collection at the Royal Crown Derby Museum – a type of decoration favoured by some other manufacturers, but evidently not at King Street.

Coloured Bodies
There is a recipe in the archives for a green body, but no examples are known in this colour. Another is headed "Mixing Mauve Ground Body", dated 1865. Four examples, all factory marked, are known of lavender/mauve, coloured bodies, all with white applied modelled flowers. These comprise two different-sized mirror frames and two vases. There has been a good deal of speculation regarding just how these were produced, as the body when deeply scratched shows no colour and the glaze is also uncoloured. A likely suggestion is that the addition of some colour to the paste then reacted chemically with the glaze when fired and this produced the colour in the finished piece.

Earthenware
Earthenware was used to model two candle extinguishers, one of the Quaker Elizabeth Fry and the other of a monk. Both bear the S and H factory mark and are known in a private collection.

The illustration below is of the Napier Coffee Apparatus. It was advertised as being available with an earthenware base decorated with a "Crown Derby Pattern". This is Old Crown Derby Witches and this is also used on the beaker. The bases, with the lamp or heater resting on the left hand side, were also available in white, white with gilt border, but the Imari decorated version was the most expensive, the whole unit costing 52/-6d. in 1863.

The date of 1863 and the wording in the literature clearly point to the bases and beakers, like the earthenware extinguishers, having come from King Street. As a recipe for earthenware body exists, dated 1865, with another for earthenware glaze, it seems likely that the factory was turning out products in earthenware, rather than buying them in from other manufacturers.

Care is always needed when assessing whether the factory was producing a certain product or buying it in from outside. This is particularly so because the factory shop was selling items other than those produced in the factory, this being borne out by an advertisement in the *Derby and Chesterfield Reporter* of 23 January, 1849. In this, which announced that manufacture will commence shortly at King Street, there is also included the statement "Dealers in Earthenware and Glass".

Napier Coffee Apparatus.
Private Collection.

Parian

Sampson Hancock recalls in his 1894 interview that he had employed John Mountford, who is said to have developed the marble like Parian whilst working for Copeland and Garrett, in Staffordshire (2). He had previously worked as a potter at Nottingham Road. No wares in Parian have yet been identified as having come from King Street, but from information unearthed, it seems likely that some items may have been produced. The following points support this view, all the information coming from the archives held at Royal Crown Derby.

a) King Street had in its possession an early recipe for Parian Body.

b) A recipe for Parian Glaze exists and is dated circa 1870.

c) Amongst the prices paid to artists for decorating wares is the following entry, "Parian figures 3/- each".

d) In the list of prices paid for finished goods is a record of wares supplied to Mr. Maurice Moses, London. From the quantity of various figures that he purchased, it is likely that Moses was a china retailer, but this has not been confirmed. Amongst these items was a Parian basket and the same item, but this time coloured. Belleek and other factories glazed and decorated some of their Parian bodied wares.

e) The Derby Crown factory at Osmaston Road was producing Parian figures in the later nineteenth century.

MATCHING

John Haslem states that the factory did "a great deal of matching", making good losses which had occurred in services made earlier at Nottingham Road (3). This would have provided welcome additional business for the factory and is mentioned in advertisements reproduced in Chapters One and Seven.

The following short announcement, in the *Derby Mercury* of 20 November 1861, records the factory's involvement in producing replacements for the service made in Derby in 1841-42, for Queen Victoria.

"Messrs. Stevenson and Co., china manufacturers, of this town, have just completed some dessert ware for Her Majesty, to match a service which was manufactured for the Queen, about twenty years since, at the old works on the Nottingham road. The dress or mounted plates are very handsome; and the pattern, which is green and gold, beautifully painted in small compartments with fruit, flowers, birds, and insects, has a rich and elegant appearance. The china will be sent to London on Friday, and, until that day, will be on view at the works, on the Duffield road."

Note: The "dress or mounted plates" (assiettes montées) refer to plates mounted in tiers of two or three and, in this case, surmounted by a container to hold flowers. The use of the word "dress" in this context simply refers to an object with which to "dress" a table, in the same way that a shop window is stated, "to have been dressed."

Haslem also records that the Queen's confectioner and table-dresser had a say in the height required for these mounted plates.

SHAPES AND PATTERNS

Examples of many shapes used for enamelled wares along with the wide range of patterns used are shown later in this chapter and these include both ornamental and useful wares. Several patterns which originated at Nottingham Road, were still in use in the 1930s, including Rose Barbeau and the Imari patterns of Witches and Garden.

Occasionally the factory broke away from the more traditional and slightly conservative patterns and became more adventurous. In the twentieth century artists occasionally tried out Art Deco type patterns. Another bold design, with stylised landscapes in black, grey and silver on a set of coffee cups and saucers, is known in a private collection.

Some artists were permitted to sign their work and many of these pieces were finely decorated and had elaborate gilding, some of which was raised. A certain number were "cabinet" pieces, rather than for more general use.

Although difficult to read, a list of prices for the 1850s and 1860s shows something like thirty patterns, but it is not possible to tell how many were in use at any one time. In contrast, about half that number were in use just prior to the factory closure.

FIGURES

Judging by the number of figures produced, their production was of some importance to the factory, and the authors have compiled the table given below. This is clearly incomplete and will remain so until additional examples appear.

Table of Figures 1

Additional information on figures, some limited, can be sourced as shown in columns 1, 2 and 3, the key to these being as follows: 1. Illustrated in this book 2. Recorded in factory catalogue/price list, in Chapter 7 3. White wares catalogue, available at sources listed in this chapter	1	2	3	FROM KING STREET			Also produced at Nottingham Road
				Unglazed Biscuit	Glazed White	Enamelled	
African Sal) A pair	1	2				X	X
Billy Waters)	1	2				X	X
Autumn, from an unusual set of Seasons			3		X	X	
Boy, holding shell dish) A pair			3		X	X	X
Girl, holding shell dish)			3		X	X	X
Boy, holding a basket) A pair			3		X	X	
Girl, holding a basket)			3		X	X	
Boy, representing night) A pair	1	2	3		X	X	X
Girl, representing morning)	1	2	3		X	X	X
Boy, reading a book) A pair			3		X		X
Girl, tatting)			3		X		X
Boy, with basket on his back	1					X	
Boy, with rosy cheeks	1					X	
Belper Joe	1					X	
Cupid candlestick	1		3		X	X	X
Cobbler	1	2		X	X	X	X
Crying Philosopher)	1					X	X
Laughing Philosopher) A pair	1	2	3		X	X	X
Coffee Season, Spring	1	2				X	X
Coffee Season, Autumn	1	2				X	X
Carpet Beater, spill vase			3		X		
Crossing Sweeper, spill vase			3		X		

Table of Figures 2

Additional information on figures, some limited, can be sourced as shown in columns 1, 2 and 3, the key to these being as follows: 1. Illustrated in this book 2. Recorded in factory catalogue/price list, in Chapter 7 3. White wares catalogue, available at sources listed in this chapter	1	2	3	FROM KING STREET Unglazed Biscuit	Glazed White	Enamelled	Also produced at Nottingham Road
Chelsea Flower Seller) Chelsea Fruit Seller) A pair	1 1	2 2	 3		X X	X X	X X
Dr. Syntax, walking		2	3		X	X	X
Dr. Syntax, up a tree	1	2	3		X	X	X
Dr. Syntax, sketching	1	2			X	X	X
Dr. Syntax, on horseback	1	2				X	X
Dr. Syntax, at Calais		2				X	X
English Shepherd) English Shepherdess) A pair	1 1	2 2	3 3		X X	X X	X X
Elements	1	2				X	X
French Shepherd) French Shepherdess) A pair	1 1	2 2	3 3	X X	X X	X X	X X
French Flower Seller) French Fruit Seller) A pair		2 2				X X	
Falstaff	1	2				X	X
Fisher Boy		2				X	
Fisher Boy, small		2				X	
Flower Girl		2				X	
Greenwich Pensioner	1					X	
Girl, with dove						X	

Table of Figures 3

Additional information on figures, some limited, can be sourced as shown in columns 1,2 and 3, the key to these being as follows: 1. Illustrated in this book 2. Recorded in factory catalogue/price list, in Chapter 7 3. White wares catalogue, available at sources listed in this chapter	1	2	3	FROM KING STREET			Also produced at Nottingham Road
				Unglazed Biscuit	Glazed White	Enamelled	
Gardener)	1	2		X		X	X
Gardener's Companion) A pair	1	2		X		X	X
Girl, with lyre)			3		X		
Girl, with book) A pair			3		X		
Girl, with grapes			3		X		
Hairdresser Group		2	3		X	X	X
Jesus Christ	1		3		X		
Milton			3		X	X	X
Madame Vestris	1		3		X	X	X
North African Solder			3		X	X	
No.8 Boy)		2	3	X	X	X	X
No.8 Girl) A pair		2	3	X	X	X	X
Old Woman)				X		X	
Old Man) A pair				X		X	
Polish Dancers Group	1			X		X	X
Paul Pry		2		X		X	X
Paul, of Paul and Virginia			3		X		
Peasant Woman			3		X	X	

Table of Figures 4

Additional information on figures, some limited, can be sourced as shown in columns 1, 2 and 3, the key to these being as follows: 1. Illustrated in this book 2. Recorded in factory catalogue/price list, in Chapter 7 3. White wares catalogue, available at sources listed in this chapter	1	2	3	FROM KING STREET			Also produced at Nottingham Road
				Unglazed Biscuit	Glazed White	Enamelled	
Putto, with fruit			3		X		
Putti, as Spring candlesticks	1		3		X		X
Soldier, with rifle	1					X	X
Snuff Taker	1	2				X	
Small masked figure			3		X		
Seasons	1	2	3		X	X	X
Shakespeare			3		X	X	X
Tinker)	1	2			X	X	
Tinker's Companion) A pair	1	2	3		X	X	
Tythe Pig Group	1	2	3		X	X	X
Tythe Pig Group - individual figures							
Parson			3		X	X	X
Farmer's Wife			3		X	X	X
Thrower	1	2	3	X			
Vineyard Worker			3		X		
Virgins, awakening Cupid	1	2		X		X	X
Welch Tailor)	1	2	3		X	X	X
Welch Tailor's Wife) A pair	1	2	3	X	X	X	X

The following animal figures were also produced:

Bears	Fox
Birds	Greyhounds
Butterflies	Hound (alcibiados)
Calves	Kittens
Camels	Lions
Cockerels	Peacock
Cows	Pigs
Crocodiles	Several different Pugs
A variety of small dogs	Tigers
Dog and Fox heads (stirrup cups)	Toads

Notes:

a) Some of the gaps in the list of figures need explanation. For example, out of the three individual figures of the Tythe Pig Group, only two are listed. Probably the figure of The Farmer was produced, but as it is not yet known, it fails to get an entry.

b) Several of the figures listed and others, not sold separately, were used to decorate comports, vases, sweetmeat dishes, bowls, inkwells, pot-pourri and frequently candle-sticks.

c) With figures there are firm links with Nottingham Road. Readers of an advertisement placed shortly before the factory closure reminded them of the King Street production of "original Old Derby figures, as modelled by Spangler, Stephan and Coffee etc", these three being very well known Derby modellers from the past (5).

SHAPE AND PATTERN NUMBERS ON WARES

In general, neither shape nor pattern numbers are found on the wares themselves. The very few numbers that have been recorded and which may not even relate to shape or patterns are listed in Chapter Three, Marks, under the heading "Numerals".

PATTERN BOOKS

Derby Pattern Book Number One

Haslem wrote in 1876:

"Mr. Sampson Hancock, the proprietor of the present small china works at Derby, has a small pattern book which belonged to the old factory; it does not, however, contain more than eighty patterns, a few of which are for dinner and dessert services, but chiefly for tea ware. They are, for the most part, a repetition of the patterns in the older books, with the corresponding numbers to them. This book contains a number of drawings of smelling bottles. The patterns are remarkably neat, and most of them have subjects in small panels, such as trophies, landscapes, birds or flowers."(4)

Aileen Dawson, the Curator of the Department of Medieval and Modern Europe, at the British Museum, is confident that the pattern book to which Haslem refers is one of two books presented by F. Howard Paget to the Museum. This Derby Pattern Book Number One, has a museum registration number of 1936 7-15 140 and was considered in detail by Aileen Dawson in 1991 (5).

Derby Pattern Book Number Two

The second book, Derby Pattern Book Number Two, which is 23cm. x19.5cm. has a museum registration number of 1936 7-15 141 and is of direct relevance to King Street. In his letter, which accompanies this Book Two and which is reproduced in full in Chapter Three, Paget suggests that patterns in the first half of this book were supplied to Nottingham Road by the Rockingham factory, based at Swinton. The patterns, mainly for cups and saucers, are neatly drawn, mainly coloured, but not as elaborate or detailed to those in Pattern Book One. The following names appear several times against the numbers used: Rothchild, Ponsonby, Clark and most frequently Alcock.

These supposedly ex-Rockingham patterns bear numbers from 150-387. These numbers do not match up with the usual published Rockingham numbers, these being:

teaware patterns 404-1566, with a break between 1000 and 1100;
dessert wares 409-822 and maybe higher (6).

A study of the contents of the first half of Book Two could be of interest to researchers of these two earlier factories. There is also the copper plate engraved with two Rockingham marks, which is illustrated and discussed in Chapter Three on Marks. In the King Street archives there is a recipe for Rockingham Glaze, most likely brought from Nottingham Road, but not a specific recipe for a Rockingham Body.

Hilda Moore makes mention of Locker, first proprietor at King Street, visiting Swinton, possibly shortly before the closure of the Rockingham works in 1842. He is reported to have brought back some Rockingham moulds with him and presumably taken them to Nottingham Road, where he was still employed (7).

The second half of Pattern Book Two, which Paget suggests was compiled at King Street, shows illustrations of patterns, some of which are not well drawn and others that are faded, those drawn in pencil having suffered most. The numbers are as follows, shown in the same order as entered in the book:

402-450
457-460
685-687
27
600-657
317-322
658-684
324-334
3029-3033

The illustrations, again mainly of teawares, are seldom given names, the following being exceptions:

Hawthorn Blossom	Stanhope
Townsend	New Shape
Wellington Shape	

254

Many of the illustrations show prices against them entered in pencil, which were paid to workers for decorating and, or gilding, a few examples being:

603   1/9 doz. – probably a price for decorating
604   2/3 doz. Gilding
617   Painting 2$^{d.}$ Gilding 3$^{d.}$ suggesting a price per piece
631   4/3 doz. Painting and gilding

The only date that is recorded in the entire book is on page forty five and is July 7, '59 which implies that these entries in the second half were made after the closure of Nottingham Road in 1848 and possibly, as Howard Paget suggests, at King Street.

King Street Pattern Book

Twenty-six illustrations of patterns, painted in watercolours on good quality paper, are now held in the Museum at Royal Crown Derby. It can be seen that these sheets were originally part of a book, but are now preserved in individual plastic wallets within a red "Nyrex" cover, which bears a typed label on the front reading: "King Street patterns 1920".

John Twitchett has provided the information that these patterns were amongst the few records remaining from King Street that were salvaged by Colin Osborn, who was a director of Royal Crown Derby in the 1950s.

The sheets of patterns bear page numbers 1-11, but thereafter the numbers are missing. Each pattern is marked in pencil with a number and these are D1-D26.

All the designs are for plates, cups and cans, and some saucers. Of the total six only are named, the Duesbury Sprig patterns and Rose Barbeau being continuations of earlier Nottingham Road patterns. They are all reproduced below and many can be seen on known twentieth century King Street wares, some of these being illustrated in this chapter.

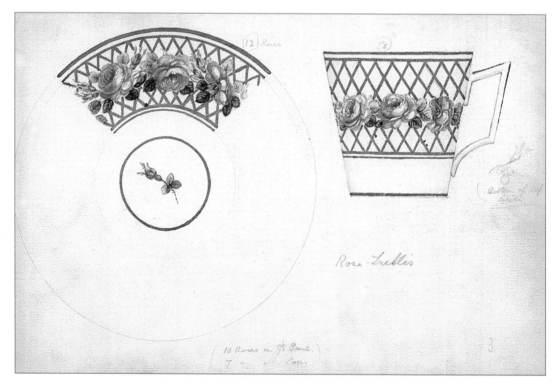

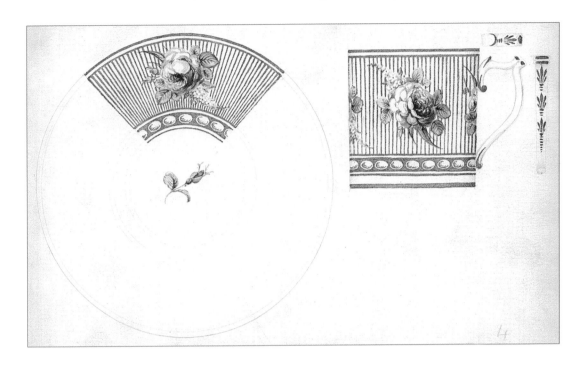

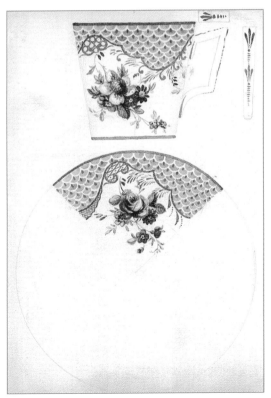

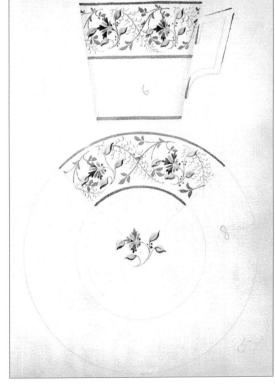

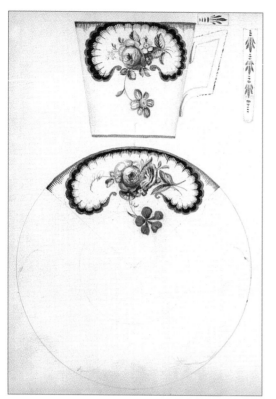

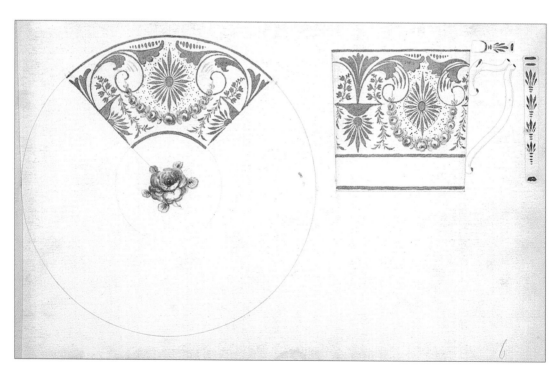

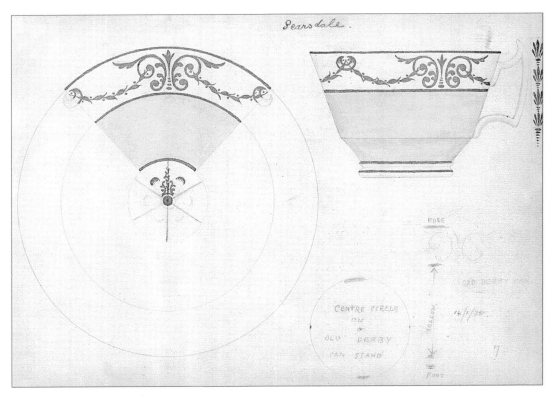

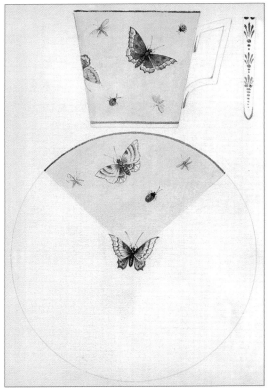

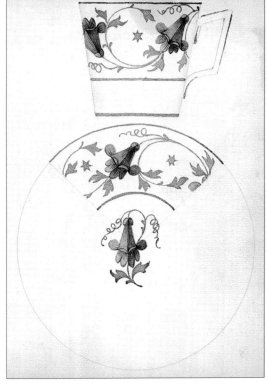

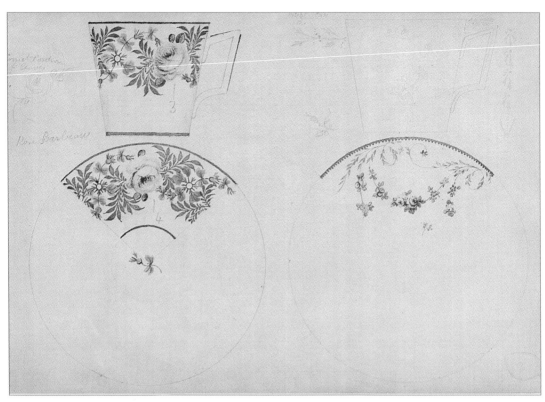

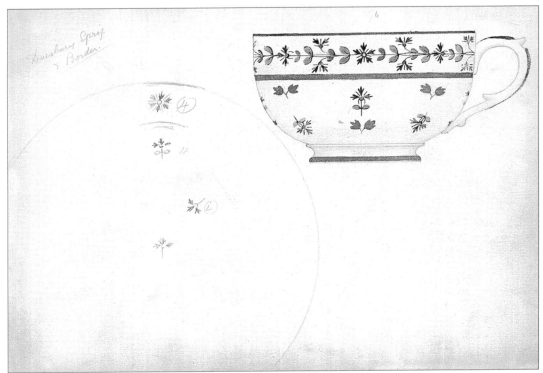

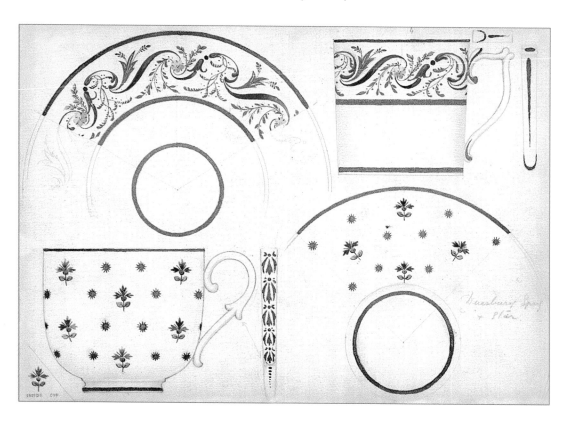

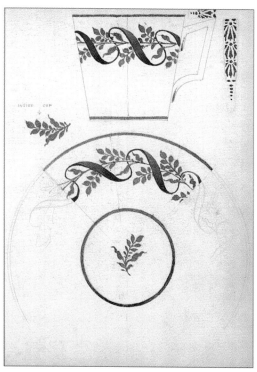

Other Sources

Although not true Pattern Books like the two in the British Museum, which have just been described, there are four other references to King Street shapes and patterns which will now be considered. Before doing this, readers should be reminded that the numbers shown in the 1934-35 catalogue and price list can fairly safely be ruled out, as they are most likely sales reference numbers, rather than relating to shapes or patterns. The remaining four sources are as follows:

Source One

As in the second half of the British Museum Pattern Book Two, further prices paid to decorators for painting and or gilding are given in a small book in the Royal Crown Derby Museum archives. This book has "Almanac 1867" on the inside of the front cover.

Many of the prices in this book, which have been dealt with in Chapter Two, are for decorating figures and ornamental wares, but a few pattern names are quoted and also thirteen pattern numbers and both are listed below: the date May 16/81 refers to the year 1881.

Numbers (listed as in the book)

No.		No.	
301	Teas.	312	Teas.
304	Teas.	320	Teas.
269	Teas.	220	Teas.
266	Teas.	279	Teas.
287	Teas.	308	Teas.
319	Teas.	289	Teas.
201	Teas.		

Names

Partridge Japan.   Lily and convulvulus.
Fancy Japan.   Embossed sprig.

There are no illustrations in this book.

Source Two

A second small book held at Royal Crown Derby also lists King Street prices, but this time for finished wares. The dates given range from 1853 to 1874. Very few of the long list of pattern names have pattern numbers against them and these with a full list of names are set out below:

Names, with numbers:

No. 6	Maitland in gold and colour.
No. 129	Pattern, Dinner and Tea Service.
No. 630	Green and Gold.
No. 642	White Leaf, crimson border and gold.

Names without numbers:

	Blue Chantilly.
1862	Blue traceing, Courtney.
	White & gold edge.
	Orchards.
	Blue branch.

	Dowell.
	Royal lily & gold.
1853	Buxtons border.
	Ramsbottom blue & gold.
	Barbo sprig & gold.
	Tekle (same as blue & gold sprig).
	Exetor Japan.
1854	Pink stripes & gilt.
	Exetor, dark blue.
	Combermere border.
	Royal lily.
	Lovegroved bell.
1861	Old Japan full.
	Rich India.
	Hancocks laurel.
	Hills flowers.
1861	Purple scrole & gold.
	Embossed Table, blue flowers.
	Blue & gold line.
	Sir M. Woods
	Partridge Japan, red blue & gold.
	Cromptons border.
1861	Witches Japan.
	Red feather.
	? Dejeune.

1853	Rose Chantilly.
1861	Goodes.
	Db, & lace or Db. & gold.
1853	Townsend.
	Maitland.
1854	Gold Star border.
1855	Roses & gold sprigs.
	Kings, gold border.
	George III.
	Band & plain ground.
1856	Queens dress
	Blue & ? sprig.
1861	Rose Japan.
1861	Blue stripe, edged gold.
	Dark blue stripe flower.
	Sprigs of Roses.
1861	Betts border, white & gold
	Horseshoe, blue & gold.
	Caledon's
	Blue ? and gold sprig
	(dark blue, pink & gold lines, same price)
	Green border and gold lines.
	Rich old Derby Tea Service, Roses, blue ground & gold.

	Gold band & blue line.
1854	Gold edge & blue dots.
1862	Grecian Japan.
	Dragon Japan.
1853	Rich India Japan.
	Lamp Arabesque.
	Green Chantilly.
	Nett Japan.
1853	Blue Rosette.
	Green border ? lines.
	Blue Vine & gilt.
	Forget me nots.
1874	Oak & acorn.
1854	Tamworth's ?
1854	Rose festoon.
1854	Flowers in Dresden style.
	Green & gold scallup.
	Embossed flowers, blue lines no gold.
	Dontill edge.
	Slight Japan.
	Turquoise border.
	Gold edge
	Combermere border.
1860	London Zigzag & red & gold wreath & sprigs.
1862	Mangles stripe, dark blue & gold.
	Duke's embossed forget me not.
	Blue band, pink line & gold do.
1864	The Old Japan.
1864	Roses and brown leaf, blue tracing ?
1865	Duke's border in all colours & gold.
	Blue band.
	New beaded edge.
	Glazed Kiln Celeste for Dresden Group.

Notes on the above patterns:

a) In this book there are no illustrations.

b) A few pages have been omitted, where they are not in any way instructive e.g. Page 11: "Various Coloured".

c) Many of the above patterns were used at Nottingham Road, some with slightly altered names. These include the various Chantilly and Japan patterns, and Purple scroll and gold. Barbo or Rose Barbo, as it became known, was originally Bourbon Rose.

Source Three

In Mrs. Willoughby Hodgson's book *Old English China*, one page is devoted to illustrations of patterns, which it is claimed were in the books originally owned by Duesbury 1st of Nottingham Road fame, who died in 1786. It is also stated that this pattern book was in the possession of Sampson Hancock. Aileen Dawson in her article confirms that the British

Museum Pattern Book One does not contain any illustrations that match those shown by Mrs. Hodgson and they do not tie up with any of the other sources of information reviewed in this chapter.

It is the opinion of the authors that Sampson Hancock was very proud of King Street's connections with the Nottingham Road factory. For this reason it was at first thought that possibly this book does not date back as far as suggested, but on the other hand Mrs. Hodgson's mention of The Derby Mark in puce suggests a date in the eighteenth century. It is certainly not King Street's own S & H mark in puce, as this had not been introduced when Mrs. Hodgson's book was published. Could this be another undiscovered pattern book? This page of patterns is shown below:

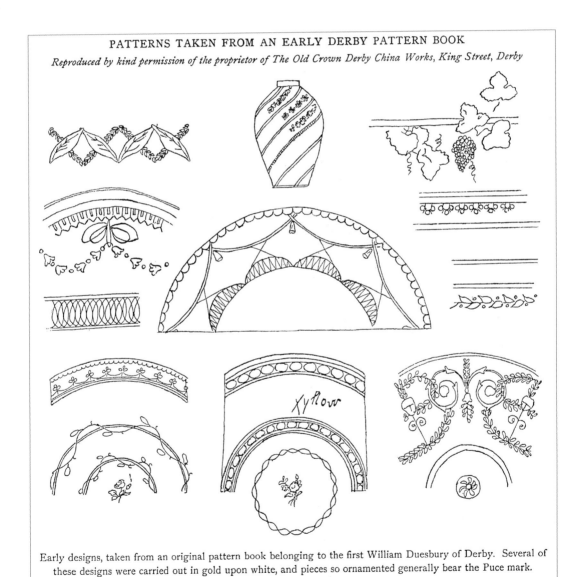

PATTERNS TAKEN FROM AN EARLY DERBY PATTERN BOOK
Reproduced by kind permission of the proprietor of The Old Crown Derby China Works, King Street, Derby

Early designs, taken from an original pattern book belonging to the first William Duesbury of Derby. Several of these designs were carried out in gold upon white, and pieces so ornamented generally bear the Puce mark.

Patterns: Mrs. Willoughby Hodgson, "Old English China."

Source Four

In an envelope in the archives there are sketches of some cups, a jug and a vase with names and sales prices written against some by Sampson Hancock. Drawn on the company's letterheaded paper, they combine shapes and patterns and are shown below:

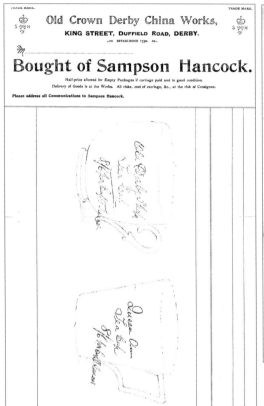

Sketches of shapes and patterns, drawn by Sampson Hancock.
Royal Crown Derby Museum Archives.

270

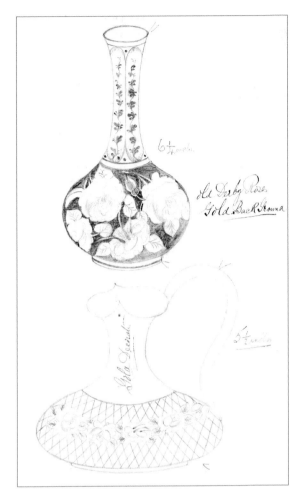

Notes on these sketches:

a) As the writing is that of Sampson Hancock these sketches will have been made prior to November 1895, the date of his death.

b) The chocolate cup and jug carry the Rose Trellis pattern that was so popular at King Street.

Patterns and Shapes Summary

Counting the British Museum Book Two having been considered separately in two parts, a total of eight sources of information on shapes and patterns have been examined. Spread over these records is a mixture of pattern names and numbers, a few shape names and some illustrations. From the information contained in these documents, the authors have not found it possible to compile a full and authoritative list of King Street patterns or shapes accompanied by their numbers.

It is hoped however that by setting out clearly in this chapter all the known information, although rather disconnected, it will provide an occasional clue to those who in the future may attempt to identify a King Street pattern, shape or figure. Unfortunately any search will not be helped by the lack of information on the wares themselves.

During a study of these eight sources of information, it has been noticed that on a few occasions, a pattern name, number or a shape appears in more than one place. These are recorded below in tabular form. The likely movement of these documents shown in the table is interesting. As it seems probable that all had King Street as their home at some time or another and with the factory's links with Nottingham Road, it is not surprising that earlier patterns and shapes were repeated by this small factory.

	BRITISH MUSEUM BOOK ONE	BRITISH MUSEUM BOOK TWO FIRST HALF	BRITISH MUSEUM BOOK TWO SECOND HALF
Possible Origins and Subsequent Movements of Records	Nottingham Road to King Street to British Museum	Rockingham Nottingham Road King Street British Museum	King Street British Museum
Approximate Dates	18th Century 19th Century	No date shown Rockingham factory closed 1842	One date shown - 1859
	315 New Cup and Saucer Lord Charles Townsend's * Pattern, dentil edge and handle, gold laurel (not illustrated)		
	Stuck into an early page a sketch of a breakfast cup inscribed "Stanhope" (no pattern shown)		406 Stanhope shape cup (a pattern is illustrated but no cup shape)
		294 Betts Border (not illustrated)	
		339 Rose Japan (not illustrated)	
		340 Witches Japan (not illustrated)	
			630 Gilding 3½ d (a green and gold pattern is illustrated)
			642 Gilding 3½ d (a leaf pattern with crimson border and gold is illustrated)
			319 ?/6 doz. possibly 2/6 but the 2 is unclear (border is illustrated, caption N10Green)
			320 Teas 2d (border is illustrated, caption N10 Green)

Alternative spelling
* Townshend

Book One
Museum Registration
Number 1936 7-15 140

Book Two
Museum Registration
Number 1936 7-15 141

ROYAL CROWN DERBY BOOK ONE	ROYAL CROWN DERBY BOOK TWO	HANCOCK'S SKETCHES	MRS. HODGSON'S PATTERNS	KING STREET PATTERN BOOK
King Street R C D Museum	King Street R C D Museum	King Street R C D Museum	Nottingham Road King Street Unknown	King Street R C D Museum
Two dates shown 1867 and 1881	Dates shown 1853 - 1874	Prior to 1895	Prior to 1848	One date shown 14.1.35.
	Townsend (1853) (not illustrated)			
	Betts border (1861) (not illustrated)			
	Rose Japan (1861) (not illustrated)			
	Witches Japan (1861) (not illustrated)			
	630 Green and Gold (not illustrated)			
	642 White leaf. Crimson border and gold. (not illustrated)			
319 Teas 2/6 doz. (not illustrated)				
320 Teas 2/6 doz. (not illustrated)				

The writers hope that the following illustrations and the details covering each piece provide a picture of the diverse range of shapes and decoration that was turned out by the King Street factory. With few details remaining of what the factory produced over a period of eighty-six years, there is little doubt that in the years ahead more previously unrecorded items will appear.

Figure of a Greyhound

Description: A greyhound lying on a rectangular base. It is decorated in enamel colours, with a spotted brown coat, grey-shaded nose and paws. It has a gilt collar and the base is a mottled green, with a gilt band around the side.

Marks: Puce crown over crossed swords and D, with two sets of three dots and initials S and H. Also the mark of two parallel lines in puce, and incised *N* 16.

Measurements: Length 13.75cm.

Date: Circa 1915-1934.

Location: In the collection of Mr. and Mrs. H. Cordwent.

Notes: 1. Also turned out undecorated in biscuit and glazed, both blue mark.
2. Minor restoration to collar and tail.

Figure of a Parrot

Description:	The bird is enamelled in bright colours and is perched on a green mound base.
Marks:	Puce crown over crossed swords and D, with two sets of three dots and initials S and H.
	Also in puce the mark ₮
Measurements:	Height 11.25cm.
Date:	Circa 1915-1935.
Location:	In the collection of Mr. and Mrs. H. Cordwent.

Figure of a Hound

Description: A figure of a hound seated on an oval grassy mound, its head facing left and upwards. It is decorated in enamel colours with a gilt band around the base.

Marks: Underglaze blue crown over crossed swords and D, with two sets of three dots and initials S and H. Also on the base incised initials that are unclear.

Measurements: Height 14.5cm.

Date: Probably later nineteenth century.

Location: In the collection of Mr. and Mrs. H. Cordwent.

Literature: D. G. Rice, *English Porcelain Animals of the 19th Century*, Antique Collectors' Club, 1989, p.185, shows a Staffordshire wolf, which appears to have come from the same mould.

Exhibition: On display in "The Factory at King Street, 1849-1935" Exhibition at The Museum and Art Gallery, Derby. Catalogue number 101.

Notes: 1. A glazed white version of this hound is known in a private collection.
2. When on display in 1991 in the Royal Crown Derby Museum, this enamelled hound carried the following caption: "A rare model alcibiados hound, taken from a bronze original. Blue mark c. 1886."

Figure of a Lamb

Description: A recumbent lamb, with gilt collar, rests on a green mound base outlined in gilt.

Marks: Red crown over crossed swords and D, with two sets of three dots and initials S and H.

Measurements: Length 7.5cm.
Height 3.5cm.

Date: Twentieth century.

Location: Royal Crown Derby Museum.

Notes: A group of three lambs, one being recumbent, is recorded as being modelled by Joseph Taylor. See Twitchett and Bailey, *Royal Crown Derby*, Antique Collectors' Club. 1988, p.14.

Figure of a Peacock

Description: A figure of a peacock, enamelled in bright colours, stands on a mound base decorated with gilt scrolls and applied flowers.

Marks: Puce crown over crossed swords and D, with two sets of three dots and initials S and H.

Measurements: Height 16.75cm.

Date: Circa 1915-1935.

Location: Royal Crown Derby Museum.

Notes: 1. Some crazing.
2. Figures of peacocks were produced earlier at the Nottingham Road factory.

Cow Cream Jug

Description:	A cream jug in the form of a horned cow standing on a base consisting of two scrolled surfaces which fan down and outwards from a central point on the cow's belly. The mouth forms the spout, its tail the handle, and there is a lift- off cover in the animal's back. The whole is decorated in enamel colours and gilding.
Marks:	Red crown over crossed swords and D, with two sets of three dots and initials S and H.
Measurements:	Height 10cm. Length 15.5cm.
Date:	Late nineteenth or early twentieth century.
Location:	Derby Museums and Art Gallery. No. 1890-241/312.
Provenance:	A gift to the Museum by the late Felix Joseph.
Literature:	A cow creamer is illustrated in the factory sales catalogue, 1934-35, number 75.

Dromedary

Description:	A free standing one humped camel decorated in enamel colours.
Marks:	Red crown over crossed swords and D, with two sets of three dots and initials S and H.
Measurements:	Height 6cm.
Date:	Late nineteenth or early twentieth century.
Location:	Private collection.
Literature:	A similar dromedary illustrated in Twitchett and Bailey *Royal Crown Derby*, Antique Collectors' Club, 1988, p.12.

Animals

Description:	A group of eleven glazed white, free standing, small animals, *Top Line*: Dachshund, Lion, Shihtzu, Foxhound. *Middle*: Rhinoceros, Fox, Pug, Elephant, Cow. *Lower*: Large and small crocodiles.
Marks:	All are marked in underglaze blue, with the S and H mark in varying degrees of clarity, according to the space available.
Measurements:	Maximum length 13cm. (large crocodile). Height from 1.75cm. to 7cm.
Date:	Probably later nineteenth.
Location:	Private collection.
Provenance:	The Fox: The estate of Derby collector the late J. Mordecai.
Exhibition:	The foxhound on display in "The Factory at King Street 1849-1935" Exhibition held in 1993 at The Museum and Art Gallery, Derby. Catalogue number 118.
Notes:	1. Some repairs and restoration, mainly to legs and tails. 2. The Pug and Shihtzu were also turned out decorated in enamel colours. 3. Much attention was paid to detail in the modelling of many of the King Street animals. At first sight, any two small pugs, similar to the one illustrated, look alike until turned over when differences can be seen, the bitch and dog versions being correctly modelled according to their sex.

Pair of Lions

Description:

A pair of glazed white recumbent male lions, each with its tail curled around it. They each rest on a plain rectangular plinth.

Marks:

Left: Underglaze blue crown over crossed swords and D, with initial S only.
Right: Underglaze blue crown over crossed swords and D, with initials S and H.
The two sets of three dots are missing from both marks.

Measurements:

Height 10cms.
Plinths: 14cm. x 6cm.

Date:

Probably later nineteenth century.

Location:

Private collection.

Pug Dogs

Description: A glazed white group of three pug dogs on an oval mound base. Each wears a studded collar. Two dogs are lying on the base facing each other. The third, in playful mood, front legs on the back of another dog, bites its left ear.

Marks: Underglaze blue crown over crossed swords and D, with one set of two dots and initials S and H.

Measurements: Height 11cm.
Length 17.5cm.
Width 14cm.

Date: Probably later nineteenth century.

Location: Private collection.

Notes: 1. Restoration to tail of one dog.
2. Worcester produced a group of three pugs very similar to this one.

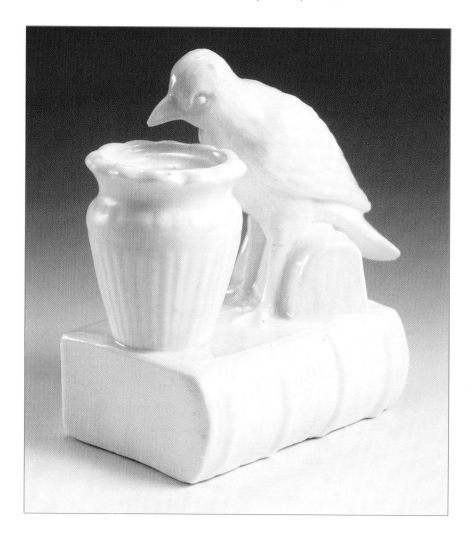

Bird

Description: A glazed white bird standing on a rectangular base, modelled as a book. A second smaller book provides support for the bird, which is studying, with interest, the contents of a vessel, which also rests on the larger book.

Marks: Underglaze blue crown over crossed swords and D, with two sets of three dots and initials S and H.

Measurements: Height 10.5cm.
Base 8.5cm. x 5.75cm.

Date: Probably later nineteenth century.

Location: Private collection.

Notes: On the inside of the vessel are a considerable number of firing blacks, both large and small.

Figure of Belper Joe

Description: The figure of a man wearing a top hat, striped trousers, a waist-coat held together with string, and an overcoat. He holds a sheet of paper in his left hand and stands on a circular base.

Marks: Inscribed "Belper Joe" in gilt around the base.
Puce crown over crossed swords and D, with two sets of three dots and initials S and H. Also mark of two parallel lines in puce.

Measurements: Height 11cm.

Date: Circa 1915-1934.

Location: Royal Crown Derby Museum.

Literature: This figure is illustrated and the story attached to Belper Joe is given in Twitchett and Bailey, *Royal Crown Derby*, Antique Collectors' Club, 1988, p.33.

Exhibition: On display in "The Factory at King Street, 1849-1935" Exhibition held in 1993 at The Museum and Art Gallery, Derby. Catalogue number 102.

Figure of African Sall

Description:	A figure of a negress with hands on her hips, standing on a circular base painted green to represent grass. The figure is painted in polychrome enamels with gilding.
Marks:	Inscribed "African Sall" in gilt around the base. In puce, crown over crossed swords and D, with two sets of three dots and initials S and H. Also the mark of two parallel lines in puce.
Measurements:	Height 9.2cm.
Date:	Circa 1915-1934
Location:	In the collection of Dr. J. R. Freeman.
Literature:	Illustrated in the factory sales catalogue, 1934-35, Number 48.
Exhibition:	On display in "The Factory at King Street, 1849-1935" Exhibition held in 1993 at The Museum and Art Gallery, Derby. Catalogue number 27.
Notes:	1. This model was made at Nottingham Road in the nineteenth century. 2. This figure and that of Billy Waters were based on the well-known theatrical figures of the 1820s, played by William Walbourn and Mr. Saunders.

Figure of Billy Waters

Description:	A figure of a Negro fiddle player with one wooden leg. He stands on a circular base painted green to represent grass. The figure is painted in polychrome enamels with gilding.
Marks:	Inscribed "Billy Waters" in gilt around the base. Puce crown over crossed swords and D, with two sets of three dots and initials S and H. Also the mark of two parallel lines in puce.
Measurements:	Height 9.5cm.
Date:	Circa 1915-1934.
Location:	In the collection of Dr. J. R. Freeman.
Literature:	Illustrated in factory sales catalogue. 1934-35, number 47.
Exhibition:	On display in "The Factory at King Street, 1849-1935" Exhibition held in 1993 at The Museum and Art Gallery, Derby. Catalogue number 27.
Notes:	1. This model was made at Nottingham Road in the nineteenth century.
	2. This figure and those of African Sall were based on the well-known theatrical figures of the 1820s, played by William Walbourn and Mr. Saunders.

287

Pair of figures of The Philosophers.

Description:	A pair of figures of the Laughing and Crying Philosophers. Both are dressed in brightly coloured clothes including striped breeches. Both stand on circular bases which are decorated with a gilt band.
Marks:	Both figures, puce crown over crossed swords and D, with two sets of three dots and initials S and H. Also mark of two parallel lines in puce on both.
Measurements:	*Laughing*: Height 11.5cm. *Crying*: Height 11.75cm.
Date:	Circa 1915-1934.
Location:	Royal Crown Derby Museum.
Literature:	The Laughing Philosopher is illustrated in the factory sales catalogue. 1934-35, number 43.
Notes:	It is strange that the King Street factory should have named this figure The Laughing Philosopher. The Nottingham Road pair of Philosophers (Haslem's list, numbers 159 and 160) are busts and in no way do the King Street figures resemble either of them (see illustration, Bradshaw, P. *Derby Porcelain Figures 1750-1848*, Faber and Faber, 1990, p.281). These figures, despite their name, resemble the pair of Topers illustrated in Bradshaw, P., *Derby Porcelain Figures 1750-1848*, Faber and Faber, 1990, p.427.

Pair of figures of Spring and Autumn

Description: A pair of figures of Spring and Autumn from The Four Seasons (see notes below). Both decorated in bright enamel colours and standing on mound bases, each with a wide gilt band. Spring carries a basket of fruit over her right arm and Autumn a satchel and a water bottle at his waist.

Marks: Puce crown over crossed swords and D, with two sets of three dots and initials S and H. Also the mark of two parallel lines in puce.

Measurements: Height 16.75cm.

Date: Circa 1915-1934.

Location: Private collection.

Literature: Illustrated in Twitchett and Bailey, *Royal Crown Derby*, Antique Collectors' Club, 1988, p.31.

Notes: In the factory sales catalogue 1934-35 these two figures are named "Coffee Season. Spring" and "Coffee Season. Autumn", probably after William Coffee, the Nottingham Road modeller. Figures representing Summer and Winter are not known in this form.

Figure of Greenwich Pensioner

Description:
The Pensioner is sitting on a tree stump and has a table at his left hand side with a jug and glass of ale upon it. He holds his purse in his left hand. His right leg is wooden. He wears a black tricorn hat and colourful clothes decorated in enamel colours, embellished with gilding.

Marks:
Red crown over crossed swords and D, with two sets of three dots and initials S and H. Also the mark of two parallel lines in red.

Measurements:
Height 13cm.

Date:
Circa 1915-1934.

Location:
Private collection.

Literature:
Illustrated in Twitchett and Bailey, *Royal Crown Derby*, Antique Collectors' Club, 1988, p.15.

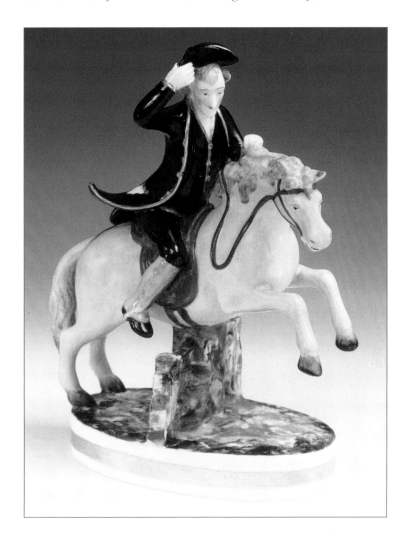

Figure of Dr. Syntax on Horseback

Description: Dr. Syntax is astride his horse Grizzle, which is jumping a fence. He is dressed in black frock-coat, waistcoat and trousers. The whole figure, decorated in enamel colours, is on an oval base which has a wide gilt band.

Marks: Puce crown over crossed swords and D, with two sets of three dots and initials S and H. Also the mark of two parallel lines in puce.

Measurements: Height 18.5cm.

Date: Circa 1915-1934.

Location: Private collection.

Literature: The story of the range of Dr. Syntax figures produced by the Derby factories is told by Valerie and Harry Cordwent in News-letter, June 1995 from the *Derby Porcelain International Society*.

Figure of a Boy

Description:	A figure of a rosy-cheeked young boy, standing on a mound base with the thumb of each hand in the pockets of his short trousers. He also wears a long-sleeved shirt and brown shoes, all decorated in enamel colours.
Marks:	Puce crown over crossed swords and D, with two sets of three dots and initials S and H. Also the mark of two parallel lines in puce.
Measurements:	Height 11cm.
Date:	Circa 1915-1934.
Location:	Private collection.

Pair of figures of English Shepherd and Shepherdess

Description:
A pair of decorated figures.

Shepherd: He is wearing a patterned shirt, jacket and breeches, and holds a dog, looking lovingly up at its master.

Shepherdess: She has her hair in a bun and wears a blue bodice and yellow skirt. With both hands she holds a lamb at her waist.

Both figures are decorated in enamel colours and gilding and rest on pierced shell bases.

Marks:
Puce crown over crossed swords and D, with two sets of three dots and initials S and H. Also the mark of two parallel lines in puce, on both.

Measurements:
Height 17cm.

Date:
Circa 1915-1934.

Location:
Private collection.

Literature:
Illustrated in the factory sales catalogue, 1934-35, the Shepherd number 71 and Shepherdess number 72.

Notes:
John Twitchett in *Derby Porcelain*, Barrie and Jenkins, 1980, p.253 explains the differences between the Nottingham Road and King Street factories in the naming of the English and French Shepherd and Shepherdess figures.

293

Candle Extinguisher

Description:
A match holder with wide gilt rim around the circular base. The underside of the holder is striated for easy striking. The extinguisher, which fits over the match holder is in the form of a female figure, decorated in enamel colours, representing Sarah Gamp from Charles Dickens' works.

Marks:
Incised on base of match holder "Gamp". Blue crown over crossed swords and D, with two sets of three dots and initials S and H.

Measurements:
Assembled Height 10.5cm.

Date:
Probably later nineteenth century.

Location:
Derby Museums and Art Gallery. No. 1959-425/1.

Provenance:
Previous owner was Miss Alice Amy Robinson, a great grand-daughter of founder partner and proprietor Sampson Hancock, and daughter of proprietor John James Robinson.

Literature:
This extinguisher and others from King Street, described and illustrated by A. J. Horsley, *Distinguished Extinguishers*, 1999, *pp.84-91*.

Figure Group: The Tythe Pig Group

Description:

Three figures standing in front of a tree, which overhangs their heads. One is dressed as a farmer and holds a pig in his right arm and leans on a crooked staff. The central figure of a woman is wearing a bonnet, cape and long dress and in her arms she carries a baby. The third figure is of a parson, hands clasped and wearing a wig and clerical clothes. These figures, decorated in enamel colours, are on an oval mound base, on which are also sheaves of corn, a pig and a basket of eggs.

Marks:

Underglaze blue crown over crossed swords and D, with two sets of three dots and initials S and H.

Measurements:

Height 16cm.
Length 22cm.

Date:

Probably later nineteenth century.

Location:

Private collection.

Literature:

A similar twentieth century group is illustrated in the factory sales catalogue, 1934-35, number 40.

Notes:

1. This group portrays the farmer's wife offering their child as tythe to the dismayed parson, in the hope that he will accept it, rather than a pig.

2. The parson and farmer's wife were produced as separate figures in the white and decorated, but the farmer is so far unrecorded.

Figure of Falstaff

Description: A figure of Falstaff holding a sword and shield, standing on a scrolled base picked out in gilt, the whole enamelled and gilt.

Marks: Red crown over crossed swords and D, with two sets of three dots and initials S and H. Also, the same mark in underglaze blue but much of it is invisible.

Measurements: Height 24cm.

Date: Probably later nineteenth century.

Location: In the collection of Dr. J. R. Freeman.

Exhibition: On display in "The Factory at King Street, 1849-1935" Exhibition held in 1993 at The Museum and Art Gallery, Derby. Catalogue number 25.

Figure of Fire

Description: A figure of Fire; one of the Four Elements. A figure of a man in eighteenth century costume. His right arm is held above his head and in his right hand is a torch and in his left hand a stick. His left foot is resting on a stone. The octagonal base is decorated with a Greek key pattern in relief, embellished with gilding. The rest of the figure is decorated with enamel colours and gilding.

Marks: Puce crown over crossed swords and D, with two sets of three dots and initials S and H. Also in puce the initials "WL" which form the monogram of proprietor William Larcombe.

Measurements: Height 17cm.

Date: Circa 1915-1917.

Location: Derby Museums and Art Gallery. No. 1999-157.

Literature: The figure illustrated in factory sales catalogue, 1934-35, number 28.

Exhibition: On display in "The Factory at King Street, 1849-1935" Exhibition held in 1993 at The Museum and Art Gallery, Derby. Catalogue number 156.

Notes: This model was made earlier, at Nottingham Road, as one of a set of Four Elements.

Pair of figures: Chelsea Flower and Fruit Sellers

Description:	Male and female seated figures, both decorated with enamel colours and gilding. The female wears a hat and long skirt and she holds in her right hand a basket of flowers. The male wears a hat and a long jerkin and holds in his left hand a basket of fruit.
Marks:	Puce crown over crossed swords and D, with two sets of three dots and initials S and H. Also initials "H.W." in puce.
Measurements:	Height 11cm.
Date:	Circa 1915-1935.
Location:	Private collection.
Literature:	Illustrated in factory sales catalogue, 1934-35, numbers 65 and 66.
Exhibition:	On display in "The Factory at King Street, 1849-1935" Exhibition held in 1993 at The Museum and Art Gallery, Derby. Catalogue number 129.

Boy in a Boat ornament

Description: A scantily dressed boy is seated in the middle of a boat, with legs in the air, giving the impression of being about to fall into the water. The boat rests on a green mound base and has two groups of modelled flowers on it. At one side of the boat is a mound representing a river bank.

Marks: Blue crown over crossed swords and D, with two sets of three dots and initials S and H.

Measurements: Height 13cm.
Length 27cm.
Width 13cm.

Date: Probably later nineteenth century.

Location: In the collection of Mr. and Mrs. H. Cordwent.

Literature: *"A Rare Piece of King Street, Two versions of a Boy in a Boat,"* Derby Porcelain International Society Newsletter, May 1996.

Notes: 1. A similar inward facing pair in glazed white (blue mark) is known in a private collection, but each boy is seated at the helm, rather than the middle of the boat.
2. Thomas Banks, an outside modeller used by King Street, supplied models of boats in 1872.

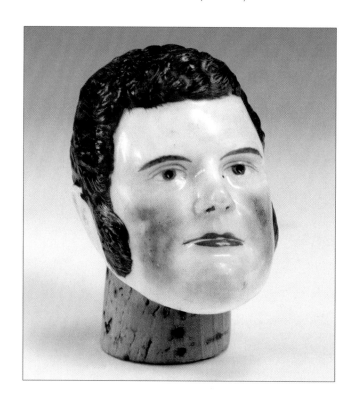

Head

Description:	The head of a man, decorated with enamel colours. He has brown curly hair, sideburns and rosy cheeks. The head is hollow and there are three small holes, two behind the ears and one at the back of the head.
Marks:	Red crown over crossed swords and D, with two sets of three dots and initials S and H.
Measurements:	Height 3cm.
Date:	Perhaps about 1900.
Location:	In the collection of Mr. and Mrs. H. Cordwent.
Literature:	Illustrated in the booklet, "The Factory at King Street, 1849-1935," by A. Bambery and R. Blackwood. Derby Museums and Art Gallery, October 1993, plate ii.
Exhibition:	On display in "The Factory at King Street, 1849-1935" Exhibition held in 1993 at The Museum and Art Gallery, Derby. Catalogue number 208.
Notes:	1. It is likely that this head represents someone well-known and the small holes suggest that it was designed to be attached to something. Suggestions have been made that the head portrays either Robbie Burns or Sampson Hancock.
	2. The head is displayed resting on a cork.

Figure group of Polish Dancers

Description:	A dancing group of Boy and Girl, arms around each other. They are dressed in brightly coloured clothes and are on a plain base with marble pattern.
Marks:	Red crown over crossed swords and D, with initials S and H. The two sets of three dots are missing.
Measurements:	Height 21cm.
Date:	Later nineteenth century
Location:	In the collection of Mr. and Mrs. H. Cordwent.
Literature:	This group illustrated by Twitchett and Bailey in *Royal Crown Derby*, Antique Collectors' Club, 1988, plate 10.
Notes:	A larger version of this group in biscuit, allegedly made at King Street from a Nottingham Road mould, was offered for sale as part of the W. Winter Collection. This sale was held in Derby on 27 June 1884.

Figure of a Soldier

Description: A figure of a soldier dressed in red jacket, brown trousers and
                   helmet, is kneeling on a grassy mound with a rifle in his hands.
                   There is no gilding.

Marks: Red crown over crossed swords and D, with two sets of three dots
                   and initials S and H. The same mark can also be seen repeated
                   faintly in blue.

Measurements: Height 10cm.

Date: Probably later nineteenth century,

Location: In the collection of Mr. and Mrs. H. Cordwent.

Exhibition: On display in "The Factory at King Street, 1849-1935" Exhibition
                   held in 1993 at The Museum and Art Gallery, Derby. Catalolgue
                   number 96.

Notes: This model was previously made at Nottingham Road and a
                   smaller version of it can be seen as a finial on a Nottingham Road
                   vase in biscuit in the collection of The Derby Museums and Art
                   Gallery.

Pair of figures of Welch Tailor and Wife

Description:

Tailor: He is mounted on a goat and is holding on to its left horn. On his back is a pair of kids in a basket. He wears a tricorn hat and green frock coat. The goat, mounted on an oval scrolled base, carries a flatiron in its mouth.

Wife: She is mounted on a nanny goat and is holding on to its left horn. In her right arm a child is cradled to her bosom. Two babies are carried in a basket on her back. She wears a pink bodice and yellow skirt. The nanny goat, mounted on an oval scrolled base, suckles a kid.

Both figures are decorated in enamel colours and gilding.

Marks: Blue crown over crossed swords and D, with two sets of three dots and initials S and H.

Measurements: Height: 13cm.

Date: Later nineteenth century.

Location: Private collection.

Figure of a Boy

Description: A figure of a boy dressed in tunic and breeches and wearing a conical shaped hat. He carries a basket of grapes on his back. The figure stands on one leg, the other kneeling on a tree stump, which is on a mound base. All in enamel colours.

Marks: Puce crown over crossed swords and D, with two sets of three dots and initials S and H.

Measurements: Height 12cm.

Date: Circa 1915-1935.

Location: In the collection of Mr. G. Orme.

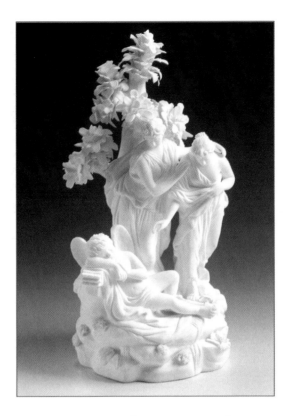

Figure group of Two Virgins Awakening Cupid

Description:	A group in unglazed biscuit. The winged figure of cupid lies on a deep rocky mound base, head resting on a quiver of arrows. The bow is at the feet of two bareheaded maidens in long flowing dresses, who stand, leaning over cupid. At the back is a tree with branches bearing modelled leaves.
Marks:	Incised crown over crossed swords and D, with two sets of three dots and initials S & H. Incised N 129.
Measurements:	Height 25cm.
Date:	Probably nineteenth century.
Location:	Private collection.
Literature:	A similar group is illustrated in the factory sales catalogue, 1934-35, p.1.
Notes:	1. This group is very similar to the one produced in biscuit at Nottingham Road. 2. It was still being produced at King Street as late as 1916, but decorated in enamels. 3. The incised number 129 on this biscuit group does not agree with the N 195 found on the earlier version. The relevance of 129 is not known.

Figures of The Gardener and Companion

Description:	A pair of figures in unglazed biscuit.
	Gardener: He stands on a rectangular base, his chin supported by his cupped right hand, and in his left hand is his spade. He is bareheaded and wears a shirt, jacket with rolled-up sleeves and breeches with bows at the knees. There are mossy tufts and leaves on the base.
	Companion: She stands on a rectangular base, left hand out-stretched, her right hand clasped to her bosom. She is looking at a plant in a pot which rests on top of a plinth. She is bareheaded and wears an ankle length dress. There are mossy tufts and leaves on the base.
Marks:	Both figures, under a specially applied dab of glaze, blue crown over crossed swords and D, with two sets of three dots and initials S & H.
Measurements:	*Gardener*: Height 13.5cm. *Companion*: Height 14cm.
Date:	Probably later nineteenth century.
Location:	Private collection.
Literature:	An enamelled pair is illustrated in the factory sales catalogue, 1934-35, numbers 1 and 2.
Notes:	1. Gardener's spade is restored. Companion has tips of four fingers of left hand missing, and restoration to flowers in pot. 2. These figures are similar to the Nottingham Road pair No. 359, but with some differences. 3. In the later nineteenth century this biscuit pair was also turned out glazed at King Street.

Figures of The French Shepherd and Shepherdess

Description: A pair of figures in unglazed biscuit.

Shepherd: He stands on a scroll base, with two groups of applied flowers and leaves upon it and a tree-stump supports the figure at the back. He holds a lamb under his right arm and in the palm of his outstretched left hand are two coins. He wears a hat with upturned brim, shirt, jacket and knee length breeches. His hair is in a ponytail.

Shepherdess: She stands on a scroll base, with two groups of applied flowers and leaves upon it and a tree-stump supports the figure at the back. In the folds of her upturned skirt is an assort ment of modelled flowers. She wears a hat with upturned brim, dress and bodice.

Marks: Both figures, blue crown over crossed swords and D with two sets of three dots and initials S and H.

Measurements: Height 17cm.

Date: Probably later nineteenth century.

Location: Private collection.

Literature: 1. An enamelled pair of French Shepherd (No.5) and French Shepherdess (No.6) is illustrated in the factory sales catalogue 1934-35. John Twitchett in *Derby Porcelain*, Barrie and Jenkins, 1980, p.253 explains the differences between the Nottingham Road and King Street factories in the naming of the English and French Shepherd and Shepherdess figures.

Notes: The fingers of the shepherd's left hand are restored.

Figure of The Cobbler

Description: A figure in unglazed biscuit. The Cobbler sits at a work bench, wearing a large soft cap, shirt with rolled-up sleeves, breeches and an apron. He has an upturned shoe in his lap and an awl in his right hand. His head is turned to the right and he is looking up at a bird in a cage on a ledge above him. The tools of his trade are scattered around his feet and at his side, on the bench on which he is sitting.

Marks: Blue crown over crossed swords and D, with two sets of three dots and initials S and H.

Measurements: Height 15.5cm.

Date: Probably later nineteenth century.

Location: Private collection.

Literature: An enamelled figure of the Cobbler is illustrated in the factory sales catalogue, 1934-35, number 33.

Notes: 1. The bird, its cage, the awl and cobbler's left hand and arm are restored.
2. The Nottingham Road factory produced a figure of the Cobbler, but the King Street figure varies considerably from this.

Figure of Jesus Christ

Description:	A glazed white figure. He has shoulder length hair, a beard and wears a flowing robe and sandals. The figure stands on a plain circular base.
Marks:	Underglaze blue crown over crossed swords and D, with initials S and H. The two sets of three dots are missing.
Measurements:	Height 37cm.
Date:	Probably later nineteenth century.
Location:	Private collection.
Exhibition:	On display in "The Factory at King Street, 1849-1935" Exhibition held in 1993 at The Museum and Art Gallery, Derby. Catalogue number 126.
Notes:	The left hand has been restored.

Holy Water Stoup

Description:	A glazed white figure of an angel, wearing a cross at the neck and with large wings, kneels on a stool and holds a container for Holy Water.
Marks:	Underglaze blue, crown over crossed swords and D, with initials S and H (the two sets of three dots are missing).
Measurements:	Height 33cm.
Date:	Late nineteenth century.
Location:	Private collection.
Provenance:	Used in two homes by a lady of Roman Catholic faith, now deceased, who lived in North Leicestershire.
Literature:	One Thing Leads to Another. An article by R. Blackwood in Newsletter, June 2002 from the Derby Porcelain International Society.
Notes:	1. Some firing cracks and restoration to base. 2. The stoup is designed to be wall mounted.

Pair of Boy and Girl figures, Morning and Night

Description:	A pair of glazed white figures.
	Morning: A girl crouching on a rectangular plinth representing a cushion, with a tassel at each corner. She is tying the laces of her left shoe.
	Night: A figure of a young boy saying his prayers, with his hands clasped in front of him. He wears a nightshirt and is kneeling on a rectangular plinth representing a cushion, with a tassel at each corner.
Marks:	Both figures, underglaze blue crown over crossed swords and D, with two sets of three dots and initials S and H.
Measurements:	Both figures: Height 8.5cm.
Date:	Probably later nineteenth century.
Location:	Private collection.
Literature:	This pair, enamelled, is illustrated in the factory sales catalogue, 1934-35, numbered 44 for Morning and 45 for Night.
Notes:	1. The head of Morning has been repaired.
	2. The arms and hands of the Morning figure, although not restored, are poorly shaped.
	3. H. G. Bradley in *"Ceramics of Derbyshire 1750-1975,"* first printing 1978, p.196 records that these figures of Morning and Night were originally modelled by George Cocker, when he had a small establishment in Friar Gate, Derby. For details concerning Cocker see John Twitchett, *"Derby Porcelain,"* Barrie & Jenkins, 1980, p.221.
	4. In the Cocker and Minton versions of Morning, the second shoe of the pair is seen adjacent to the one that is being tied, but is not modelled on the King Street version.

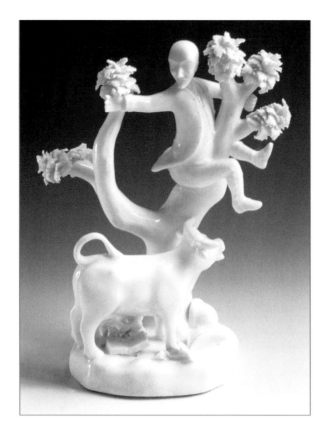

Figure of Dr. Syntax up a tree

Description:	A glazed white figure of Dr. Syntax, legs in the air, clinging to the boughs of a tree. Underneath the tree, on a simple mound base, is a bull. Also on the base is the Doctor's sketch pad and tricorn hat.
Marks:	Unmarked. (See note 2)
Measurements:	Height 17cm.
Date:	Probably early twentieth century.
Location:	Private collection.
Literature:	1. An enamelled version is illustrated in the factory sales catalogue, 1934-35, number 4. 2. The story of the range of Dr. Syntax figures produced by the Derby factories is told by Valerie and Harry Cordwent in Newsletter, June 1995, from the Derby Porcelain International Society.
Notes:	1. Small chip in base and on one finger of his right hand. 2. This figure closely resembles the twentieth century King Street enamelled figure, but differs in detail from the earlier Nottingham Road figure. Due to its exceptionally clean appearance it is suggested that it is a twentieth century figure, left undecorated and unmarked.

Pair of figures, Tinker and Companion

Description:
A pair of glazed white figures.

Tinker: He has long hair and carries a saucepan in his left hand and in his right hand he holds a piece of rope on which is secured a larger pan resting on his back. He wears a hat with upturned brim, shirt, apron, jacket and trousers with gaiters. The figure rests on a circular pierced scroll base, with a tree stump to support it.

Companion: She stands on a circular pierced scroll base and carries a bucket on her left arm. In her right hand is a saucepan and hanging at her waist is another saucepan. She wears a scarf over her head, bodice, apron and ankle length skirt.

Marks:
Both figures, underglaze blue crown over crossed swords and D, with two sets of three dots and initials S and H. In the case of the Companion the mark is very faint.

Measurements:
Both figures: Height 22cm.

Date:
Probably later nineteenth century.

Location:
Private collection.

Literature:
A later enamelled pair illustrated in factory sales catalogue, 1934-35, numbers 31 and 32.

Notes:
Tinker: He has one small restoration, but is heavily crazed and with discolouration and many kiln blacks is not a good example of a quality product.

Figure of The Thrower

Description: This glazed white figure is barefooted and wears a cap, tunic with the sleeves rolled up and knee length breeches. He sits on a narrow plank and using both hands is modelling a small pot at the potter's wheel. His working utensils are at his right hand side. All is mounted on a deep circular scroll base.

Marks: Underglaze blue crown over crossed swords and D, with two sets of three dots and initials S and H.

Measurements: Height 19.5cm.

Date: Probably later nineteenth century.

Location: Private collection.

Literature: A later enamelled version of this figure is illustrated in the factory sales catalogue, 1934-35, number 41.

Exhibition: On display in "The Factory at King Street, 1849-1935" Exhibition held in 1993 at The Museum and Art Gallery, Derby. Catalogue number 115.

Notes: 1. The Thrower's working utensils are not always identical on every figure.
2. Meissen produced a figure named The Potter (one of a pair with The Blacksmith) and as the King Street model is similar, it is likely that it was based on this earlier example.

Plate

Description: An octagonal plate with gilt rim. Decorated with five reserves of mixed flowers in enamel colours.

Marks: Red crown over crossed swords and D, with two sets of three dots and initials S and H. Also the mark of two parallel lines in red.

Measurements: Diameter 22cm.

Date: Late nineteenth or early twentieth century.

Location: Private collection.

Notes: Small crack at rim.

Plate

Description: A dessert plate with gadroon rim, the border lavishly gilded and decorated with eight colourful birds in flight, each one chasing an insect. A similar bird is painted in the centre of the well.

Marks: Red crown over crossed swords and D, with two sets of three dots and initials S and H. Also in red the initials "WL"which form the monogram of proprietor William Larcombe and the mark of two parallel lines in red.

Measurements: Diameter 22cm.

Date: Circa 1915-1917.

Location: In the collection of Dr. J. R. Freeman.

Provenance: The P. Ann Hayes collection. Number 16.

Notes: A crack in the rim.

Plate

Description:	A dessert plate with gadroon rim and wide gilt border. The centre is decorated with mixed flowers surrounded by gilt decoration and a further border of mixed flowers in enamel colours.
Marks:	Red crown over crossed swords and D, with two sets of three dots and initials S and H. Also the mark of two parallel lines in red.
Measurements:	Diameter 22cm.
Date:	Early twentieth century.
Location:	Private collection.
Notes:	Some firing cracks and crazing.

Plate

Description: A tea plate with gilt rim, decorated in enamel colours with butterflies and insects.

Marks: Red crown over crossed swords and D, with two sets of three dots and initials S and H. Also in red the mark of two parallel lines and the initials "WL" which form the monogram of proprietor William Larcombe.

Measurements: Diameter 14cm.

Date: Circa 1915-1917.

Location: Private collection.

Basket

Description:	A circular open weave basket of flared shape with two twisted rope handles. It is filled with brightly coloured modelled flowers, with one butterfly resting on the rim.
Marks:	On a pad on the base, in puce, crown over crossed swords and D, with two sets of three dots and initials S and H. Also the mark of two crossed parallel lines in puce.
Measurements:	Diameter 13.5cm. Height 10cm.
Date:	Circa 1915-1935.
Location:	Royal Crown Derby Museum.
Literature:	A pair of these baskets illustrated in Twitchett and Bailey, *Royal Crown Derby*, Antique Collectors' Club, 1988, plate 12.

Plate

Description:	A dessert plate with gadroon rim, decorated in enamel colours and gilding in the "Rose Barbeau" pattern.
Marks:	Inscription in gilt on the reverse. "Presented to Councillor and Mrs. Raynes on the occasion of their Silver Wedding from the Workers of Derby. April 3, 1918." Red crown over crossed swords and D, with two sets of three dots and initials S and H. Also in red the initials "W L P" which form the monogram of proprietors William Larcombe and Howard Paget.
Measurements:	Diameter 15cm.
Date:	Circa 1917-1933.
Location:	Private collection.
Exhibition:	On display in "The Factory at King Street, 1849-1935" Exhibition held in 1993 at The Museum and Art Gallery, Derby. Catalogue number 146.
Notes:	1. Alderman W. R. Raynes, J.P., was later elected the first Labour Mayor of Derby in November 1921. 2. This and a second similar plate are included in a part tea service and were probably used for bread and butter or cake. 3. The present owner also has in her possession the Mayor and Mayoress's oval medallions each of which has mounted in the centre a small circular china plaque. Both are decorated with a "Buck in the Park", the crest of Derby, in enamel colours with a gilt border. These may have been produced at King Street. They are most likely the medallions that were presented to retiring Mayors and Mayoresses, a practice that ceased in 1974, when the status of County Borough was lost. This information supplied by the present Mayor of Derby and obtained by The Principal Curator of Derby Museums and Art Gallery. 4. The plate is crazed.

Plate

Description:	A dessert plate with indented border, decorated with a band of orange enamel between gilt lines. In the centre is a simple spray of pansies. Part of a dessert service.
Marks:	Stevenson, Sharp and Co. in puce.
Measurements:	Diameter 23.5cm.
Date:	Circa 1859-c.1861.
Location:	In the collection of Dr. J. R. Freeman.

Tea Plate

Description:	A tea plate painted in unusually strong colours. The decoration consists of poppies and leaves in enamel colours.
Marks:	Puce crown over crossed swords and D, with two sets of three dots and initials S and H. Also on the reverse the initials "H.W." and separately the initial "P.", both in puce.
Measurements:	Diameter 15cm.
Date:	Circa 1915-1935.
Location:	Royal Crown Derby Museum.

Plate

Description:	A cabinet plate with gadroon rim, the whole surface richly decorated with gilding and panels of blue ground. In the centre, a roundel depicting a landscape in enamel colours.
Marks:	Inscription in brown near footrim: "Dromana". Green crown over crossed swords and D, with two sets of three dots and initials S and H. Impressed mark: "Derby XI". Impressed mark: "028" or "C28".
Measurements:	Diameter 22.5cm.
Date:	Probably late nineteenth or early twentieth century.
Location:	Private collection.
Exhibition:	On display in "The Factory at King Street, 1849-1935" Exhibition held in 1993 at The Museum and Art Gallery, Derby, Catalogue number 73.
Notes:	1. The factory mark in green has not been found on any other piece of King Street china. 2. The impressed mark, "Derby", suggests that the plate was bought in undecorated from Royal Crown Derby. 3. The Royal Crown Derby mark was used in green at times at Osmaston Road between the 1920s and some date in the 1960s.

Plate

Description:	Bread and butter plate, in "Rose Trellis" pattern, with single rose in the central panel.
Marks:	Red crown over crossed swords and D, with two sets of three dots and initials S and H.
Measurements:	26.5cm. x 23cm.
Date:	Probably late nineteenth century.
Location:	Private collection.

Dish

Description: An oval dish with a lobed border and deep well. The border
                   decorated with gilding. The centre panel painted in enamel
                   colours, with a scene of five children in regency dress, in a
                   farmyard, feeding chickens.

Marks: Red crown over crossed swords and D, with two sets of three dots
                   and initials S and H.

Measurements: 23.75cm x 19.75cm.

Date: Probably late nineteenth or early twentieth century.

Location: Derby Museums and Art Gallery. No. 1970-198.

Exhibition: On display in "The Factory at King Street, 1849-1935"
                   Exhibition held in 1993 at The Museum and Art Gallery, Derby.
                   Catalogue number 194.

Notes: Dish restored and decoration retouched.

Tray

Description:	A rectangular tray with gilt moulded scroll edge and large central floral bouquet in enamel colours.
Marks:	Red crown over crossed swords and D, with two sets of three dots and initials S and H.
Measurements:	15.5cm. x 11.25cm.
Date:	Early twentieth century.
Location:	Derby Museums and Art Gallery. No. 1982-485/1.

Dish

Description: A fan shaped dish painted in enamel colours and gilding in the Imari pattern "Old Crown Derby Witches", with variations.

Marks: Red crown over crossed swords and D, with two sets of three dots and initials S and H.

Measurements: 18cm. x 13cm.

Date: Late nineteenth or early twentieth century.

Location: Private collection.

Notes: Some crazing.

Dish

Description:	A small oval dish with scalloped rim decorated in enamel colours and gilding in the Imari pattern of "Old Crown Derby Witches".
Marks:	Red crown over crossed swords and D, with two sets of three dots and initials S and H.
Measurements:	Length 22cm. Width 13cm.
Date:	Twentieth century.
Location:	Private collection.

Basket of Flowers

Description: An oval basket, with two single loop handles, rests on four semi-circular feet. The basket is filled with modelled flowers in enamel colours with touches of gilding. A single butterfly rests on a rose.

Marks: Puce crown over crossed swords and D, with two sets of three dots and initials S and H. Also in puce the initials WLP which form the monogram of proprietors William Larcombe and Howard Paget.

Measurements: Length 29cm.
Width 22cm.
Height 15cm.

Date: 1917-1933.

Location: Private collection.

Leaf Dish

Description: A glazed white dish in the form of a leaf, with a single ring handle, on which rests a butterfly. The dish has an oval foot-rim.

Marks: Underglaze blue crown over crossed swords and D, with two sets of three dots and initials S and H.

Measurements: Height 8.5cm.
Length 21cm.
Width   16cm.

Date: Probably later nineteenth century.

Location: Private collection.

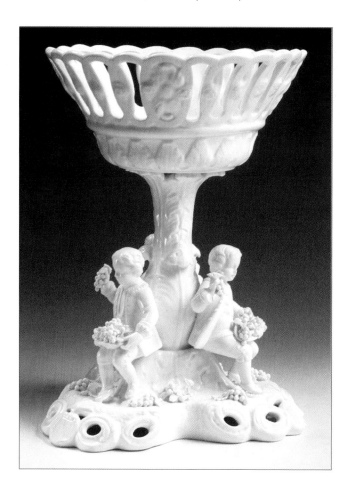

Comport

Description:	Three figures of "No. 8" Boys are seated around a central column, which supports a pierced bowl with moulded decoration. The trilobed, pierced shell base is decorated with applied grapes and vine leaves. The whole is in glazed white.
Marks:	A faint blue crown over crossed swords and D, with initials S and H. The two sets of three dots are missing and the mark is not underglaze.
Measurements:	Height 28.5 cm.
Date:	Probably later nineteenth century.
Location:	Private collection.
Notes:	1. There is some discolouration. 2. The name of "No.8" Boys given to the figures at King Street probably arose as similar figures were produced earlier at the Nottingham Road factory and are listed as "No.8" in Haslem's list of figures dated c.1876.

Basket

Description: A small circular glazed white basket, which flares out towards the rim on which are two water lilies with buds and leaves.

Marks: On a pad applied to the base, underglaze blue crown over crossed swords and D, with two sets of three dots and initial H. The S is missing.

Measurements: Diameter 12.5cm.

Date: Probably later nineteenth century.

Location: Private collection.

Notes: This is the first basket of this shape and size to be recorded which has no handles. Twisted rope handles are usually found on them.

Basket

Description: A large glazed white circular trellis work basket with double branch and twig ring handles. Decorated with four groups of modelled flowers and leaves around the rim, positioned at each side of the handles. It stands on four semi-circular feet at the centre of the base, with a single flower and two leaves at each corner.

Marks: On a pad applied to the centre of the base, underglaze blue crown over crossed swords and D, with two sets of three dots and initials S and H.

Measurements: Height 12.5cm.
Diameter 22.75cm.

Date: Probably later nineteenth century.

Location: Private collection.

Notes: 1. Minor chips to flowers and leaves. Firing crack in rim, under one handle.
2. The glaze is so thickly applied that it can be seen in places between the trellis work, resembling a spider's web.

334

Trio

Description:	A tea cup, saucer and tea plate decorated in enamel colours with sprays of mixed flowers on a green ground.
Marks:	Red crown over crossed swords and D, with two sets of three dots and initials S and H. Also the mark of two parallel lines and two crossed parallel lines in red on cup, saucer and plate.
Measurements:	*Cup*: Height 4.5cm. *Saucer*: Diameter 14cm. *Plate*: Diameter 15cm.
Date:	Twentieth century.
Location:	Private collection.

Cup and Saucer

Description: A tea cup and saucer, each lavishly decorated with a band of flowers in enamel colours and gilding.

Marks: Red crown over crossed swords and D, with two sets of three dots and initials S and H. Also the marks of two parallel lines and two crossed parallel lines in red on cup and saucer.

Measurements: *Cup*: Height 6.5cm.
       Saucer: Diameter 14cm.

Date: Early twentieth century.

Location: Private collection.

Cup and Saucer

Description: A cup and saucer from a tea service. Cobalt blue ground colour and lavish gilding on both. The saucer has a central panel decorated in enamel colours with mixed flowers and insects and this flower decoration is repeated on the cup, but only on the interior.

Marks: Red crown over crossed swords and D, with two sets of three dots and initials S and H on both cup and saucer. Also the mark of two parallel lines in red.

Measurements: *Cup*: Height 4.5cm.
Saucer: Diameter 14cm.

Date: Twentieth century.

Location: Royal Crown Derby Museum.

Coffee Cup and Saucer

Description:	A bucket-shaped coffee cup with an angular handle with gilt decoration. Cup and saucer decorated with panels of mixed flowers in enamel colours and the cup also has a single rose and leaves at the base of the interior.
Marks:	Both Cup and Saucer: Red crown over crossed swords and D, with two sets of three dots and initials S and H. Also the mark of two crossed parallel lines in red.
Measurements:	*Cup*: Height 5cm. *Saucer*: Diameter 11cm.
Date:	Twentieth century.
Location:	Private collection.
Notes:	Saucer heavily crazed.

Coffee Can and Saucer

Description: The cylindrical cup and its saucer both decorated in enamel colours and gilding, with a band of orange and turquoise leaves in gilt compartments.

Marks: On both can and saucer, in red, crown over crossed swords and D, with two sets of three dots and initials S and H. Also the mark of two parallel lines in red.

Measurements: *Cup*: Height 6.5 cm.
Saucer: Diameter 13.5cm.

Date: Late nineteenth or early twentieth century.

Location: Private collection.

Exhibition: On display in "The Factory at King Street, 1849-1935" Exhibition held in 1993 at The Museum and Art Gallery, Derby, Catalogue number 148.

Child's mug

Description: A cylindrical mug with angular handle, decorated in enamel colours with, on the exterior, flowers, insects and butterflies and on the interior, fishes. The name "Betty" is painted within garlands of flowers on the exterior.

Marks: The name "Betty" on the exterior of the mug. Red crown over crossed swords and D, with two sets of three dots and initials S and H. Also in red the initials WL which form the monogram of proprietor William Larcombe, and the mark of two parallel lines in red.

Measurements: Height 7.5cm.

Date: Circa 1915-1917.

Location: Royal Crown Derby Museum.

Literature: Twitchett and Bailey, *Royal Crown Derby*, Antique Collectors' Club, 1988, p.249. The authors state that this mug was commissioned by proprietor Paget as a gift for his young daughter Elizabeth. The fishes inside the mug were revealed as the mug was emptied; an inducement for "Betty" to drink up her milk.

Exhibition: On display in "The Factory at King Street, 1849-1935" Exhibition held in 1993 at The Museum and Art Gallery, Derby. Catalogue number 88.

Loving Cup

Description: A small two-handled, bucket-shaped cup, on four claw and ball feet. The exterior of the cup is decorated in enamel colours with flowers on one side and butterflies and fruit on the other. The whole is embellished with gilding.

Marks: Red crown over crossed swords and D, with two sets of three dots and initials S and H. Also the mark of two parallel lines in red.

Measurements: Height: 8.25cm.

Date: Probably twentieth century.

Location: Derby Museums and Art Gallery. No. 1947-63/4.

Exhibition: On display in "The Factory at King Street, 1849-1935" Exhibition held in 1993 at The Museum and Art Gallery, Derby. Catalogue number 155.

Drinking Vessels

Description:

The above illustrations show some of the many different sizes and shapes of drinking vessels produced during the nineteenth and twentiety centuries. They also demonstrate the wide variety of different handle shapes that were used.

Marks:

Mainly crown over crossed swords and D, with two sets of three dots and initials S and H, in red or puce.

Measurements:

In the group: Maximum height 11cm.
                Minimum height 3.3cm.

Date:

1861-1935.

Location:

Private collection.

342

Cup and Saucer

Description:	A teacup and saucer with a simple border of gold and green harebells. They both bear the rare Locker, late Bloor mark.
Marks:	Locker, Late Bloor, in puce on both.
Measurements:	*Cup*: Height 6.5cm.
	Saucer: Diameter 14cm.
Date:	Circa 1849-c.1859.
Location:	Royal Crown Derby Museum.
Notes:	Gilding rubbed.

Cup and Saucer

Description:

The cup of London shape. The cup and saucer each decorated with a single reserve surrounded by a gilt border and containing passion flowers in enamel colours.

Marks:

Red crown over crossed swords and D, with two sets of three dots and initials S and H, on both the cup and saucer.

Measurements:

Cup: Height 5.5cm.
Saucer: Diameter 14cm.

Date:

Twentieth century.

Location:

In the collection of Dr. J. R. Freeman.

Cup and Saucer

Description: A small cup and saucer, the cup with a loop handle, the saucer plain and deep. The exterior of the cup and upper surface of the saucer decorated with a band of yellow ground, framed by two narrower bands of a gilded pattern. In the centre of the cup interior and in the centre of the saucer, a gilt flower spray.

Marks: Red crown over crossed swords and D, with two sets of three dots and initials S and H. Impressed or incised in script "Derby", on base of saucer.

Measurements: *Cup*: Height 4.25cm.
Saucer: Diameter 12cm.

Date: Probably early twentieth century.

Location: Private collection.

Exhibition: On display in "The Factory at King Street, 1849-1935" Exhibition held in 1993 at The Museum and Art Gallery, Derby. Catalogue number 135.

Cup and Saucer

Description:	Cup and saucer, lavishly gilded on a cobalt blue ground.
Marks:	Red crown over crossed swords and D, with two sets of three dots and initials S and H on both. Also in red, the initials "WL", which form the monogram of proprietor William Larcombe on both cup and saucer. The zeppelin mark of gilt moon and black zeppelin is also painted on the reverse.
Measurements:	*Cup*: Height 6.5cm. *Saucer*: Diameter 14cm.
Date:	31 January 1916.
Location:	Royal Crown Derby Museum.
Notes:	Gilding worn. Cup discoloured on the interior.

Cup and Saucer

Description: The border of the saucer and body of the cup ground-laid with pale turquoise green. The cup has four oval reserves each containing a waterscape. The saucer has five similar reserves. Gilt fronds project into the border.

Marks: Red crown over crossed swords and D, with two sets of three dots and initials S and H, only on cup.

Measurements: *Cup*: Height 6.5cm.
Saucer: Diameter 14cm.

Date: Probably later nineteenth century.

Location: In the collection of Dr. J. R. Freeman.

Exhibition: On display in "The Factory at King Street, 1849-1935" Exhibition held in 1993 at The Museum and Art Gallery, Derby. Catalogue number 15.

Coffee Can and Saucer

Description:	The can with simple loop handle, decorated in enamel colours and gilding with stylised acorns and leaves on both exterior and interior. The saucer with similar decoration.
Marks:	On saucer only, both impressed and painted in red, crown over crossed swords and D, with two sets of three dots and initials S and H. Also impressed "Derby". No marks on can.
Measurements:	*Cup*: Height 6cm. *Saucer*: Diameter 13.5cm.
Date:	Late nineteenth century.
Location:	Private collection.
Notes:	1. Handle of cup is riveted. 2. It is unusual to find an impressed S and H mark on tablewares.

Coffee Cup and Saucer

Description: Bucket-shaped cup with an angular handle. Both cup and saucer decorated in enamel colours with tulips, sunflowers and roses. A single moss rose is painted on the base of the interior of the cup and the centre of the saucer.

Marks: Red crown over crossed swords and D, with two sets of three dots and initials S and H, on both cup and saucer. BCM/PUG in red inside the footrim, this being the firm's telegraphic address, on saucer only.

Measurements: *Cup*: Height 5.25cm.
Saucer: Diameter 11cm.

Date: Circa 1930.

Location: Private collection.

Exhibition: On display in "The Factory at King Street, 1849-1935" Exhibition held in 1993 at The Museum and Art Gallery, Derby. Catalogue number 50.

Notes: 1. The cup restored.
2. Cup and saucer crazed, with one extremely large blob of glaze on base of the saucer.

Coffee can

Description: A slightly tapered coffee can with wishbone handle. Moulded panels, outlined in gilt, are decorated with the upper side picked out in blue.

Marks: Courtney, Late Bloor, in puce.

Measurements: Height 6cm.

Date: Circa 1849- c.1862.

Location: In the collection of Dr. J. R. Freeman.

Coffee Set

Description:	A coffee set consisting of six cups and saucers, coffee pot, sugar bowl and cream jug. All pieces have eight faceted sides and are decorated in enamel colours with the "Old Crown Derby Witches" pattern. The set is in a baize-lined wooden box with a lock.
Marks:	Red crown over crossed swords and D, with two sets of three dots and initials S and H.

Measurements:

Coffee pot:	Height 18.5 cm.
Jug:	Height 7.5 cm.
Basin:	Height 6.5 cm.
Cups:	Height 6.5 cm.
Saucers:	Diameter 13.5 cm.

Date:	Probably twentieth century.
Location:	Derby Museums and Art Gallery. No. 1979-563/113.
Provenance:	Gertrude Whittaker bequest.
Exhibition:	On display in "The Factory at King Street, 1849-1935" Exhibition held in 1993 at The Museum and Art Gallery, Derby. Catalogue number 164.

Tyg

Description:	A three-handled tyg with angular handles and three main panels of flowers decorated in enamel colours, each surrounded with scroll gilding.
Marks:	Red crown over crossed swords and D, with two sets of three dots and initials S and H.
Measurements:	Height 12.5cm. Body, without handles: Diameter 12.5cm.
Date:	Early twentieth century.
Location:	Private collection.

Teapot

Description: A one-cup teapot with globular body, short straight tapering spout and high loop handle. The lid is circular with a button knop. Decorated with gilt scrolls and foliage and with groups of blue petals.

Marks: Red crown over crossed swords and D, with two sets of three dots and initials S and H.

Measurements: Height 9cm.

Date: Twentieth century.

Location: In the collection of Dr. J. R. Freeman.

Teapot

Description:	A teapot and cover with a bellied body, gilt rim top and bottom, and decorated in Imari colours with "Old Crown Derby Witches" pattern.
Marks:	Red crown over crossed swords and D, with two sets of three dots and initials S and H.
Measurements:	Height 16cm.
Date:	Late nineteenth century.
Location:	Private collection.
Notes:	Cracks in body.

Roman Lamp

Description:	Ornamental vessel with short pointed spout and circular cover, the handle in the form of a tall scroll rising from the body. The body and cover decorated with applied modelled flowers and leaves in enamel colours. All embellished with gilding.
Marks:	On body only: Red crown over crossed swords and D, with two sets of three dots and initials S and H.
Measurements:	Height 11.5cm.
Date:	Twentieth century.
Location:	Private collection.
Literature:	A similar Roman Lamp illustrated in the factory sales catalogue, 1934-35, number 67.
Notes:	1. Minor chips to flowers. 2. Having perforations at the base of the spout, it is suggested that what King Street called a "Roman Lamp" was based on a vessel originally used for tea tasting.

Wine Taster

Description: A ribbed wine taster with gilt rim, pierced flat handle and a single enamelled rose in the centre of the bowl.

Marks: Red crown over crossed swords and D, with two sets of three dots and initials S and H.

Measurements: Bowl: Diameter 6.5cm.

Date: Probably twentieth century.

Location: Royal Crown Derby Museum.

Sorbet Cups

Description:	Two glazed white sorbet cups and stands. The cups are of inverted bell shape, set on low domed feet. The scroll handles are set between two groups of applied flowers, one simple and one more elaborate. The stands have applied flowers and leaves around their rims.
Marks:	*Left cup*: Underglaze blue crown over crossed swords and D, with one set of three dots and no initials S and H. *Left stand*: Unmarked. *Right cup and stand*: Underglaze blue crown over crossed swords and D, with two sets of three dots and initials S and H.
Measurements:	Both cups with stands: Height 9cm.
Date:	Probably later nineteenth century.
Location:	Private collection.
Notes:	1. Minor damage and some discolouration. 2. Similar cups and stands, with enamelled applied flowers, were produced at Nottingham Road.

Miniature Teawares

Description: This group of glazed white jug, sucrier (centre) and teapot all have applied flowers on them and the sucrier and teapot also have them on the covers.

Marks: All, underglaze blue crown over crossed swords and D, with two sets of three dots and initials S and H.

Measurements: *Jug*: Height 5.75cm.
Sucrier: Height 5.5cm.
Teapot: Height 6cm.

Date: Probably later nineteenth century.

Location: Private collection.

Notes: Minor chips to flowers on teapot cover.

Pair of Ewers

Description:	A pair of small ewers, of Stanhope shape, each decorated in enamel colours with two panels of flowers on an apple green ground and standing on gilded acanthus feet.
Marks:	Both, puce crown over crossed swords and D, with two sets of three dots and initials S and H. Also the mark of two parallel lines in puce.
Measurements:	Height 16.5cm.
Date:	Circa 1915-1934.
Location:	Private collection.

Vase

Description:	A small vase and domed cover decorated with bold orange flowers on a gilt ground.
Marks:	Red crown over crossed swords and D, with two sets of three dots and initials S and H. Also the mark of two parallel lines in red on base of body.
Measurements:	Height 12.5cm.
Date:	Probably twentieth century.
Location:	Royal Crown Derby Museum.
Notes:	Similar decoration can be seen on a cup from the Bloor period on display in Royal Crown Derby Museum.

Small Jug

Description:	A jug of "toby" style, the figure modelled as the Snuff Taker. He wears brightly coloured clothes, painted in enamel colours. His top hat is formed as a stopper and is detachable. There is a handle at the back.
Marks:	Puce crown over crossed swords and D, with two sets of three dots and initials S and H. Also the mark of two parallel lines in puce.
Measurements:	Height, with hat: 11.5cm.
Date:	Circa 1915-1934.
Location:	In the collection of Mr. G. Orme.
Literature:	Illustrated in factory sales catalogue, 1934-35, number 30.

Ewer

Description:	A ewer decorated in enamel colours. One main panel depicts a woman and child and on the reverse a still life, incorporating fruit, flowers and a tankard.
Marks:	Red crown over crossed swords and D, with two sets of three dots and initials S and H.
Measurements:	Height 17cm.
Date:	Probably late nineteenth or early twentieth century.
Location:	Royal Crown Derby Museum.
Literature:	llustrated in the booklet "The Factory at King Street 1849-1935" by A. Bambery and R. Blackwood, Derby Museums and Art Gallery, October 1993, plate i.
Notes:	Heavily crazed.

Vase

Description:	A small posy vase, with squat bulbous body and short wide neck. The body decorated in enamel colours with flowers and butter flies.
Marks:	Red crown over crossed swords and D, with two sets of three dots and initials S and H.
Measurements:	Height 5 cm.
Date:	Twentieth century.
Location:	Private collection.

Spill Vase

Description: A spill vase with fluted gilt rim with turquoise studs and
                   fleur-de-lys gilding at the foot. Cupids in relief, decorated in
                   enamel colours, are harvesting grapes.

Marks: Red crown over crossed swords and D, with two sets of three dots
                   and initials S and H.

Measurements: Height 11.75 cm.

Date: Probably late nineteenth century.

Location: Royal Crown Derby Museum.

Vase

Description:	A small vase with flattened circular body and tall narrow neck. Decorated with a yellow ground and two reserve panels, one painted in enamel colours with flowers, the other with fruit. The yellow ground is decorated with raised gilding.
Marks:	Puce crown over crossed swords and D, with two sets of three dots and initials S and H. Also in puce the initials "WL" which form the monogram of proprietor William Larcombe.
Measurements:	Height 9.75cm.
Date:	Circa 1915-1917.
Location:	Private collection.
Literature:	Illustrated in the booklet "The Factory at King Street, 1849-1935", by A Bambery and R. Blackwood, Derby Museums and Art Gallery, 1993, plate iii.
Exhibition:	On display in "The Factory at King Street, 1849-1935" Exhibition held in 1993 at the Museum and Art Gallery, Derby. Catalogue number 134.

Vase

Description: A vase with round body and tall narrow neck having an everted rim. Two large single roses, with branches and leaves, are applied to the body. These and butterflies and insects all in enamel colours. There are gilt lines at the rim and footrim.

Marks: Red crown over crossed swords and D, with two sets of three dots and initials S and H.

Measurements: Height 15.75cm.

Date: Later nineteenth or early twentieth century.

Location: Private collection.

Notes: This vase is one of a pair. Two similar vases, in the white, are known in a private collection (blue mark).

Vase

Description:	A vase with round body and a tall narrow neck, having an everted rim. The lavender coloured body is decorated with applied white flowers.
Marks:	Underglaze blue crown over crossed swords and D, with initials S and H. The two sets of three dots are missing.
Measurements:	Height 15.75cm.
Date:	Probably later nineteenth century.
Location:	Private collection.
Notes:	1. Lavender coloured bodies on King Street wares are uncommon, only four having been recorded, these being another vase and two mirror frames, all with applied white flowers. 2. The colour in the body is blotchy. Damage to applied flowers.

Miniature Jug and Basin

Description:	A matching miniature jug and octagonal basin, both with gilt rims and decorated in Imari colours of "Old Crown Derby Witches" pattern. The decoration is continued on the interior of the basin.
Marks:	On both: Red crown over crossed swords and D, with two sets of three dots and initials S and H.
Measurements:	*Jug*: Height 5.5cm. *Basin*: Diameter 8cm.
Date:	Late nineteenth or early twentieth century.
Location:	Private collection.
Literature:	Two similar bowls, but without jugs and decorated in different Imari patterns illustrated in factory sales catalogue, 1934-35, numbers 55 and 60. The captions read "Octagonal Tray".

Miniature Jardinière

Description: A bucket-shaped vessel, with two fixed ring handles. A moulded bow, embellished with gilding is shaped beneath each handle. The whole is decorated in the "Rose Barbeau" pattern.

Marks: Red crown over crossed swords and D, with two sets of three dots and initials S and H.

Measurements: Height 6cm.
At rim: Diameter 7.5cm.

Date: Probably later nineteenth century.

Location: Private collection.

Toby Jug

Description:	A miniature jug with a Toby figure, arms folded and wearing a black tricorn hat, red coat and black shoes. A single loop handle is attached to the back of the figure.
Marks:	Red crown over crossed swords and D, with two sets of three dots and the initials S and H.
Measurements:	Height 4cm.
Date:	Probably twentieth century.
Location:	In the collection of Dr. J. R. Freeman.
Literature:	Illustrated in factory sales catalogue, 1934-35, number 4.

Jug

Description: A green ground jug with two circular reserves, each showing a
moulded classical head in the white. There are moulded masks at
the spout and where the handle joins the top of the body.

Marks: Red crown over crossed swords and D, with two sets of three dots
and initials S and H.

Measurements: Height 18.5 cm.

Date: Probably later nineteenth century.

Location: In the collection of Mr. and Mrs. H. Cordwent.

Notes: Cracks in handle.

Jug

Description: A sparrow beak jug of eighteenth century form, with gilt handle.
                     Decorated fully inside and out in the Imari pattern "Old Crown
                     Derby Rose".

Marks: Red crown over crossed swords and D, with two sets of three dots
                     and initials S and H.

Measurements: Height 7cm.

Date: Twentieth century.

Location: In the collection of Dr. J. R. Freeman.

Literature: Ilustrated in the factory sales catalogue, 1934-35, number 59.

Bottle and Stopper

Description:	A bottle with wide gilt rim at the base and at the neck. The body profusely decorated with applied garden flowers, leaves and tendrils in enamel colours. The stopper is decorated with a single modelled rose and leaves, and has a wide gilt border.
Marks:	Underglaze blue crown over crossed swords and D, with two sets of three dots and initials S and H on the base of the bottle only.
Measurements:	Height 47cm.
Date:	Later nineteenth century.
Location:	Private collection.
Notes:	Firing crack and minor chips to flowers.

Bottle and Stopper

Description: A bottle of bulbous shape with a long neck and deep stopper. Both are decorated in blue enamel around applied white flowers. These are in two swags on the body and the stopper has a central single rose.

Marks: Underglaze blue crown over crossed swords and D, with initials S and H. The two sets of three dots are missing.

Measurements: Height 27.5 cm.

Date: Probably later nineteenth century.

Location: Private collection.

Notes: This method of decoration is unsatisfactory, as inevitably the white flowers are marked with blue enamel.

374

Bough Pot

Description:	An oval shaped bough pot with two holes for wall hanging if required. The upper surface is pierced with openings for flowers. Decorated on the exterior with sprays of flowers painted in underglaze blue.
Marks:	Underglaze blue crown over crossed swords and D, with two sets of three dots and initials S and H.
Measurements:	Length 21cm. Height 16cm.
Date:	Later nineteenth century.
Location:	Royal Crown Derby Museum.
Literature:	Twitchett and Bailey, *Royal Crown Derby*, Antique Collectors' Club, 1988, p.22.
Exhibition:	On display in "The Factory at King Street, 1849-1935" Exhibition held in 1993 at The Museum and Art Gallery, Derby. Catalogue number 99.
Notes:	1. Underglaze blue decoration on its own is unusual at King Street. 2. Also turned out glazed but undecorated and also fully decorated.

Vase, with figure of a Girl

Description:	A bucket-shaped vase, with two rope loop handles, rests on a deep rocky base. Beside the vase is seated a girl with flowers in her lap, a posy in her right hand and roses in her hair. The rocky base is mounted on an oval stand, on which is a small basket and modelled branches and flowers. The whole is in glazed white.
Marks:	Underglaze blue crown over crossed swords and D, with two sets of three dots and initials S and H.
Measurements:	Height 18.25 cm.
Date:	Probably later nineteenth century.
Location:	Private collection.
Literature:	Illustrated in the booklet "The Factory at King Street 1849-1935", by A. Bambery and R. Blackwood, Derby Museums and Art Gallery, October 1993, plate i.
Exhibition:	On display in "The Factory at King Street 1849-1935" Exhibition held in 1993 at The Museum and Art Gallery, Derby. Catalogue number 106.
Notes:	The vase was sold on its own in glazed white.

Small Jugs

Description: Two small glazed white ornamental jugs with bodies of baluster shape and standing on scrolled bases. Both models have applied flowers. On the right hand jug the loop handle rises above the body before joining the rim which is scalloped on both jugs.

Marks: Both jugs, underglaze blue crown over crossed swords and D, with two sets of three dots and initials S and H.

Measurements: *Left Jug*: Height 12.75cm.
Right Jug: Height 13.5cm.

Date: Probably later nineteenth century.

Location: Private Collection.

Literature: These jugs illustrated by John Twitchett in *In Account with Sampson Hancock, 1860s – 1880s*, DJC Books, 1996, plate 21.

Notes: 1. Two cracks in loop handle.
2. A jug with a loop handle and decorated in the Rose Trellis pattern is in the collection of The Derby Museums and Art Gallery.

Jardinière

Description:
A glazed white oblong vessel, with irregular shaped pierced rim, which is on a scrolled base. At each end stands a scantily clad putto holding a cornucopia filled with fruit and flowers. Between the main vessel and the base there is a further narrow ornamental bowl at each side.

Marks:
Underglaze blue crown over crossed swords and D, with two sets of three dots and initials S and H.

Measurements:
Height 20cm.
Length 28cm.
Width 17cm.

Date:
Probably later nineteenth century.

Location:
Private collection.

Notes:
Minor restoration to applied flowers.

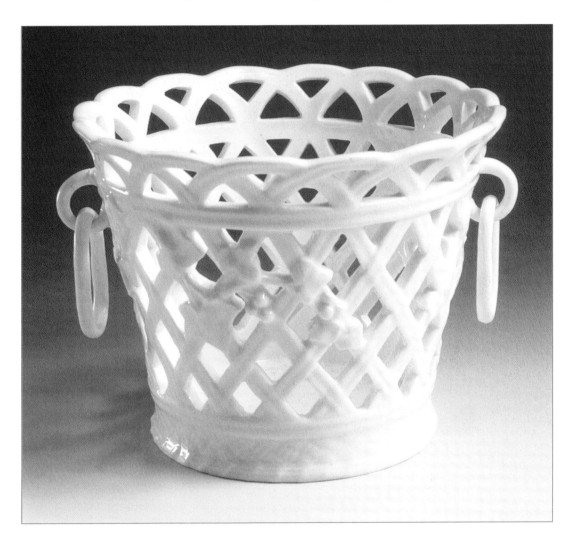

Cachepot

Description:	Circular pierced glazed white cachepot of flaring form with two oval ring handles.
Marks:	Underglaze blue crown over crossed swords and D, with two sets of three dots and initials S and H.
Measurements:	Height 13.75cm. Diameter 17.5cm. At base Diameter 12cm.
Date:	Probably later nineteenth century.
Location:	Private collection.
Notes:	1. One handle is repaired. 2. There is no hole in the base.

Pair of Moulded Candlesticks

Description:	A pair of glazed white moulded candlesticks with modelled flowers and leaves.
Marks:	Both candlesticks, underglaze blue crown over crossed swords and D, and initials S and H. The two sets of three dots are missing.
Measurements:	Height 20.5cm.
Date:	Probably later nineteenth century.
Location:	Private collection.
Provenance:	Estate of the late The Rt. Hon. The Viscount Scarsdale.
Notes:	Minor chips to leaves and flowers.

Pair of Chamber Candlesticks

Description: A pair of scantily dressed putto, with garlands of small flowers and leaves in their hair, are seated in mirror positions on scrolled mound bases. There is bocage each side of the figures. The candle sconces are mounted at the side of each figure. Each putto has a posy in one hand, whilst the other is around the bocage that carries the sconce. At the back of each candlestick is a carrying handle mounted on the base. The whole is in glazed white.

Marks: Both candlesticks, faint underglaze blue crown over crossed swords and D, with two sets of three dots and initials S and H.

Measurements: Height 19cm.

Date: Probably later nineteenth century.

Location: Private collection.

Literature: There is a close resemblance between this pair of candlesticks and the earlier Spring Candlesticks illustrated by Peter Bradshaw in *Derby Porcelain Figures 1750-1848*, Faber and Faber, 1990, p.336.

Exhibition: This pair on display in "The Factory at King Street, 1849-1935" Exhibition held in 1993 at The Museum and Art Gallery, Derby. Catalogue number 128.

Notes: 1. Minor restoration to bocage.
2. The bocage used to decorate these candlesticks has not been seen on any other glazed white figures from King Street.

Candlestick

Description:

A glazed white candlestick consisting of a scantily dressed winged Cupid seated on a deep scrolled base. Both arms are outstretched and close to the two branch-like arms on which are mounted the candle sconces.

Marks:

Underglaze blue crown over crossed swords and D, with initials S and H. The two sets of three dots are missing.

Measurements:

Height 22cm.
Span 27cm.

Date:

Probably later nineteenth century.

Location:

Private collection.

Notes:

1. Both wings and the pan of the sconce on the figure's right are restored.
2. This candlestick is based on the Cupid Candlestick (sconces missing) illustrated by Peter Bradshaw in *Derby Porcelain Figures, 1750-1848,* Faber and Faber, 1990, p.359. The Nottingham Road candlestick was one of a pair, the other being Flora. If King Street also produced a Flora candlestick, this is unknown, but mention of "1 Bust of Flora" is made in an invoice from the outside modeller, William Hopkinson.

Framed Plaque

Description: An unglazed biscuit plaque of an arrangement of raised modelled mixed flowers and leaves, mounted in a gold leaf frame.

Marks: Faint blue crown over short crossed swords and D, with one set of three dots and initials S and H.

Measurements: The portion of the plaque visible within the oval gilt mount:
Height 22cm.
Width 15.5cm.

Date: Probably later nineteenth century.

Location: Private collection.

Notes: It is suggested that this plaque was not from normal production and may have been produced for the 1870 Exhibition, held in Derby. The frame maker Henry Moseley of Derby, whose label is on the back, was in business between 1840 and 1890.

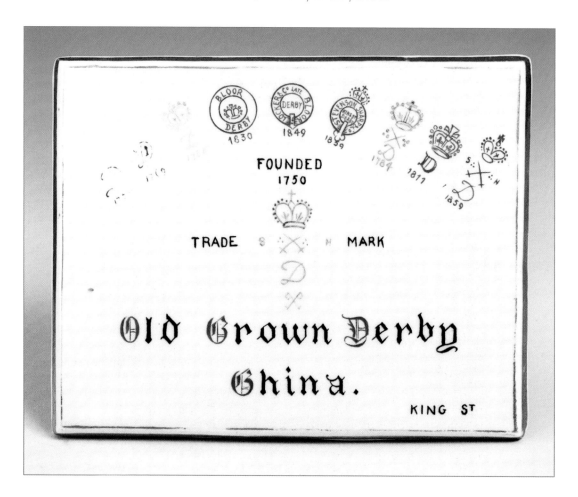

Plaque.

Description:	A rectangular plaque showing Derby marks from 1750-1934 and probably used as an advertisement. There is a rest at the back.
Marks:	On the back of the plaque in puce, crown over crossed swords and D, with two sets of three dots and initials S and H. Also in puce the crossed Ps mark of the proprietor Paget and his wife.
Measurements:	10cm. x 8.5cm.
Date:	Circa 1933-1935.
Location:	In the collection of Mr. and Mrs. H. Cordwent.
Provenance:	Godden Reference Collection.
Notes:	Wear to the gilding and first three marks in the top left corner.

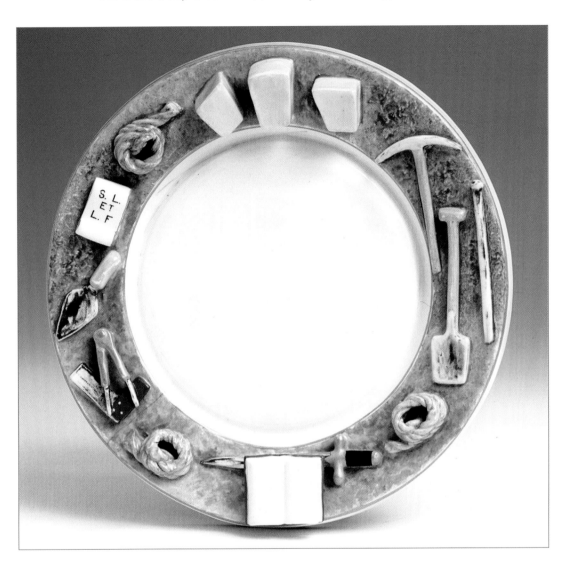

Plaque

Description: An unusual circular plaque bearing the symbols of Royal Arch Masonry around the rim.

Marks: A paper label attached to the reverse reads "Royal Arch Masonry". Puce crown over crossed swords and D, with two sets of three dots and initials S and H. Also in puce the crossed Ps of proprietor Paget and his wife.

Measurements: Diameter 20cm.

Date: Circa 1933-1935.

Location: Royal Crown Derby Museum.

Notes: One crack at rim.

Plaque

Description:
A rectangular plaque painted in enamel colours with mixed flowers and leaves.

Marks:
Red crown over crossed swords and D, with two sets of three dots and initials S and H.

Measurements:
14cm.x10cm.

Date:
Late nineteenth or early twentieth century.

Location:
In the collection of Sheila Williams.

Notes:
1. This plaque is usually framed. There is no other means of support.
2. A line of kiln blacks runs down the left edge.

386

Plaque

Description: A circular framed plaque depicting in enamel colours a basket of flowers and fruit on a marble plinth.

Marks: Red crown over crossed swords and D, with two sets of three dots and initials S and H.

Measurements: Diameter 12cm.

Date: Late nineteenth century.

Location: Private collection.

Inkwell and Stand

Description:

A circular inkwell comprised of four pieces. The body has holes for three pens, a separate well and cover and a stand. The whole decorated in Rose Barbeau pattern.

Marks:

Red crown over crossed swords and D, with two sets of three dots and initials S and H on the body and stand.

Measurements:

Body with cover: Height 7cm.
Stand: Diameter 15cm.

Date:

Early twentieth century.

Location:

Private collection.

Ornamental Pen Holder

Description: A holder for four pens in the form of a crown, lavishly decorated in gilt and enamel colours.

Marks: Red crown over crossed swords and D, with two sets of three dots and initials S and H.

Measurements: Height 9cm.

Date: Twentieth century.

Location: Royal Crown Derby Museum.

Notes: Possibly made for the coronation of 1911.

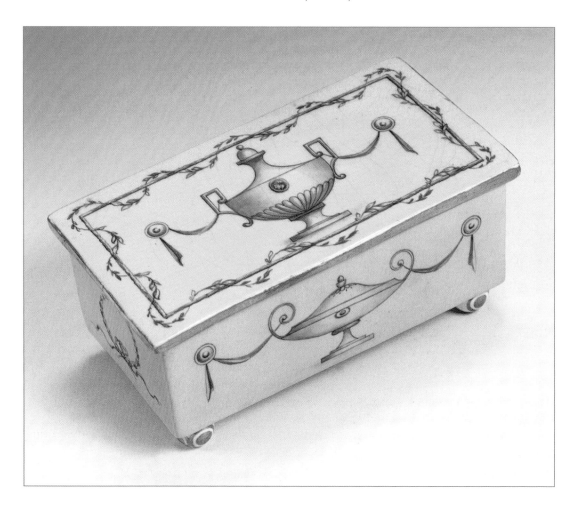

Box and Cover

Description:	A rectangular box and cover resting on four ball feet. The classical Adam style decoration is on a yellow ground.
Marks:	On both body and cover, red crown over crossed swords and D, with two sets of three dots and initials S and H. A painted mark of "M" also appears on the base of the body.
Measurements:	Height 12.5cm. Width 7cm.
Date:	Probably early twentieth century.
Location:	In the collection of Mr. and Mrs. H. Cordwent.

Pair of Trinket Boxes

Description: A pair of glazed white inward facing oval trinket boxes, with rounded ends and moulded pattern around the sides. On the covers are figures of a boy and girl wearing shawls or animal skins. Each holds a basket of fruit.

Marks: Underglaze blue crown over crossed swords and D, with two sets of three dots and initials S and H. Marks on the bodies only, one having the mark applied twice.

Measurements: Height 9cm.
Length 9cm.
Width 6.5cm.

Date: Probably later nineteenth century.

Location: Private collection.

Notes: 1. The head of the girl figure has been repaired.
2. Both pieces are thickly potted and heavy and the lids a poor fit.
3. The usual practice at King Street was for boys to display fruit and girls shown with flowers, but as seen here this rule does not always apply.

Egg Cup

Description: An egg cup and stand, the two joined, decorated in the "Rose Barbeau" pattern.

Marks: Red crown over crossed swords and D, with two sets of three dots and initials S and H.

Measurements: Height 5.5cm.
Base Diameter 10cm.

Date: Early twentieth century.

Location: Derby Museums and Art Gallery. No. 1999-154.

Egg Ring

Description: An egg ring in the white, with gilt rim top and bottom and gilt inscription.

Marks: Inscribed in gilt:
"Duke of Devonshire
Easter Sunday 1889
Many Happy Returns."
Red crown over crossed swords and D, with two sets of three dots and initials S and H.

Measurements: Height 5cm.

Date: Circa 1889.

Location: In the collection of Mr. and Mrs. H. Cordwent.

Pastille Burner

Description: A pastille burner and cover standing on four claw feet, decorated with gilding and brightly enamelled modelled flowers applied to the body and pierced cover.

Marks: Puce crown over crossed swords and D, with two sets of three dots and initials S and H. Also the mark of two parallel lines in puce.

Measurements: Height 15.5cm.

Date: Circa 1915-1934.

Location: On loan to Royal Crown Derby Museum.

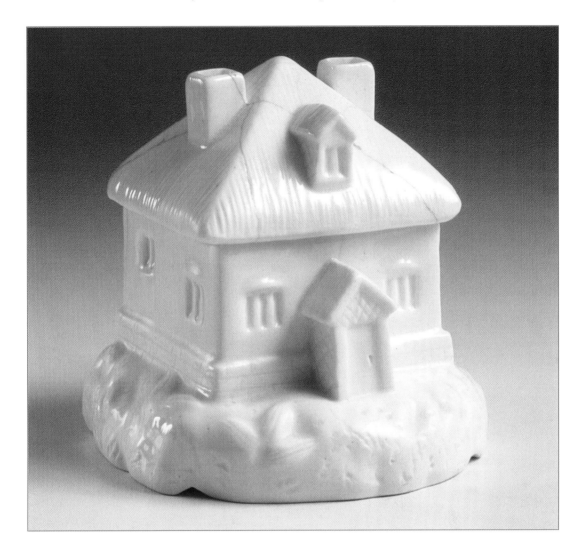

Pastille Burner

Description:

A glazed white pastille burner in the form of a cottage on a mound base. The cover, in the form of the cottage roof, has two open chimneys. There are five circular perforations in the base.

Marks:

Underglaze blue crown over crossed swords and D, with two sets of three dots and initials S and H.

Measurements:

Height 8.75cm.

Date:

Probably later nineteenth century.

Location:

Private collection.

Notes:

1. Several cracks in cottage roof.
2. An enamelled version is known in a private collection and this bears the S and H mark in red.

Pot- pourri

Description: A large two handled pot-pourri decorated with an Imari pattern similar to "Old Crown Derby Witches". It has a solid inner cover with gilt knop and rim and a pierced outer cover.

Marks: Indistinct underglaze blue crown over crossed swords and D, with two sets of three dots and initials S and H, on base of the body only.

Measurements: Height 23cm.

Date: Probably later nineteenth century.

Location: Royal Crown Derby Museum.

Scent Bottle

Description: A small scent bottle, the body decorated with insects and flowers in triangular panels outlined in blue. The top is silver gilt, with hallmark for 1902.

Marks: Red crown over crossed swords and D, with two sets of three dots and initials S and H. Also the mark of two parallel lines in red.

Measurements: Height 6.5cm.

Date: Circa 1902.

Location: In the collection of Mr. and Mrs. H. Cordwent.

Brooch

Description: A ring of modelled enamelled flowers and leaves on a circular base, with two holes for the fitting of a pin.

Marks: Red crown over crossed swords and D, with two sets of three dots and initials S and H.

Measurements: Diameter 3.5 cm.

Date: Probably early twentieth century.

Location: In the collection of Mr. and Mrs. H. Cordwent.

Notes: Minor chips to flowers.

Hair Tidy

Description:	A hair tidy box with cover, decorated with roses in enamel colours.
Marks:	The cover inscribed "Hair Tidy" in gilt. Red crown over crossed swords and D, with two sets of three dots and initials S and H.
Measurements:	Box and cover: Height 10.5cm.
Date:	Late nineteenth or early twentieth century.
Location:	Derby Museums and Art Gallery. No. 1959-425/3.
Provenance:	Previous owner was Miss Alice Amy Robinson, a great grand daughter of founder partner and proprietor Sampson Hancock, and daughter of proprietor John James Robinson.

Thimble

Description:	A thimble with indentations on the domed top and extending halfway down the sides. Plain white, with a gilt rim, and just above the rim, painted in enamel colours, three single flowers placed at intervals around the circumference: a rose, a pansy and a forget-me-not, each with leaves.
Marks:	Puce crown over crossed swords and D, with two sets of three dots and initials S and H. Also worker's mark "I" in puce inside the thimble.
Measurements:	Height 2.5cm.
Date:	Circa 1915-1935.
Location:	Derby Museums and Art Gallery. No. 1953-188/4.
Exhibition:	On display in "The Factory at King Street, 1849-1935" Exhibition held in 1993 at The Museum and Art Gallery, Derby. Catalogue number 168.

Mirror

Description:	A small circular mirror frame decorated with mixed flowers and leaves in enamel colours, applied within two beaded borders. The mirror has a mahogany back and brass ring for hanging.
Marks:	Underglaze blue crown over crossed swords and D, with two sets of three dots and initials S and H.
Measurements:	Diameter 16cm.
Date:	Probably later nineteenth century.
Location:	Private collection.
Notes:	Minor damage to applied flowers. Glass probably replaced.

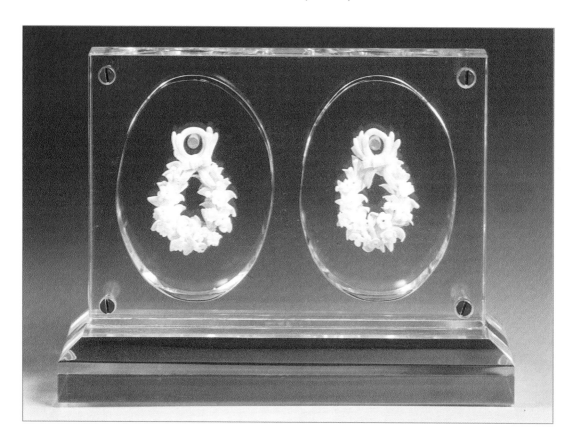

Earrings

Description: A pair of glazed white pendant earrings, with clusters of very small modelled flowers, leaves and buds, formed into an oval shape. The applied decoration is on both sides of the earrings. At the top of each oval is a bow surmounted by a ring, decorated with buds.

Marks: Unmarked (see note 2).

Measurements: Height 4.5cm.
Width 3.25cm.

Date: Probably later nineteenth century.

Location: Private collection.

Notes: 1. Repair to one earring and a little discolouration.
2. Although unmarked, the present owner is confident that the origin of these earrings is the King Street factory. The flowers, leaves, buds and bows match those known on other wares. These were purchased at auction in Derbyshire, in a lot of ten items, including a decorated brooch and many of the items were factory marked. The vendor, who wishes to remain anonymous, had previously worked at the factory.
3. Earrings are illustrated in their acrylic display stand.

6. REFERENCES

(1)   Haslem, J., *The Old Derby China Factory*. G. Bell, 1876, p.238

(2)   Bradbury, E., "The Story of Old Crown Derby China," reprinted from the *Yorkshire Weekly Post*, 12 May1894, published by High Peak News, Buxton 1894, p.10

(3)   Haslem, Op, Cit., p.237

(4)   Haslem, Op. Cit., p.199

(5)   Dawson, A., "A Derby Pattern Book in the British Museum," *DPIS Journal II*, 1991, pp. 73-78. Aileen Dawson is the Curator, Department of Medieval and Modern Europe, at the British Museum.

(6)   Cox, Alwyn & Angela, *Rockingham Pottery and Porcelain, 1745-1842*. Faber and Faber, 1983, p.230

(7)   Moore, H., "A Note about the Derby (King Street) China Works," an article in *DPIS Newsletter*, September, 1985

(8)   Mrs Willoughby Hodgson, *Old English China*. G. Bell and Sons Ltd., 1913, opposite p.194

7. SALES

The only known printed sales catalogue and separate price list are for 1934-35. In the archives there are hand-written prices for a wide variety of items and these cover a period in the 1850s and 1860s. Just three sales invoices for finished goods exist in a private collection. There is no trace of the factory having employed salesmen.

Although the factory had links with the London Showrooms of Thomas Courtney, which appear to have ended around 1862, it was not until 1917 that it had its own showrooms in the West End of London. This interval must have placed great reliance on sales being achieved through the factory shop. These would have been assisted by advertising, word of mouth recommendation, the execution of special commissions and manufacture of replacements.

These and other aspects related to sales are considered in this chapter and it closes with a copy, in full, of the 1934-35 catalogue and price list, with some comments on nineteenth century prices.

ADVERTISEMENTS

Advertisements were placed in a variety of publications local to Derby and some of these are reproduced below, showing that they became a little more enterprising as the years progressed (1).

WILLIAM LOCKER AND CO.
(LATE R. BLOOR, ESQ.)
CHINA MANUFACTURERS,
Opposite St. Helen's House,
26, KING STREET, DERBY,

Advertisement, 1852.
Derby Local Studies Library. (D.L.S.L.)

1852
A very simple advertisement placed in Freebody's Directory.

DERBY CHINA MANUFACTORY,
26 KING STREET,
OPPOSITE ST. HELEN'S HOUSE.

MESSRS. WILLIAM LOCKER AND CO.,
SUCCESSOR TO THE LATE ROBERT BLOOR, ESQ.,

Return their sincere thanks to the Nobility, Clergy, Gentry, Innkeepers, and Public generally, for the patronage they have received, and beg to solicit a continuance of past favors, assuring all who may wish either to renovate their old sets, or purchase new ones, they will be as well suited both in quality and price, at the above establishment, as at any China Manufactory in the kingdom.

N.B.—THE TRADE SUPPLIED ON LIBERAL TERMS.

Advertisement, 1858.
D.L.S.L.

1858
 Placed in Glover's Directory, it is the one advertisement to mention that trade discounts are available and that a service is provided for customers, "to renovate their old sets", suggesting repairs to broken pieces, or the making of replacements.

Who hasna heared ov the Darby Cheney, | Hancock ah know con please heigh or low,
 Meyd ov the finest ov cley, | Soo caw wen yore gooin that wey.

S. HANCOCK, China Manufacturer,
KING STREET, DERBY.

BREAKFAST, TEA, DINNER, AND DESSERT SERVICES.
ELEGANT VASES, ANTIQUE AND MODERN FIGURES.
OLD DERBY PATTERNS ACCURATELY MATCHED.

Advertisement, 1870
D.L.S.L.

1870
This advertisement appeared in "Owd Sammy Twitcher's Christmas Bowk" for the year 1870. This light-hearted book was written by Joseph Barlow Robinson, who was a well-known

sculptor. It is written in what the author terms "Derbyshire dialect", hence the style of wording at the top of the King Street entry.

Robinson's words of advice on the subject of advertisements, also given in his "Christmas Bowk", are worth recording:

A WORD TUT PUBLIC
Now matter wot may be sed in an Advertisement, yo
conna buy a gud article wiaat peyin a fair price for't,
An yo'll foind that t'cheapest it long run.

S. HANCOCK,
CHINA MANUFACTURER,
KING STREET, DERBY.

BREAKFAST, TEA, DINNER, AND DESSERT SERVICES.
ELEGANT VASES, ANTIQUE AND MODERN FIGURES.
OLD DERBY PATTERNS ACCURATELY MATCHED.

Advertisement, 1870.
D.L.S.L.

1870

This advertisement appeared in the catalogue of the 1870 Exhibition held in Derby. An account from Richard Keene, printer and publisher, dated Christmas 1870 and rendered quarterly, shows that the cost of placing this in the catalogue was 7/6d, the account being settled on 22 March 1871.

SAMPSON HANCOCK,
CHINA MANUFACTURER,
KING STREET,
DERBY.

Breakfast, Tea, Dinner, and Dessert Services.
ELEGANT VASES.
ANTIQUE AND MODERN FIGURES.
OLD DERBY PATTERNS ACCURATELY MATCHED.

Advertisement, 1871.
D.L.S.L.

1871

A year later, Richard Keene's Almanack for 1871 included the advertisement on the previous page, with slightly more attention having been given to presentation.

DO YOU WANT TO MAKE A PRESENT?

THEN GO TO THE

DERBY CHINA WORKS,

AND EXAMINE THE BEAUTIFUL PRODUCTIONS OF CHOICE
PORCELAIN NOW ON VIEW.

NO STRANGER VISITING DERBY SHOULD OMIT MAKING A PURCHASE.

Breakfast, Tea, Dinner, and Dessert Services.

ELEGANT VASES AND TAZZAS RICHLY PAINTED AND GILT.

ANTIQUE AND MODERN FIGURES.
Old Derby Patterns accurately matched.

REMEMBER THE ADDRESS—

S. HANCOCK,
CHINA MANUFACTURER.

KING STREET (Opposite the Derby School), DERBY.

Advertisement, 1881.
D.L.S.L.

1881

The above advertisement was included in Bemrose visitors' guide and handbook to the Derby and Royal Agricultural show of 1881. In it, encouragement is given to pay a visit to the works, the first occasion on which this has appeared.

Post 1915

The first mention of visitors being shown over the works and yet another reference to continuity between Duesbury's Old Derby China Factory and King Street.

Advertisement, post 1915.
D.L.S.L.

TRADE  MARK.

DO YOU WANT TO MAKE A PRESENT?

THEN GO TO THE

OLD CROWN

DERBY CHINA WORKS,

AND EXAMINE THE BEAUTIFUL PRODUCTIONS OF CHOICE
PORCELAIN NOW ON VIEW.

No stranger visiting Derby should omit making a purchase.

Breakfast, Tea, Dinner, and Dessert Services.

ELEGANT VASES AND TAZZAS
RICHLY PAINTED AND GILT.

ANTIQUE & MODERN FIGURES.

Old Derby Patterns accurately matched.

REMEMBER THE ADDRESS—

S. HANCOCK,

CHINA MANUFACTURER,

KING STREET (Opposite the Derby School), DERBY.

Visitors are shown over the Works which, although but small, are a
direct offshoot of Duesbury's Old Derby China Factory.

Advertisement, post 1915
D.L.S.L.

*" Heard melodies are sweet, but
those unheard
Are sweeter, therefore, ye soft pipes,
play on."*

French Shepherd and Shepherdess

Old Crown Derby China

William Duesbury first made it in
1750, and his original Wheel is
still used.

. . . Creating something exquisite,
unsurpassable !

To be treasured by Kings : to pass
into the great collections and museums
of the world.

To set a standard in English craftsmanship to which the eyes of every
present day craftsman must turn.

To be part of a world enshrined,
enchanted, where only Colour, only
Grace, only Beauty hold sway.

To be superior to mere " Period."

To delight all who regard it . . .

THIS TIMELESSNESS, THIS
WORLDLESSNESS, THIS LOVE-
LINESS, THIS OLD CROWN
DERBY CHINA!
THIS FROZEN MUSIC !

A booklet descriptive of the China's history, with
coloured illustrations of selected examples, will
be sent to you free upon request.

The Old Crown Derby China Works

King Street Established
DERBY 1 7 5 0

"Hark ! I hear the sound of coaches !"
—Beggar's Opera.

Old Crown Derby Tea-Cups

William Duesbury first made them in 1750

—When tea came to London by the East
Indian Argosies, and was distributed by pack-
horse to the country-houses far and wide.

—When even the fashionable host would
count the leaves prudently (the popularity of
price and flavour being yet to come).

—When Horace Walpole " was pleased
with his costly tea-cups and with his
costly tea."

—When George the Third took tea with
Mrs. Delany. (And Dr. Johnson, Lamb,
and Sir Joshua Reynolds were alive).

—When Souchong, Twankay, Orange
Pekoe in the tea-cups of Old Crown Derby
must have inspired much of the immortal
" gossip" of those days. (Their gossip,
their pictures, their books—their Old Crown
Derby tea-cups—are treasured still).

. . . .

*William Duesbury first made them
in 1750—and his original Wheel
is still used. Tea-cups of Old
Crown Derby China! And round
the tea-cups are gathered the aristo-
crats of each Age.*

A booklet descriptive of the China's history, with
coloured illustrations of selected examples, will
be sent to you free upon request.

The Old Crown Derby China Works

King Street Established
DERBY 1 7 5 0

*Advertisement, post 1915.
Dr. John Freeman Collection.*

*Advertisement, post 1915.
Dr. John Freeman Collection.*

Advertisement, post 1915.
Dr. John Freeman Collection.

410

These final four advertisements, the most elaborate so far, were probably produced shortly before closure in 1935. In the first of these a telephone number is given for the first time. The rather indistinct illustration in the central oval panel is of the group of Two Virgins Awakening Cupid, which was turned out both in biscuit and fully enamelled. This advertisement was included in a publication called "Derby City of Vital Industries", produced by *Derby Corporation Publicity Committee.*

The source of the last three slightly flowery advertisements is not known, but the paper on which they were printed suggests it was probably a magazine.

LETTERHEADS

As these include some advertising materials, two which are of interest, are discussed below:

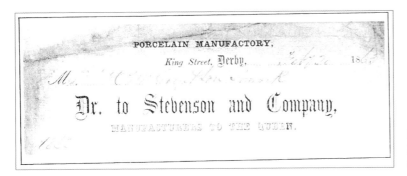

Letterhead, dated 1863. Twitchett & Bailey, "Royal Crown Derby."

1863

The above letterhead appears on an invoice dated 20 July 1863. John Twitchett tells us that circa 1862 the firm was trading as Stevenson and Co. (2). This is perhaps another pointer to Stevenson's partner Samuel Sharp having left the business by 1861.

The mention on the letterhead of royal patronage could have arisen from the replacements that King Street turned out to make good losses that had occurred in the dessert service originally made at Nottingham Road in 1841-1842 for Queen Victoria (3). Jewitt offers the opinion that, because of these replacements, the owners of King Street "are still therefore as fully entitled to the name of "royal" works as any of their predecessors". (4)

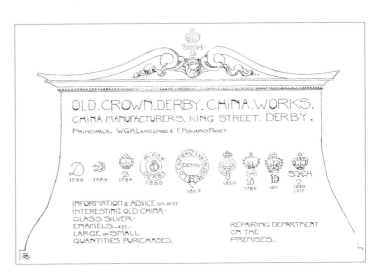

Letterhead, dated 1918. Private Collection.

411

1918

The letterhead shown on the previous page is from a letter dated June 1918, from Howard Paget to a customer. The marks that are reproduced date from 1750, ending with the S and H mark giving a period of use from 1859 up to 1917, a date near to when the letter was written. 1859 is a little earlier than the generally accepted date of 1861 for the introduction of the S and H mark.

The information service that is now offered includes glass and silver, reflecting Larcombe's general interest in antiques. "Large or small quantities purchased" indicates some second-hand business being carried on.

A business card, now in a private collection, was in use around 1923, with a layout very similar to that used on the above letterhead.

FACTORY SALES SHOP

Several authors, when writing about the King Street factory, make specific mention of the sales shop. The writers hold the view that this shop played a prominent role in sales of the output from this small works. The shop, which was part of the factory buildings, faced onto the road. A picture of its contents is shown below. The large number of mirror frames that can be seen, probably in the white, suggests that this was taken in the late nineteenth century (5).

Factory Sales Shop.
Royal Crown Derby Museum
archives.

412

In 1995 Neville Colwyn Evans wrote an article for the Derby Porcelain International Society, in which he described his visits to the shop, first as a boy and later as an adult. He has kindly agreed to allow these memories of his to be reproduced in this chapter (6).

"My first contact with the King Street Factory and shop was in the late 1920's and involved the shop only as their purpose was usually to take china that had been broken to be repaired. This was carried out in the factory, and pieces were nearly always with metal strap rivets attached.

My main interest in the establishment was in the early 1960s by which time, of course, the factory had closed. The shop was run by the two Misses Sadler sisters from at least the 1920s but by 1960 one sister had died. These ladies were also friends of the Phillip Robinson family. Miss Sadler used to visit the Osmaston Road factory every Tuesday morning to collect her wares.

Premises lay out: Through the front door into the front shop with a counter, behind which was a staircase to the upper floor, and a sitting room which had an open fire place, and this usually had a coal fire burning. In the room was a bow-fronted Hepplewhite chest of drawers always full of china.

Miss Sadler used to collect, and build up dinner and tea services for orders for her clients, and this chest of drawers was used for housing these. The room upstairs was used to store china, but I never saw this; indeed this would not have been possible as the stairs were always piled high with china. Beyond this sitting room was a long narrow room facing on to the yard at the rear of the premises. This might have been part of the old factory. It was only just possible to walk from one room to another as the whole place was piled high with china, some even being on the floor of the front shop.

Up to the 1960s Miss Sadler used to say that her shop was the only place permitted to sell "seconds." The stock was very large indeed, "perfects" and "seconds," modern manufacture from Osmaston Road, and a quantity of older pieces. In spite of this enormous stock she usually had a very good idea of what she had in stock at the time, and where to find it from.

A wide variety of designs and patterns were held, including the old "Wilmot" pattern. She also had a quantity of figures, including the old four-inch King Street ones.

Miss Sadler was a petite lady with a good sense of humour. She died sometime between 1969 and 1975"

Postcript by John Twitchett:

I had known that the Sadlers had sold King Street items, but not much about their family friendships with the Robinsons of Royal Crown Derby, and had not realized the quantity of Royal Crown Derby products sold in their shop.

The story of repairs in paragraph 1 told by the boy sent on errands to have china riveted, and the switching to the adult visits in the 1960's adds great charm to this rare little insight into the shop.

I am, however, not sure that Miss Sadlers' claim to be the only place to sell "seconds" could be verified as they would have been available at Osmaston Road!

LONDON SHOWROOMS

Bond Street
Courtney, of 34 Old Bond Street, was Robert Bloor's London agent. Jewitt wrote in January 1862 that Courtney "still does a good trade with the present firm of Stevenson and Hancock". (7)

As King Street was marking pieces with Courtney's own mark, it seems likely that sales through this London retailer were mostly of an "own brand" nature, with the factory having little or no control over the activities of these showrooms.

An undated list of around 1860, which is in the King Street archives, records the price of around twenty items of tableware supplied to Thomas Courtney in the white. These may have been for use by "outside" decorators.

The demise of the Courtney Late Bloor mark in the 1860s suggests the end of this association.

Brook Street

There was an interval of around sixty years between the factory's association with Courtney in London and having a new outlet through the showroom shared with Howard Paget's other business, The Dorking Brick Company. The use of this showroom is proudly shown on the letterhead below, which is on correspondence between Larcombe and a customer (8). Note that the lifespan of the S and H mark has been updated to 1923 from a previous letterhead, where it was 1917.

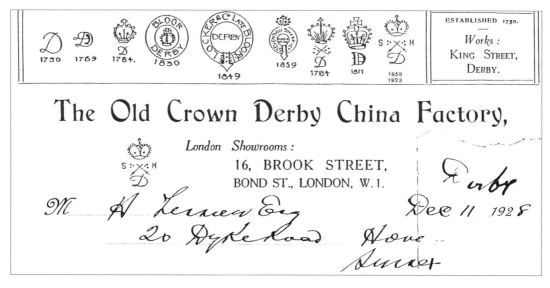

Letterhead, incorporating address of London Showrooms.
G. A. Godden.

Larcombe recalls in notes that he made in the later 1930s, that the factory had use of this London shop for nine years.

EXHIBITIONS

Derby

The factory exhibited in the Midland Counties Exhibition, held in May 1870 at the Drill Hall, Derby, which was an exhibition of Works of Art and Industrial Products. Only one entry has been identified without doubt, as having been turned out by King Street, although it is recorded in the guide to the exhibition, that Sampson Hancock had a "stall".

Exhibit 4674, loaned by Mr. W. Bemrose, jun is listed as:

"PAIR OF DERBY PLAQUES, raised Flowers in Biscuit,
on lavender ground, by Shufflebottom."

This guide to the exhibition, produced by *"A Commiteee man"*, gave high praise to these plaques, saying:

"The delicate modelling of a pair of Bisquet (sic.) China flower- pieces, hanging on the next girders, by Shufflebottom, while in the employ of Mr. Hancock of the present China Works in Derby, is equal probably to anything ever done in the material. — They are exquisitely beautiful."

Haslem recalls that Lady Crewe of Calke Abbey, near Derby, purchased several of the best pieces of biscuit with applied flowers (9). A fine vase with pierced cover is still on display there.

Wembley
King Street exhibited at the British Empire Exhibition, held in June 1924 at Wembley. The family of Hilda Moore's husband was related to the King Street modeller Edward Swainson and she tells us that he demonstrated his skills at this exhibition, before members of the Royal Family and the King and Queen of Denmark(10).

FIRE HEARTH INSPECTION

The press announcement, which is shown below, inviting visitors to view an impressive china fire hearth, was surely a good public relations exercise. Its display may well have encouraged those who saw it, to consider the purchase of something that was readily available in the Sales Shop.

"We have been favoured with the sight of a novel and beautiful china hearth, now manu-facturing by Messrs. Wm. Locker and Co. It is made in sections or parts, and painted with the following views:- Chee Tor; Ferry over the Derwent, Matlock; Castle of the Peverels of the Peak; Dovedale; High Tor; Heights of Abraham. When finished it is intended to form part of a splendid fire grate now in progress of manufacture in Derby, and can be seen at the china manufactory until Saturday next.
January 1857.

The publisher of this press release is not known, but it was amongst other cuttings from *The Derby Reporter* (11).

OWN BRAND

Although two retailers' names have been recorded on King Street wares, only one of them, Thomas Courtney, was strictly an own brand customer. The other, Thomas Goode, the well-known London retailer, allowed the factory to place its own mark close to their name. Un-fortunately, Goode's records do not show what this firm purchased from King Street.

Business was carried on between the factory and Courtney in the mid-nineteenth century, Thomas Courtney having been the London sales agent for the Nottingham Road factory, prior to its closure in 1848.

In the records of prices charged by the factory for finished goods, are just a few entries for the supply of decorated wares to Courtney. In the entry shown below, dated 1854, perhaps the wording "finished for Courtney", indicates that these bottles bore his own brand mark of "Courtney Late Bloor". The order, priced £2/16/0, was for the supply of "Bottles finished for Courtney, 1 pair, Insects and flowers, gold vermicelli".

SPECIAL COMMISSIONS

Numerous examples exist of wares being commissioned for special occasions, such as presentations and birthdays, and correspondence exists showing the making of a complete tea service to a customer's requirements.

Out of many, probably the most interesting example to record here, is that of a plate commissioned around 1918. This plate exists in a private collection and the front and back are shown below, and the relevant part of a hand-written letter from Howard Paget to this customer is reproduced and transcribed below.

The request to paint the moon and zeppelin on this plate is strange. As seen earlier, in the chapter on marks, this was only used on 31 January 1916 and yet here it is requested some two years later. The relevance of the bee and wording "lighter than Air" is unknown. The standard S and H mark and the WL monogram of Larcombe and worker's mark of two parallel lines, appear below the painted bee, all being in puce.

Specially commissioned plate – front.
Private Collection.

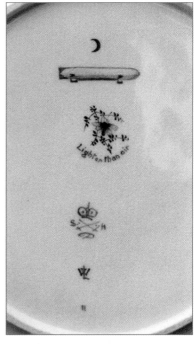

Specially commissioned plate – reverse.
Private Collection.

Paget's Letter

May 12th 1918
I have told my partner to make you an octagonal plate of Bow shape and pattern, birds and festoons of flowers, which I am always very fond of. We bought Bow 1776 or there-abouts so have the right to use it. The Zep. Will be beneath it with the Moon. I hope you will like it. The painter is Harry Hancock great great grandson of Duesbury's first apprentice in 17—?*

Note: *The date mentioned refers to 1769 the year John Hancock (1757-1847) was apprenticed.

FACTORY COSTING

Tucked away amongst various recipes dated 1865 is the only factory costing yet to be seen and this is as follows:

12 pieces	Price of Labour and Gold for White Service.	
	Gold for 12 pieces	1/3d.
	Gilding	6d.
	Burnishing	4d.
	Firing	8d.
		2/9.
	Profit	1/4½d.
		4/1½d.
	White ware	7/-
	Price for Service	11/-

The figures do not add up exactly, but no doubt a selling price of 11/- for the service was more attractive than 11/1½d.

PRICES OF FINISHED GOODS

Invoices
One of the three customer sales invoices known to exist is reproduced on the right. It is for goods supplied in 1896.

Note:The final single item priced 1/- may be the figure of a fowl. King Street produced figures of a cockerel.

Factory Prices, 1850s - 1860s
In the King Street Archives there are hand-written records of the prices charged in the 1850s and 60s for items painted in about

Sales Invoice for 1896.
Private Collection.

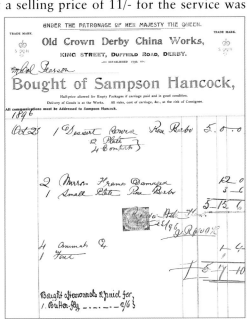

417

thirty different patterns. They are not easy to read therefore could not be accurately reproduced here, but there are five entries worthy of a separate mention.

a) The prices of wares decorated with "Hill's Flowers" are dated 1861. James Hill was known for his "Hills Flowers" at Nottingham Road and, as covered earlier, was a founder partner at King Street. He died in 1854, but this shows that the pattern bearing his name continued in use well after his death.

b) A coffee cup and saucer with "Goodes" pattern was charged at 1/8d. This is most likely one of the items mentioned in the chapter on Marks and was supplied, as Own Brand, marked T. Goode & Co.

c) Sampson Hancock had his own pattern shown as "Hancock's Laurel", for which some prices are given and these are also dated 1861. Under this heading the price of a dessert plate is decipherable as 2/6d. and a cream jug is priced at 1/9d.

d) A number of pattern names, for which prices are given in the 1850s and 1860s, still appear in the 1934-35 price list. A comparison of prices for similar items is of interest.

PATTERN	ITEM	1850-60s PRICE	1934-35 PRICE
Purple Scroll	Tea Cup and Saucer	5/10d.	18/0d.
Witches Japan	Tea Cup and Saucer	6/8d.	£1.0.0d

e) A heading reading "2nds." is only found once in the lists of prices. It was most likely prepared in the 1860s and shows prices for six items, but it is unclear to what these refer, but other prices on the same page are for tablewares.

CATALOGUE AND PRICE LIST, 1934-35

Despite extensive enquiries made over the last few years the authors have not been able to trace any sales catalogues, other than the one dated 1934-35. They have an original copy of this catalogue and, as part of their aim of providing a full picture of the activities at King Street, have reproduced it at the end of this chapter. This also includes six pages of text at the start of the catalogue, which form an introduction and are not known to have been published elsewhere.

As there is now no record of an original 1934-35 price list to go with the catalogue, John Twitchett has kindly agreed to allow the use of the one published in his book *Royal Crown Derby*.

Turn, turn, my wheel!
This earthen jar
A touch can make,
A touch can mar.
LONGFELLOW "KERAMOS."

*S*eventeen hundred and fifty! *With George II. still on the Throne.* 1 7 5 0
When Sir Joshua Reynolds, Goldsmith and Dr. Johnson were very much
alive. . . . The eyes of the Graces must have shone with excitement,
for Old Crown Derby China was about to be born.

*   *   *

It was born into an England as yet innocent of a single railway track, "*Hark! I hear the*
when Derby was a day-and-a-half's journey from London, when men *sound of coaches!*"
wore wigs, and letters were written by candle-light with quill pens. —BEGGAR'S
Into an age of sedan chairs and link extinguishers, with the spinning-wheel OPERA.
and the tinder-box as articles of everyday use. Into the days of powder, "*Things that per-*
patches, and brocade. Into these it was born, and has lived right on *sist — and things*
into our modern "post-war" world. *that change.*"

1750

Page One

419

About 1745, a French refugee (there were many in England at the time)—was it Thomas Briand or Andrew Planché?—made small china figures—" birds, cats, lambs and other animals "—in Lodge Lane, a humble quarter of Derby, and fired them in a pipe-maker's oven nearby. John Heath, an Alderman of Derby, who with his brother Christopher owned pot works in Cock Pit Hill, then commenced—" with the possible help of Planché "—to make porcelain figures that were either sold in the white or sent to London to be decorated. A number of these figures were so decorated by William Duesbury at his enamelling establishment in Chelsea.

In 1756, William Duesbury entered into an agreement with Heath, and came to live at Derby, and the porcelain side of the Cock Pit Hill works was transferred to Nottingham Road, near St. Mary's Bridge. (Planché is also mentioned in the document, though it is not clear that he fulfilled his part.)

In 1780 the brothers Heath became bankrupt, and the Cock Pit Hill stock was sold. Duesbury then carried on alone at Nottingham Road.

The chief productions from 1750 to 1780 were unmarked figures, that have since, and wrongly, been attributed to Bow or Chelsea, but are now being replaced in their proper category. " It is doubtful if Duesbury used any mark before he purchased the Chelsea works in 1770." If he did, it was " 𝒟 " neatly drawn and generally in blue. With the year 1770 began the Chelsea-Derby period.

" There's a joy without canker or cark,
There's a pleasure eternally new,
'Tis to gloat on the glaze and the mark
Of China that's ancient and blue;
Unchipp'd all the centuries through
. . . ."
—ANDREW LANG.

The first documentary evidence of the manufacture of porcelain in England is in the nature of a patent specification taken out in the year 1744 by Edward Heylyn and Thomas Frye, but though china was made before that date, it is very difficult to identify. The specification refers to certain white clays, and a manufactory was either established at Stratford-by-Bow to work the patent, or, the works already being in existence, negotiations were entered into for the sole rights of its use. The establishment of the Chelsea works took place probably in the succeeding year (1745), and for the next five or six years practically the only porcelain manufactured in England came from Chelsea.

Page Two

420

State Room.
By courtesy of Chatsworth House.

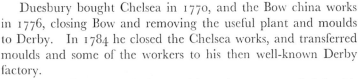

Duesbury bought Chelsea in 1770, and the Bow china works in 1776, closing Bow and removing the useful plant and moulds to Derby. In 1784 he closed the Chelsea works, and transferred moulds and some of the workers to his then well-known Derby factory.

William Duesbury died in 1786, and was succeeded by his son William, who carried on alone until 1795, when, because of ill-health, he took into partnership a miniature painter, an Irishman, Michael Kean.

Duesbury the Second died in 1796 (and Kean over-promptly married the widow), and there closed a period in English china which, in technical excellence and exquisite refinement of taste, has set a standard to which the eyes of every present-day craftsman and artist must turn.

*   *   *

Burns, Wordsworth, Coleridge, Southey, Turner, Jane Austen, Charles Lamb, Constable were in their prime ; Scott, Byron and Shelley were born ; Wolfe had taken Quebec ; Nelson was to beat the French at Trafalgar. As a setting, as a background, to these great things and these great people, the brothers Adam, Chippendale, Sheraton, built and furnished for them Harewood House, Kenwood, Kedlestone. Their portraits were painted by Raeburn, Hoppner, Romney, Van Dyck, Gainsborough and the supreme Sir Joshua.

*   *   *

In 1811 the works passed to Bloor, who had been a clerk and a salesman at the works, and it would appear that he tried to carry on the old tradition until 1821, after which he used much of the accumulated white stock for various Japan patterns, now generally known as Crown Derby.

Owing to the illness of Bloor the Nottingham Road works were closed in 1848, but a group of employees (generally referred to as " old Derby hands ") pooled their resources to transfer the bulk of the models, moulds, body and colour receipts and pattern books, together with the goodwill and trade marks, to the present china works in King Street. The old wheel of William Duesbury was included, and it remains to-day the most important memento of the birth of the china industry in this country.

No. 2.
Companion Gardener

No. 3.
Syntax Sketching

No. 1.
The Gardener.

No. 4.
Syntax up Tree.

No. 6.
French
Shepherdess.

No. 5.
French Shepherd.

"The years recede, the years advance. . . ."

S ·×· *H*

Although some of the working moulds at this time found their way to the Staffordshire potteries, the craftsmanship remained with the " old Derby hands," who continued to use the old marks, although occasionally the mark " Locker late Bloor," and " Stevenson & Sharp " and " Stevenson & Hancock," who were all of the old works, are found.

It was in the year 1862 that Professor Llewellyn Jewitt, who at that time was making a special study of the ceramic art of Great Britain, suggested that a period mark should be included ; and to do this the letters " S.H." were added, the letters being suggested by " Stevenson & Hancock." In most cases it is impossible to tell which ware was late Bloor and which was King Street before the " S.H." was added at that date. Sampson Hancock carried on alone, as the remaining survivor of the little band of craftsmen, until his death in 1898, when the works were taken over by his grandson, Mr. James Robinson, for a further period of eighteen years. In 1916 they passed to Mr. Larcombe, who took, as partner, Mr. F. Howard Paget, in the following January.

Mr. Paget now controls the works, and, as a connoisseur of Derby china, uses his collection as a guide and inspiration to the present-day artists.

It is interesting to recall that the Hancocks were associated with the china trade of Derby from its inauguration. Harry Sampson Hancock—whose flower and landscape paintings rank with such well-known Derby painters as Billingsley, Pegg, Brewer, Thomas and Steele—died in April, 1934.

* * *

The men, the artists, who created something so beautiful and so English as Old Crown Derby china, have been—for over a century —well known among appreciators of fine things :—Billingsley, " the exquisite flower painter," who, apprenticed to Duesbury in 1774, during the next four years established his reputation in Derby ; Edward Withers, another flower painter ; Banford, who painted figure subjects ; William Pegg, who gave up painting even flowers for religious scruples ; George Robertson ; the brothers Brewer ; Cuthbert Lawton, who painted hunting scenes with a spirit that must have been appreciated by Surtees and other good hunting men ; Samuel Keys, a gilder, " one of the best of his days " . . . . And the later ones :—Moses Webster, " who

" You have heard of Billingsley's roses ? "

" One shade the more, one ray the less, Had half impair'd the nameless grace."

No. 7.
Dessert Plate.

No. 11.
Three-handled
Loving Cup.

No. 12.
Dog
Flower Holder.

No. 25.
Heart-shaped Dessert Dish.

No. 13.
Incensor.
Rose Trellis.

No. 14.
Altar Vase.

No. 9.
Dessert Plate.

No. 10.
Tea and Saucer.

painted roses so naturally that you could actually smell them " ; Thomas Steele, whose fruit painting on china was unsurpassed. And the modellers and figure makers :—Spangler, Stephan, Coffee, who advanced china figures " at one bound from the merely quaint to the truly beautiful " ; and the Hancocks, whose services to Old Crown Derby china, generation by generation, extend back unbroken to the time of the first Duesbury.

"The mill, they say, cannot grind with the water that is past, but this also we know : that what we have been makes us what we are."
" What's past is prologue."

* * *

Planché, Duesbury, Billingsley, Coffee, Stephan, Spangler, Bloor, the Hancocks—their genius, and the genius of the artists who work for us now, is associated with every piece of Old Crown Derby china that you see.

* * *

THE OLD CROWN DERBY CHINA WORKS remain to-day the only well-known china factory where no mechanical process of decoration is used Each piece portrays the hands of the craftsman and artist, and no two pieces are alike unless specially required. It is due to this individuality that our products have been in demand by the connoisseur for over one-and-a-half centuries.

In using Old Crown Derby china for gift purposes—and what could be more eminently beautiful and serviceable ?—you have the satisfaction of knowing that you are giving the finest craftsmanship ; and, in addition to its imposing charm, it carries a name that has been, and still is, the pride and envy of the Western world. The value of Old Crown Derby china has always been enhanced by the passing of years ; and in many homes to-day there is still a treasured figure or service —probably incomplete. Such service can be made up, or added to.

The illustrations in this book form part only of our manu-factures. We have many other models, and numerous and varied designs in tea, coffee and dessert services, particulars of which we shall be pleased to supply on request. If it is desired to have services of a personal and distinctive pattern— particularly for presentation purposes— we can submit designs, such as local views, personal silhouettes, paintings, miniatures, etc., suitably inscribed for any specific occasion.

Any piece can be purchased separately, and this enables a complete service to be built up, or, in case of breakage. a set need never remain incomplete.

Page Eight

426

No. 15.
Small Bouquet.

No. 19.
Violet Basket.

No. 16.
Large Bouquet.

No. 17.
Flower Spray.

No. 20.
Derby Peacock.

No. 18.
Basket of Flowers.

No. 21.
Spring.

No. 24.
Winter.

No. 22.
Summer.

"No. 8"
Boy.

"No. 8"
Girl.

No. 23.
Autumn.

No. 26.
Earth.

No. 30.
Snuff Taker.

No. 27.
Air.

No. 31.
Tinker.

No. 32.
Companion Tinker.

No. 28.
Fire.

No. 33.
The Cobbler

No. 29.
Water.

Page Eleven

No. 34.
Scalloped Dish.
Game.

No. 35.
Scalloped Dish.
Chelsea Birds.
(Ground laid border.)

No. 36.
Dessert Plate.
Landscape.

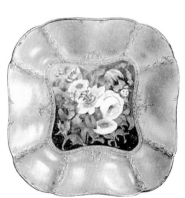

No. 37.
Square Dish. Flowers.
(Ground laid border.)

No. 38.
Dessert Plate.
Bird and Flower Panels.
(Ground laid border.)

Page Twelve

No. 42.
Toby Jug.

No. 43.
The Laughing Philosopher.

No. 39.
The Hairdresser.

No. 45.
"Night."

No. 44.
"Morning."

No. 40.
The Tythe Group.

No. 46.
African Sall.

No. 47.
Billy Waters.

No. 41.
The Thrower.

Page Thirteen

431

No. 48.
Heart-shaped Dessert Tray.
Old Crown Derby Witches.

No. 51.
Bottle Vase.
Old Crown Derby Witches.

No. 52.
Pot Pourri. Fruit.

No. 50.
Shell Gadroon Dish.
Old Crown Derby Rose.

No. 49.
Oval Dessert Dish.
Old Crown Derby Witches.

No. 58.
Pastille.
Old Crown Derby Witches.

No. 53.
Tea, Saucer and Plate.
Old Crown Derby Witches.

No. 54.
Square Tray.
Old Crown Derby Witches.

No. 59.
Tea, Saucer and Plate.
Old Crown Derby Rose

No. 60. Octagonal Tray.
Old Crown Derby Rose

No. 55. Octagonal Tray
Old Crown Derby Witches.

No. 61.
Tea, Saucer and Plate.
Old Crown Derby Garden.

No. 56.
Watering Can.
Old Crown Derby Witches.

No. 57.
Cigarette Box.
Old Crown Derby Witches.

No. 62.
Tea, Saucer and Plate.
Old Crown Derby.

Page Fifteen

433

No. 63.
Coffee Season.
Spring.

No. 67.
Roman Lamp.

No. 68.
Paul Pry.

No. 64.
Coffee Season.
Autumn.

No. 66.
Chelsea.
Flower Seller.

No. 69.
Mother Gamp.

No. 65.
Chelsea.
Fruit Seller

No. 71.
English
Shepherd.

No. 70.
Falstaff.

No. 72.
English
Shepherdess.

No. 74.
Welch Tailoress.

No. 73.
Welch Tailor

No. 75.
Cow Cream Jug.

The Virgins awakening Cupid.

No. 76.
Cabinet Cup.
Rose Trellis.

No. 78.
Green Vase.
Flowers.

No. 79.
Spills.

No. 77.
Pot Pourri.
Rose Trellis.

No. 80.
Pastille.
Flowers.

No. 81.
Gipsy Kettle.
Raised Flowers.

No. 14.
Altar Vase.
Flowers.

No. 82.
Menu Holder.

No. 83.
Trinket Box.
Flowers.

No. 84.
Small Vase.
Flowers.

Page Nineteen

437

No. 85.
Bridge Set in Case.
Old Crown Derby Witches.

No. 88.
Coffee and Saucer.
Old Crown Derby Rose

No. 87.
Coffee and Saucer.
Old Crown Derby Garden.

No. 90
Coffee and Saucer.
Butterfly.

No. 91.
Coffee and Saucer.
Green Star.

No. 92.
Coffee and Saucer.
Duesbury Sprig and Porder.

No. 93.
Coffee and Saucer
Purple Scroll.

No. 94.
Coffee and Saucer
Rose Barbeau.

No. 86.
Coffee Pot.
Old Crown Derby Witches.

No. 89.
Coffee and Saucer.
Old Crown Derby Bramble.

No. 95.
Coffee and Saucer
Sprig and Star

Page Twenty

PRICE LIST to King Street Catalogue 1934-35

			£	s.	d.
Page 3	Large size centrepiece comport	(Not illustrated)	16	16	0
18	The Virgins awakening Cupid	(Not illustrated)	6	14	6
No. 1	Gardener		2	10	6
2	Companion Gardener		2	10	6
3	Syntax Sketching..		1	16	0
4	Syntax up Tree		2	10	6
	Syntax on Horseback	(Not illustrated)	3	7	6
	Syntax Walking	(Not illustrated)	0	15	0
	Syntax at Calais	(Not illustrated)	1	0	0
5	French Shepherd..		2	10	6
6	French Shepherdess		2	10	6
7	Dessert Plate. Flowers		3	7	6
8	'No. 8' Boy		1	16	0
8	'No. 8' Girl		1	16	0
9	Dessert plate. Ground laid border		2	0	0

Flower Groups by various artists

			£	s.	d.
No. 10	Tea and saucer		0	14	0
	Coffee and saucer		0	12	6
	Breakfast and saucer		0	19	0
	4 in. plate..		0	8	6
	5 in. plate..		0	9	0
	6 in. plate..		0	10	5
	7 in. plate..		0	14	0
	Cream jug		0	14	0
	Sugar		0	14	0
	Cake plate		1	8	0
	Hot water jug		0	19	9
	Open jug, 1 pint		0	14	0
	Open jug, 1½ pints		0	16	10
	Open jug, 2 pints		0	19	9
	Tea pot or coffee pot, 1 pint		1	5	3
	Tea pot or coffee pot, 1½ pints		1	10	9
	Tea pot or coffee pot, 2 pints		1	16	3
	Tea set, 21 pieces		10	2	6
	Tea set, 40 pieces		18	17	0
	Morning set, 2 persons		4	10	3
	Breakfast set, 29 pieces		16	15	0
11	Three-handled loving cup		3	7	6
12	Dog flower holder		1	13	6
13	Incensor. Rose Trellis		1	13	6
	Incensor. Flowers		1	8	0
14	Altar vase. Large size, 9 in.		1	16	0
	Altar vase. Medium size, 7 in.		1	8	0
	Altar vase. Small size, 4½ in.		1	0	0
15	Small Bouquet		4	0	0
16	Large Bouquet		8	0	0
17	Flower Spray		0	17	0
18	Basket of Flowers		2	10	6
19	Violet Basket		1	0	0
20	Derby Peacock		6	0	0
21	The Seasons: Spring		3	7	6
22	Summer		3	7	6
23	Autumn		3	7	6
24	Winter		3	7	6
	Fitted with electric flame light, complete, as Nos. 23 and 24, each figure extra		1	1	0
25	Heart-shaped dessert dish. Flowers		2	10	6
	8 in. gadroon dessert plate. Flowers		2	2	0
26	The Elements: Earth		2	16	0
27	Air		2	16	0
28	Fire		2	16	0
29	Water		2	16	0
30	Snuff-taker		1	16	0
31	Tinker		2	16	0
32	Companion Tinker		2	16	0
33	The Cobbler		3	12	0
34	Scalloped dish. Game		3	7	6
35	Scalloped dish. Chelsea Birds. Ground laid border ..		2	12	0
36	8 in. gadroon dessert plate. Landscape		3	7	6
Page 3	8 in. gadroon dessert plate. Fruit		3	7	6
	8 in. gadroon dessert plate. Fruit and Flowers ..		3	7	6
	8 in. gadroon dessert plate. Fish		3	7	6
	8 in. gadroon dessert plate. Game Birds		3	7	6
	8 in. gadroon dessert plates. Seascapes		3	7	6

*1934-35 Price List.
Twitchett & Bailey,
"Royal Crown Derby".*

Page 3	8 in. gadroon dessert plates. Garden Scenes	3	7	6
	8 in. gadroon dessert plates. Cottage Gardens	3	7	6
	Low comports and dishes	4	0	0
	Tall comports	6	0	0
	Bon-bon dishes. Shell or leaf shape	2	5	0
	8 in. dessert plates. Flower sprays and gold *(Not illustrated)*	0	19	0
	Low comports and dishes. Flower sprays and gold			
	(Not illustrated)	1	2	9
	Tall comports. Flower sprays and gold *(Not illustrated)*	1	14	0
	Bon-bon dishes. Shell or leaf shape. Flower sprays and gold			
	(Not illustrated)	0	12	6
	8 in. Salad Bowls. Roses and gold leaves *(Not illustrated)*	2	16	0
	8 in. Salad Bowls. Flowers .. .. *(Not illustrated)*	3	7	6
No. 37	Square dish. Flowers. Ground laid border	2	16	0
38	8 in. dessert plate. Bird and flower panels. Ground laid border	2	16	0
	Low comports and dishes. Bird and flower panels. Ground			
	laid border .. .. *(Not illustrated)*	3	7	6
	Tall comports. Bird and flower panels. Ground laid border			
	(Not illustrated)	5	0	0
No. 39	The Hairdresser	5	0	0
40	The Tythe Group	6	14	6
41	The Thrower	3	0	0
42	Toby jug	0	4	6
43	Laughing Philosopher	1	16	0
	Crying Philosopher .. .. .. *(Not illustrated)*	1	16	0
44	'Morning'	0	12	6
45	'Night'	0	12	6
46	African Sall	0	15	0
47	Billy Waters	0	15	0
52	Pot pourri. Fruit	2	4	0

OLD CROWN DERBY PATTERNS

Witches. Rose. Garden. Old.

No. 48	Heart-shaped dessert tray	2	0	0
49	Oval dessert dish	2	0	0
50	Shell gadroon dish	2	4	0
	Dessert plate	1	13	9
	8 in. salad bowl	3	7	6
	Bon-bon dishes. Shell or leaf shape	1	2	6
51	Bottle vase	4	0	0
53	Tea and saucer	1	0	0
59	Tea and saucer	1	0	0
61	Tea and saucer	1	0	0
62	Tea and saucer	1	0	0
87	Coffee and saucer	0	18	6
88	Coffee and saucer	0	18	6
	Breakfast and saucer	1	8	0
53	4 in. plate	0	12	6
59	4 in. plate	0	12	6
61	4 in. plate	0	12	6
62	4 in. plate	0	12	6
	5 in. plate	0	13	6
	6 in. plate	0	15	6
	7 in. plate	1	0	0
	Cream jug	1	0	0
	Sugar	1	0	0
	Hot water jug	1	8	0
	Open jug. 1 pint	1	0	0
	Open jug. 1½ pints	1	4	0
	Open jug. 2 pints	1	8	0
86	Coffee pot or tea pot. 1 pint	1	16	0
	Coffee pot or tea pot. 1½ pints	2	4	0
	Coffee pot or tea pot. 2 pints	2	12	0
	Cake plate	2	0	0
	Tea set, 21 pieces	14	13	0
	Tea set, 40 pieces	27	6	0
	Morning set, 2 persons	6	9	6
	Breakfast set, 29 pieces	24	5	0
54	Square tray	0	7	9
55	Octagonal tray	0	10	0
60	Octagonal tray	0	10	0
56	Toy watering can	0	12	6
57	Cigarette box	1	0	0
58	Pastille	2	10	6
	Small size Gipsy kettle	0	12	6
	Small size pot pourri	0	8	6

No. 58	Small size vase	..	..	..	..	..	..	0	7	6
	Round powder or trinket box	..	..	..	..	..		1	0	0
85	Bridge set, in case. (4 coffees and saucers, 4 ash trays,									
	cigarette box)	..	..	..	..	..	..	6	17	6

Old Crown Derby Bramble

No. 89	Coffee and saucer	..	..	..	..	..	..	0	14	0
	Tea and saucer	..	..	..	..	..	..	0	15	6
	Breakfast and saucer	..	..	..	..	..	..	1	1	3
	4 in. plate..	..	..	..	..	..	..	0	9	6
	5 in. plate..	..	..	..	..	..	..	0	10	0
	6 in. plate..	..	..	..	..	..	..	0	11	8
	7 in. plate..	..	..	..	..	..	..	0	15	6
	Cream jug	..	..	..	..	..	..	0	15	6
	Sugar	..	..	..	..	..	..	0	15	6
	Hot water jug	..	..	..	..	..	..	1	1	9
	Open jug, 1 pint ..	..	..	..	..	..	..	0	15	6
	Open jug, 1½ pints	..	..	..	..	..	..	0	18	9
	Open jug, 2 pints	..	..	..	..	..	..	1	2	0
	Tea pot or coffee pot, 1 pint	..	..	..	..	..	..	1	8	0
	Tea pot or coffee pot, 1½ pints ..	..	..	..	..	..	1	14	3
	Tea pot or coffee pot, 2 pints	..	..	..	..	..	2	0	0
	Cake plate	..	..	..	..	..	..	1	11	0
	Tea set, 21 pieces	..	..	..	..	..	..	11	5	0
	Tea set, 40 pieces	..	..	..	..	..	..	20	19	0
	Morning set, 2 persons	..	..	..	..	..	4	19	9
	Breakfast set, 29 pieces ..	..	..	..	..	..	18	12	6
63	Coffee's Season, 'Spring'	..	..	..	..	..	2	8	0
64	Coffee's Season, 'Autumn'	..	..	..	..	..	2	8	0
65	Small size Chelsea Fruit Seller ..	..	..	..	..	1	8	0
66	Small size Chelsea Flower Seller	..	..	..	..	1	8	0
	Medium size French Fruit Seller		(Not illustrated)		3	7	6
	Medium size French Flower Seller	..	(Not illustrated)		3	7	6
	Small size Fisher Boy	..	..	..	(Not illustrated)		1	8	0
	Small size Flower Girl	..	..	..	(Not illustrated)		1	8	0
	Small size Fisher Boy	..	..	..	(Not illustrated)		1	0	0
67	Roman Lamp	..	..	..	..	..	..	1	8	0
68	Paul Pry ..	..	..	..	..	..	..	0	11	9
69	Mother Gamp, match holder	..	..	..	..	..	3	12	0
70	Falstaff	..	..	..	..	..	..	2	10	6
71	English Shepherd	..	..	..	..	..	..	2	10	6
72	English Shepherdess	..	..	..	..	..	4	4	0
73	Welch Tailor	..	..	..	..	..	..	4	4	0
74	Welch Tailoress ..	..	..	..	..	..	1	0	0
75	Cow cream jug ..	..	..	..	..	..	0	10	0
76	Cabinet cup. Rose trellis	..	..	..	..	..	0	10	0
77	Pot pourri. Rose trellis ..	..	..	..	..	..	1	0	0
78	Green vase, 7 in. Flowers	..	..	..	..	..	1	0	0
79	Spills, 4½ in.	..	..	..	..	..	..	0	16	9
	Spills, 3¼ in.	..	..	..	..	..	..	2	4	0
80	Pastille. Flowers ..	..	..	..	..	..	0	9	0
81	Gipsy kettle, raised flowers	..	..	..	..	..	0	6	6
	Gipsy kettle, raised flowers, small size..	..	..	..	0	9	0
	Gipsy kettle, small size, painted flowers	..	..	..	0	10	6
82	Menu holder. Flowers and butterflies ..	..	..	..	1	4	0
	Menu holder. Pair, in case	..	..	..	..	..	0	7	6
	Serviette ring. Flowers	..	..	..	(Not illustrated)		0	19	0
	Serviette ring. Pair, in case	..	..	..	..	..	1	8	0
83	Round powder or trinket box. Flowers	..	..	..	1	0	0
	Round powder or trinket box. Flower posies	..	..	0	8	6
84	Small vase. Flowers	..	..	..	..	..				

Butterflies

No. 90	Coffee and saucer	..	..	..	..	..	0	12	6

Green Star, or Purple Star

No. 91	Coffee and saucer	..	..	..	..	..	..	0	12	6
	Tea and saucer	..	..	..	..	..	..	0	14	0
	Breakfast and saucer	..	..	..	..	..	..	0	19	0
	Tea set, 21 pieces	..	..	..	..	..	..	10	2	6
	Morning set, 2 persons ..	..	..	..	..	..	4	10	3
	Breakfast set, 29 pieces ..	..	..	..	..	..	16	15	0

Duesbury Sprig and Border

No. 92	Coffee and saucer	..	..	..	..	..	..	0	11	8

No. 92	Tea and saucer ..	..	..	..	..	..	..	0	12	6
	Breakfast and saucer	..	..	..	..	..	..	0	16	9
	Tea set, 21 pieces	..	..	..	..	..	..	9	0	0
	Morning set, 2 persons ..	..	..	..	..	..	4	0	0
	Breakfast set, 29 pieces ..	..	..	..	..	..	14	17	6

Purple Scroll

No. 93	Coffee and saucer	..	..	..	..	..	..	0	15	3
	Tea and saucer ..	..	..	..	..	..	..	0	18	0
	Breakfast and saucer	..	..	..	..	..	..	1	5	0
	Tea set, 21 pieces	..	..	..	..	..	..	13	2	6
	Morning set, 2 persons	..	..	..	..	..	..	5	16	0
	Breakfast set, 29 pieces ..	..	..	..	..	..	21	15	0

Rose Barbeau

No. 94	Coffee and saucer	..	..	..	..	..	..	0	18	6
	Tea and saucer ..	..	..	..	..	..	..	1	0	0
	Breakfast and saucer	..	..	..	..	..	..	1	8	0
	Tea set, 21 pieces	..	..	..	..	..	..	14	13	0
	Morning set, 2 persons ..	..	..	..	..	..	6	9	6
	Breakfast set, 29 pieces ..	..	..	..	..	..	24	5	0

Sprig and Star

No. 95	Coffee and saucer	..	..	..	..	..	..	0	10	10
	Tea and saucer ..	..	..	..	..	..	..	0	14	0
	Breakfast and saucer	..	..	..	..	..	..	0	19	0
	Tea set, 21 pieces	..	..	..	..	..	..	10	2	6
	Morning set, 2 persons ..	..	..	..	..	..	4	10	3
	Breakfast set, 29 pieces ..	..	..	..	..	..	16	15	0

Bloor Rose. (*Not illustrated*)

	Tea and saucer ..	..	..	..	..	..	..	0	14	0
	Breakfast and saucer	..	..	..	..	..	..	0	19	0
	Tea set, 21 pieces	..	..	..	..	..	..	10	2	6
	Morning set, 2 persons ..	..	..	..	..	..	4	10	3
	Breakfast set, 29 pieces ..	..	..	..	..	..	16	15	0

Roses and Forget-me-nots. (*Not illustrated*)

	Coffee and saucer	..	..	..	..	..	..	0	12	6
	Tea and saucer ..	..	..	..	..	..	..	0	14	0
	Breakfast and saucer	..	..	..	..	..	..	0	19	0
	Tea set, 21 pieces	..	..	..	..	..	..	10	2	6
	Morning set, 2 persons ..	..	..	..	..	..	4	10	3
	Breakfast set, 29 pieces ..	..	..	..	..	..	16	15	0

Rose Trellis. (*Not illustrated*)

	Coffee and saucer	..	..	..	..	..	..	0	18	6
	Tea and saucer ..	..	..	..	..	..	..	1	0	0
	Breakfast and saucer	..	..	..	..	..	..	1	8	0
	Tea set, 21 pieces	..	..	..	..	..	..	14	13	0
	Morning set, 2 persons ..	..	..	..	..	..	6	9	6
	Breakfast set, 29 pieces ..	..	..	..	..	..	24	5	0

Roses and Gold Lines. (*Not illustrated*)

	Coffee and saucer	..	..	..	..	..	..	1	6	6
	Tea and saucer ..	..	..	..	..	..	..	1	8	0
	Breakfast and saucer	..	..	..	..	..	..	1	19	3
	Tea set, 21 pieces	..	..	..	..	..	..	20	18	0
	Morning set, 2 persons ..	..	..	..	..	..	9	3	3
	Breakfast set, 29 pieces ..	..	..	..	..	..	33	19	6

| | Fitted case for six coffees and saucers .. | .. | .. | .. | 0 | 12 | 6 |

	A collection of small animals, including dogs, pigs, cows, calves, lambs, etc. .. .. each (*Not illustrated*)	0	4	6
	Greyhound, on base .. .. .. (*Not illustrated*)	1	0	0
	Fox (sitting), on base .. .. .. (*Not illustrated*)	1	0	0
	Stirrup cups. Dog or Fox Head .. (*Not illustrated*)	1	0	0
	Christening mug. Flowers. With initial in flowers (*Not illustrated*)	1	1	0
	Christening mug. Flowers. With name in flowers (*Not illustrated*)	1	4	0

7. REFERENCES

(1)   Advertisements extracted from various publications held in the Local Studies Library, Derby.

(2)   Twitchett, J., & Bailey, B., *Royal Crown Derby.* Antique Collectors' Club, 1988, p15

(3)   Haslem, J., *Old Derby China, a history of the Derby China Works.* G. Bell, 1876, p p.205-206

(4)   Jewitt, L., "Old Derby China, a history of the Derby China Works," *The Art Journal*, London, 1 January 1862, p.4

(5)   The original photograph is in the Museum, Royal Crown Derby.

(6)   This article in *DPIS Newsletter*, June 1995, p.24

(7)   Jewitt, Op. Cit., p.4

(8)   Copy of a letter in the possession of G. Godden.

(9)   Haslem, Op. Cit., p.155

(10) Moore, H., "Porcelain manufacture in King Street Derby", *Antique Collecting Magazine*, The Antique Collectors' Club, September 1983, p.43

(11) A newspaper cutting, dated in handwriting January 1857, in Pamphlet Box 7, Local Studies Library, Derby.

8. QUALITY CONTROL

It has been reported by people who worked at or visited the factory, that quality control was carried out in a small room at the back of the sales shop. Sometimes this operation was effective and pieces with faults were left unmarked and probably sold as seconds. However, there were occasions where the system broke down and marked pieces with faults found their way on to the market. A few of the main faults are examined in this chapter, along with some of the possible causes.

Lighting
Poor lighting would have been a problem. Hilda Moore recalls that the modeller Edward Swainson, who started work at the factory around 1880, at first worked by the light of candles and when oil lamps were introduced, he said that "it was a great innovation". With oil lamps in wide use from the 1840s and gas lighting becoming common in town houses by 1840 the factory was perhaps a little slow in upgrading its lighting.

Faults
a)   Little effort seems to have been made to "match" component tablewares that were bought in prior to being decorated at King Street. Had this been done, some of the quite major differences within the same service might have been avoided.

b)   The miscellaneous debris that settled on wares and is so noticeable on glazed white wares of the later nineteenth century, was a considerable problem, along with occasional specks of blue enamel. As these faults do not appear on biscuit wares, the problem is likely to be connected with the glaze.

c)   Examples of patchy light brown discolouration can be found on wares in the white, both biscuit and glazed, perhaps indicating a problem with the components in the body, rather than any defect in the glaze.

d)   Firing cracks are seen on nineteenth century figures, but this does not appear to have been a major problem. Collapse in the kiln was a failing from which the factory suffered and made modifications to overcome. Illustrated below is a figure of Dr. Syntax Sketching, but instead of the figure sitting upright, it tilts forward because the whole centre of the base has collapsed. It is probable that the small bridges shown on the right, on a figure of a greyhound, were introduced to overcome this problem.

Opposite page top: Collapsed figure.
Private Collection.

Opposite page below: Remedial bridges.
Private Collection.

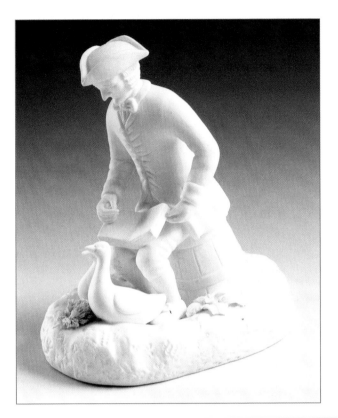

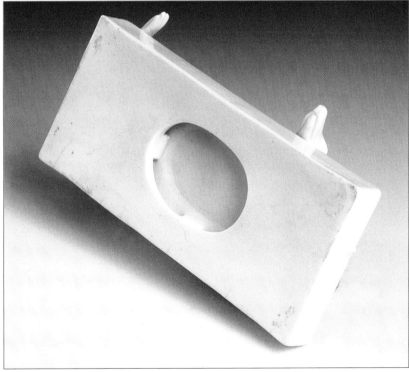

BIBLIOGRAPHY

Published Books/Booklets

Bambery, A. and Blackwood, R. *The Factory at King Street 1849-1935*. Derby Museums & Art Gallery, supported by the Derby Porcelain International Society, October 1992.

Bradley, H. G. *Ceramics of Derbyshire 1750-1975*. Maslands Ltd., 1978.

Challand, M. *Derby China through three centuries*. J. H. Hall & Sons Ltd., 1987.

County Borough of Derby Museum & Art Gallery. *Derby China*. 1973.

Gibson, H. *A Case of Fine China*. The Royal Crown Derby Porcelain Company Ltd., 1993.

Gilhespy, F. Brayshaw, *Crown Derby Porcelain*. F. Lewis, 1951.

Gilhespy, F. Brayshaw and Budd, D. *Royal Crown Derby China*. C. Skilton Ltd., 1964.

Godden, G. *Encyclopaedia of British Porcelain Manufacturers*. Barrie & Jenkins, 1988.

Godden, G. *The revival of Derby Porcelain*. Country Life Annual, 1962.

Godden, G. *Victorian Porcelain*. Herbert Jenkins Ltd., 1961.

Haslem, J. *The Old Crown Derby China Factory*. G. Bell & Sons, 1876.

Jewitt, L. *Ceramic Art of Great Britain*. Virtue & Co., 1878.

Sargeant, M. *Royal Crown Derby*. Shire publications, 2000.

Twitchett, J. *The Story of Royal Crown Derby China from 1750 to the present day*. Royal Doulton Tableware Ltd., 1978.

Twitchett, J. and Bailey, B. *Royal Crown Derby*. Barrie & Jenkins, 1976; revised edition Antique Collectors Club, 1988.

Willoughby Hodgson, Mrs., *Old English China*. Benn, 1913.

Periodicals and Journals

Bambery, A. "Derby Porcelain; the factory at King Street, 1849-1935." *Antiques Bulletin*, 6-12 November 1993

Blackwood, R. "An English Vase and a Continental Figure," *Derby Porcelain International Society (DPIS) Newsletter*, January 1995.

Blackwood, R. "Another Link with a Sculptor," *DPIS Newsletter*, May 1996.

Blackwood, R. "Decorative baskets from the Old Crown Derby China Works," *DPIS Newsletter*, May 1999.

Blackwood, R. "Dining Table Centrepieces," *DPIS Newsletter*, November 1997.

Blackwood, R. "Extending the range at King Street," *DPIS Newsletter*, December 1999.

Blackwood, R. "A Figure of Dubious Age," *DPIS Newsletter*, October 1996.

Blackwood, R. "Flowers or Fruit today?" *DPIS Newsletter*, December 2001.

Blackwood, R. "For Professional and Amateur Artists – a blank plaque for use by amateur artists," *DPIS Newsletter,* December 1998.

Blackwood, R. "Some Unusual Decoration," *DPIS Newsletter*, October 1995.

Blackwood, R. "Striking a Balance – types of decoration," *DPIS Newsletter,* June 1995.

Blackwood, R. "Twelve Years of Mistaken Identity," *DPIS Newsletter*, June1995.

Blackwood, R. "An Ugly Jug," *DPIS Newsletter*, December 1998.

Blackwood, R.   "The White Period at King Street," *DPIS Newsletter*, October 1996.

Blackwood, R.   "Why did they do that? Altered marks," *DPIS Newsletter*, January 1997.

Bradbury, E.   "The Story of Old Crown Derby China." Reprinted from the *Yorkshire Weekly Post*, 12 May 1894, by the High Peak News, Buxton.

Bradley, H. G.   "The King Street Factory," *DPIS Newsletter*, May 1996.

Bradley, H. G.   "Exhibition: King Street Factory, October 1993." *DPIS Newsletter*, January 1994.

Cordwent, H. & C. and Blackwood, R. "A rare piece of King Street," *DPIS Newsletter*, May 1996.

Dawson, A.   "A Derby Pattern Book in the British Museum," *DPIS Journal II*, 1991.

Dawson, A.   "The F. Howard Paget Collection in the British Museum," *DPIS Newsletter*, January 1988.

Gibson, H.   "Exhibition: The King Street Factory," *DPIS Newsletter*, January 1994.

Head, C.   "I was born in China so to speak, (the life story of Sampson Hancock)," *DPIS Journal 4*, 2000.

Head, C and Blackwood, R. "A Link with Sampson Hancock," *DPIS Newsletter*, December 1998.

Jewitt, L.   "Old Derby China, a history of the Derby China Works," *Art Journal*, 1 January 1862.

Kelland, G. and Blackwood, R. "Restoration," *DPIS Newsletter*, June 2001.

Moore, H.   "A note about the Derby (King Street) Works," *DPIS Newsletter*, September 1985.

Moore, H.   "The Old Crown Derby China Works," *DPIS Newsletter*, April, 1987.

Moore, H.   "Porcelain manufacture in King Street, Derby," *Antique Collecting Magazine*, Antique Collectors' Club, September 1983.

Tharp, L.   "19th Century Derby Porcelain," *Antique Collecting*, May 1993.

Twitchett, J.   "Another look at King Street," *DPIS Newsletter*, June 1986.

Wells, A.   Book Review: "The factory at King Street 1849-1935," *DPIS Newsletter*, January 1994.

Wharf, C. & F. and Blackwood, R. "Across the Divide," *DPIS Newsletter*, January 1994.

Williamson, F. "Derby China – King Street Factory." An article in *Derbyshire Advertiser*, 13 February 1925.

Catalogues
Sales Catalogues

Property of the late Mr. J. Haslem, 1884.

W. Winter Collection, 1884.

Property of the late Sampson Hancock, including his personal collection together with stock from the King Street factory, 1895.

William Bemrose Collection, 1909.

Exhibition Catalogue

"The factory at King Street 1849-1935." Derby Museums and Art Gallery, 1993.

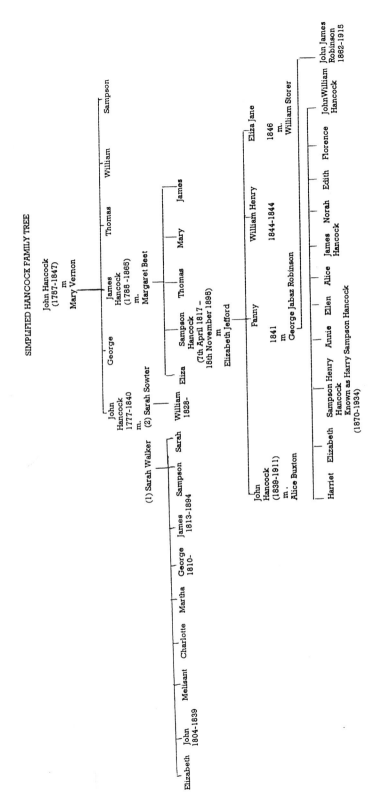

SIMPLIFIED HANCOCK FAMILY TREE

Conversion Table for Linear Measures

For those who work in imperial measures, the following table may be helpful.

Centimetres.		Inches.
7.6	=	3
8.9	=	$3^{1/2}$
10.2	=	4
11.4	=	$4^{1/2}$
12.7	=	5
14	=	$5^{1/2}$
15.2	=	6
16.5	=	$6^{1/2}$
17.8	=	7
19	=	$7^{1/2}$
20.3	=	8
21.6	=	$8^{1/2}$
22.9	=	9
24.1	=	$9^{1/2}$
25.4	=	10
25.7	=	$10^{1/2}$
27.9	=	11
29.2	=	$11^{1/2}$
30.5.	=	12
31.7	=	$12^{1/2}$
33	=	13
34.3	=	$13^{1/2}$
35.6	=	14
36.8	=	$14^{1/2}$

INDEX

(Page numbers in **bold***Italic* type refer to illustrations)

341,345,352,359,360,362,363,365,375,387,397
& cover;
  anemones, *193;*
  clematis, *194;*
  dahlias *143;*
  flowers & foliage, *58,161;*
  forget-me-nots, *73,165,400;*
  garden flowers & leaves, *95,98,100,122;*
  gloxinias, *142;*
  harebells, *343;*
  hollyhocks, *101;*
  mixed *flowers, 123,125,146,149,177;*
  315,317,335,337,338,386;
  pansies, *165,322,400;*
  passion flowers, *99,344;*
  poppies, *323;*
  roses, *73,78,93,102,111,114,*140,
  191,325,338,349,356,372,399,400;
  sunflowers, *349;*
  tulips, *90,349;*
  wildflowers, 153;
fruit, *62,*71,131,*144,145,*248,*341,362,365,387;*
fruit & foliage, 72
*insects, 112,144,*183,248,*316,318,337,340,*
366,397
insects & butterflies, *94,95,101,104,112,*199,*318,*
331,340,341,363,366 & cover
ladybird, *101*
Imari wares, 70,82,*84*
Japan patterns, 33,44,46,153,200
landscapes, 57,*84,85,*91,*97,*146,155,156,*158-162,*
169,216,248,253,*324*
leaves, 84,*339*
milkmaid, *169*
shells, *94*
still life, 71,*362*
sporting scenes, 133,*174*
stags, 199
views
  alpine scenes, *192;*
  "Ashford Mill, Derbyshire", *108;*
  "Chepstow Castle", *146;*
  "Derby from Burton Road", *103;*
  Derbyshire scenes, 140,216-217,415;
  ducks swimming on a lake, *106;*
  farmyard, *326,*
  "Fountains Abbey", *85;*
  "Haddon Hall", *63,162;*
  "High Tor, Matlock", *157;*
  historic buildings, 60;
  "Ilam Rock, Dovedale", 216-217;
  "Iona", *148;*
  "St Mary's Bridge, Derby", *147;*
  landscape with children, *146;*
  landscape with gun dog & dead game, *174;*
  "Littleover Hollow, Derbyshire", *109;*
  "The Long Bridge, Derby ", *110;*

"Morley Churchyard, nr Derby", *105;*
"Netherby Hall", *161;*
"Nidpath Castle", *148;*
"Raglan(d) Castle ", *160;*
"Remains of Dinas Bren/Bron", *158;*
"Rhuddlan Castle ", *159;*
"Salisbury Cathedral ", *96;*
"School Arch leading to Repton College,
Derbyshire", *108;*
  waterscapes, *347;*
  woman & child, *175,362;*
Paperweights, 223
Par, Cornwall, auction at, 148
Paragon China Works, Staffs, 71
Parian ware, 65,68,152-153,198,247
Parwich, Elizabeth, burnisher, 154
Pastille burner, 219,*394,395*
Patent Office, 217
Patent Silvering Co Ltd, London, 225
Pates, Alice, china painter, 154
Pattern Books, 9,27,214,215,253-273,*255-265,*
269-271
Patterns, 183,244-403;
  Adam style, *390;*
  Art Deco-style patterns, 164,248;
  Bourbon Rose *see* Rose Barbeau/Barbo;
  Bow shape & pattern, 416-417,*416;*
  Broseley, 223,237;
  Chantilly, 268;
  Derby patterns on earthenware, 246;
  dessert wares, 183,254;
  Duesbury Sprig, 255;
  Garden, 248;
  Goode's pattern, 418;
  Hancock's laurel, 418;
  Hill's flowers, 418;
  Imari decoration/patterns, 33,70,75,*84,*212,221,
  246,248,*329,354,368,372,396;*
  Islamic style, *163;*
  Japan patterns, 33,44,46,153;
  Kedleston shape, 176;
  Landscapes, 253;
  List of patterns & names, 254,266-268;
  London shape, *344;*
  No.320, 146,148;
  No.393, 131;
  No.770, 131;
  Old Crown Derby Rose, *372;*
  Old Crown Derby Witches, 246,*328,329,351,*
  354,368,396;
  Old Japan, *84;*
  Partridge Japan, 200;
  Purple scroll, 418;
  Rose Barbeau/Barbo, 248,255,*320,369,388,392;*
  Rose trellis, 271,*325,*377;
  Sèvres style, 183,199;
  Sketches of patterns, *255-265,269-271;*

461